Cal Finnigan worked as a journal  France, finishing up on the politi and Rosheen lived for many yea and settling in Constable country on the Essex-Suffolk border. They spend a lot of time in France and in New Zealand, where their daughter runs a lively beachside café near Wellington and have a son who lives by Lake Constance, in Germany.

Praise for *Letters From the Suitcase*:

'An enthralling love story, which splices vintage detail with David and Mary's surprisingly frank and modern attitudes on everything from sex to politics' *Daily Mail*

'A remarkable love story' *Irish Times*

'An incredible story' Judy Finnigan

'Deeply personal and provides a picture of day to day life during a war' *neverimitate*

ROSHEEN AND CAL FINNIGAN

LETTERS FROM THE SUITCASE

A Wartime Love Story

TINDER
PRESS

Image from page 454 © Niki Francis

First published in Great Britain in 2017 by Tinder Press
An imprint of HEADLINE PUBLISHING GROUP

First published in paperback in 2018 by Tinder Press
An imprint of HEADLINE PUBLISHING GROUP

1

Cataloguing in Publication Data is available from the British Library

ISBN 978 1 4722 4399 7

Typeset in 10.56/13.6 pt Bembo MT Pro by Jouve (UK), Milton Keynes

Printed in Great Britain by Clays Ltd, St Ives plc

Headline's policy is to use papers that are natural, renewable and
recyclable products and made from wood grown in well-managed forests
and other controlled sources. The logging and manufacturing processes
are expected to conform to the environmental regulations
of the country of origin.

HEADLINE PUBLISHING GROUP
An Hachette UK Company
Carmelite House
50 Victoria Embankment
London EC4Y 0DZ

www.tinderpress.co.uk
www.headline.co.uk
www.hachette.co.uk

This book is dedicated with love to the memory of David and Mary and the 'doomed generation'

'I received your airgraph dated Dec 18th this morning. <u>How</u> I wish you could have surprised me on Christmas Eve. Do you remember how my legs collapsed once before when you arrived unexpectedly? I have been cleaning up papers over in Elgin Crescent and reading letters, letters, letters that you have sent me during these past years. Some fiendishly casual that have the power to make me hopping mad, others, that by their intensity and sincere love, still make me happy in a mournful sort of way, you know. But the whole makes an interesting documentary history of our time – the doomed generation; we who carried the can back and found ourselves in a battle.'

CONTENTS

CONTENTS

PROLOGUE

The letters lay in a trunk in the attic throughout my childhood – the neglect and mystery of them proving an almost-tangible barrier, forbidding prying. Out of sight because my mother's new husband had fearsome nightmares about the sudden reappearance of my dead sailor father – her passionate lover. But not out of mind. For although all other traces of my father rapidly disappeared – photos, records, and Griselda, his wonderful gramophone with its huge leather horn – the letters she kept with her for the rest of her life, and in her old age in Dublin she would tantalise me with them, a few glimpses, a few given – and then taken back. Then, finally, before her death, she gave me them all, and in doing so she gave me my father.

And what letters. From their meeting in May 1938 until his death in India in May 1943 they wrote constantly; in their first year sometimes only hours after parting, such was the intensity of the relationship, with extra thoughts about love and life. The letters flowed whether they lived in borrowed flats or on borrowed floors, in training camps or on ships at sea. They married secretly weeks before war broke out but, apart from eleven months of living together when David was based in Swansea, theirs stayed a love affair untrammelled by domestic bliss.

They fell in love in terrible times with war and death an ever-present reality – terrible, but because they were so young (he was twenty, she twenty-one), and so idealistic and so passionate, wonderful also. And for that first year, London, if you were on the left and in love, was the place to be. Films, literature and music continued throughout to be their sustenance, and politics their passion.

In many ways they were an odd match; Irish immigrant meets English toff. But, of course, it never is as simple as that. True, she was born in Dublin – Irish mother, English soldier father – but she won a scholarship to the Notting Hill and Ealing High School and could have gone on to Oxford; and although he was privately educated and articled to a chartered accountant, at nineteen he was the secretary of the Finsbury and Shoreditch branch of the Communist Party.

Their meeting ran like a film script. A party given by friends at Angel House, on Pentonville Road, Mary sent upstairs to borrow glasses from the young man in the flat above. She knocks, David opens the door, she makes her request, he replies yes, but only if he can come to the party. He does . . . *coup de foudre*. In a daze they find themselves wandering in the early hours on Hampstead Heath. And the letters began.

Rosheen Finnigan (née Francis)

INTRODUCTION

The three hundred surviving letters between Mary Moss and David Francis have a particular poignancy, not only because of the fraught period over which they were written, but because they are the record of a relationship that did not end in joyous reunion or loss of love, but was brutally terminated, almost in mid-sentence, by a death 7,000 miles away.

The letters are not sad, however. They are strikingly modern, bursting with life and energy and evoking a vivid picture of the mood and events of those times with a span and maturity that quite belie the youth of the authors. From London to Delhi via Skegness, Portsmouth, Scotland and Madagascar their correspondence flows, with wit and vitality, affection and serious thought.

Angel House is still there, a nondescript 1930s apartment block in north central London situated between the Angel, Islington, and Sadler's Wells theatre. Close to the busy junction of Pentonville Road and City Road, a major artery into the City, a single-bedroom flat will leave little change out of half a million pounds nowadays.

In 1938, when Mary Moss and David Francis met there and fell in love, its fifty-odd low-rent flats were occupied mainly by young people of a radical and artistic bent and refugees from across Europe. Mary, then aged twenty, described the fateful meeting (she went to borrow glasses from David and invited him to the party at a friend's neighbouring flat) in an unpublished novel.

That they were immediately drawn to each other was not sur-prising; they had so much in common: a love of films, books, music and art, and, crucially – like many idealistic young intellectuals of the time brought up amid the mass unemployment of the 1930s and haunted by the fear of fascism, the rise of Hitler and the drama of the Spanish Civil War – progressive political views which had led them independently to join the British Communist Party and become enthusiastic supporters of its newspaper, the *Daily Worker*.

Their backgrounds were very different, however. Mary was brought up in Notting Hill, one of two children of an Irish mother and an English father who met when he was serving in the British army in Ireland. They married in Dublin and left their young daughter behind with her grandmother when they moved to London in the 1920s to seek work and a home. It was the grandmother who imbued in the little girl the myths and legends of Ireland and a sense of Irishness that stayed with her always and is often reflected in the letters.

Mary was six when she rejoined her parents and younger brother, Tom, in London. When she was eleven she won a schol-arship to the Notting Hill and Ealing High School, where she flourished. With a quick, intuitive intelligence and an all-consuming love of literature and poetry, she could have gone to Oxford or Cambridge and indeed was among the first wave of recruits to Winston Churchill's newly established Bletchley Park in 1939, an experience she did not particularly enjoy. But the need to earn a living forestalled further education and it was a chal-lenging young woman – demanding, witty, romantically intense but emotionally volatile and given to moods and introspection – who left school to seek work in the uncertain job market of pre-Second World War London.

David, aged nineteen, came from a comfortable background, one of four brothers and a sister brought up in Bushey. His father was a director of Davidson, a well-known glass firm, his upbringing conventional apart from one factor, which was to have a fatal bearing on later events: his mother, Kit, a strong-minded woman, was a committed Christian Scientist who imparted the same principles to her family.

David was educated at Paxton Park, a private boarding school in Cambridgeshire with a Christian Science ethos, and was a good athlete and a keen, county-standard hockey player. A personable, self-confident young man of considerable charm, David made friends easily and was a good organiser. He left school and in 1937 moved to London, where he was articled to a firm of chartered accountants in the City, a job arranged by his father.

Whether by chance or choice, he moved to Angel House, on Pentonville Road. Only a stone's throw from the City, the Finsbury and Clerkenwell area was then a shabby district of down-at-heel Victorian and Georgian housing and print and watchmakers' workshops, with a long history of radicalism and leftist activism. Coffee houses and working men's clubs had flourished there in earlier times. Lenin had lived in nearby Percy Circus while in exile in 1905. There, he produced tracts from a building in Clerkenwell Green, which in the 1920s and 1930s became the venue for British Communist Party meetings and in 1933 the home of the Marx Memorial Library and Workers' School.

Not far away in Cayton Street, off City Road, was the office of the *Daily Worker*, the official newspaper of the Communist Party of Great Britain established eight years earlier and regarded by the Establishment and many others on both right and left as a deeply subversive pro-Soviet organ whose aim was to undermine the social fabric by sowing unrest and discord. However, the paper and the party attracted the same writers, artists, architects, musicians and playwrights of a radical bent who helped set up the workers' theatre movement, the Unity Theatre, and the left-wing Book Club, which were founded in 1936.

It was the *Daily Worker*, referred to as 'D.W.' in the letters, that brought David and Mary into each other's orbit. Since its inception in 1930, the paper had been boycotted by wholesalers, and its distribution was organised by a network of volunteers who collected editions at local stations and took them to newsagents and pitches or sold them outside factory gates and Tube stations. Such 'capitalist censorship and repression', particularly in the febrile political and economic climate of the 1930s, inevitably appealed to a certain kind of young, romantic idealist. Its attraction for Mary, especially given her Irish background, was straightforward. She was a natural revolutionary, not overly interested in the nuts and bolts, but always ready to man the barricades.

The letters do not explain the paradox of how an engaging product of a bourgeois, private-school background in a respectable City accountancy job embraced communism to the extent that he joined the party and indeed became the secretary of the Finsbury branch. However, they show an eminently decent young man with a strong social conscience, self-confident and mature beyond his years. While obviously reacting against his roots, he made no attempt to dig them up and the letters show his continuing, if somewhat exasperated, affection for his family, although he did distance himself later.

Whatever David's political views and his frustration with the British government's attempts to deal with Hitler and fascism, when war and the call to arms came he had no hesitation in volunteering for the Royal Navy. He had an impressive service record, becoming a valuable part of Louis Mountbatten's Combined Operations staff and playing an important planning role in the invasion of Vichy-held Madagascar in 1942, the first major combined-operations assault of the war. He was mentioned in despatches for his 'distinguished service' before his untimely death from smallpox in 1943 while serving as an intelligence officer in India. It was a disease against which he had no protection because his mother's Christian Science beliefs had led her to neglect having him vaccinated.

CHAPTER 1

—

'I have taken Auden to bed with me'

Wednesday.

Dear David,

My rucksack was missing this morning and so I have asked Hetty to lend you theirs. It is superior to mine, anyway.

About Friday ~ I will have to work until 7. at least, and so, could you book from 8 - 9.?

I woke up this morning thinking about you. Last night had some lovely moments to add to the pattern you are making for me. I shall remember you with the melodramatic cigarette, and an uncertain expression always, when more tangible moments are forgotten.

I love you very much. I am going to love you much more. It's wonderful, but it scares me, because I am frightened of you sometimes. You're such a <u>superior</u> swine. On this loving note I leave you.

Till Friday, as thou.

Mary

Please write me a note before Friday (P.T.O)

The letters divide into the several distinct periods of David and Mary's relationship, dominated ultimately by the war. Some are typed, some handwritten in a more leisurely fashion, others are dashed off hurriedly in pencil. Despite their number, they are not complete and there are gaps in which some imagination is needed to follow their story.

They begin in the late spring of 1938 after the first fateful meeting at Angel House. Mary was living with her parents in Elgin Crescent, Notting Hill Gate, and was leading a busy life as an independent young working woman in the capital.

The first letter opens with a debate about the loan of a rucksack and a reference to a close friend, Hetty Goodman, at whose party they met and who, with her husband, Dick, a writer, was to feature strongly in their lives.

The relationship flourishes with a refreshing and often amusing candour after the initial *coup de foudre*. 'I have written your name seven times on the blotting paper this morning. This is becoming serious!' writes Mary. And again, when David has gone off alone on a pre-planned holiday to Normandy, she teases him about 'landlord's daughters' and tartly reprimands him for always 'writing of double beds . . . Seeing you are not available, I have taken Auden to bed with me, T. S. Eliot is on the floor . . .'

In late July, Mary's unspecified secretarial job comes to an end. After some panic and talk of having to go to Paris to find work, she gets a typing job with Stratstone, the celebrated purveyor of luxury vehicles at 27 Pall Mall, which supplied Daimlers to King George V and where butlers served champagne to clients at a given time each morning. This was obviously not much to her taste. The agony doesn't last long. In the autumn she lands a clerical job at the Passport Control Office in Whitehall.

Not so many of David's letters from this period have survived. Those that have show an amused admiration for his volatile companion.

★

1938

Wednesday. [15 June 1938]

Dear David,

My rucksack was missing this morning and so I have asked Hetty to lend you theirs. It is superior to mine, anyway.

About Friday – I will have to work until 7 at least, and so, could you book from 8–9?

I woke up this morning thinking about you. Last night had some lovely moments to add to the pattern you are making for me. I shall remember you with the melodramatic cigarette, and an uncertain expression always, when more tangible moments are forgotten.

I love you very much. I am going to love you much more. It's wonderful, but it scares me, because I am frightened of you sometimes. You're such a <u>superior</u> swine.

On this loving note I leave you.

Till Friday, asthore*

Mary

Please write me a note before Friday.

---

* Irish for 'loved one'. 'Remember, asthore, you are not just from Ireland but from Connaught,' her grandmother would tell her – and she did.

Wednesday [22 June 1938, the day after Midsummer's Eve]

Dear David,

I won't be able to come tonight as I have to go home and do a million odd jobs that I have been neglecting – and then see Tich* and find out if his job has materialised, and when he goes, etc. I shall miss you very much – it's almost a physical ache – and please see me again soon. I can come to see you on Friday, about seven, and stay until you go to sell your late Daily's†; if this is O.K. leave me a note with Hetty or ring me up, but let me have some message as Friday seems an unconscionably long way off.

I have written your name seven times on the blotting paper this morning. This is becoming serious!

    Mary

Wednesday evening [22 June 1938]

Darling,

I missed you too, but the ache was not qualified by an 'almost'! Yes, do come on Friday; I'll redouble my efforts at the Branch meeting to get sufficient sellers without me.

The bus whisked you away so quickly yesterday that before I had time to say goodbye, you were gone. Thank you for contributing so much to a well-nigh perfect evening – perfect even without the so ardently desired consummation. A lovely evening, Mary, in which even the Midsummer fantasy seemed in the world of reality – or were we in the world of dreams? Maybe.

---

* A friend.
† David sold the *Daily Worker* at the Angel Tube station on Fridays.

Beware, lest I am accused of counter revolutionary activities by depleting the D.W. stationery supply!

Yes Friday seems an unconscionable time-a-coming. I want to see you again so much – now more than ever – if that were possible.

G'night, Dave

72 Elgin Crescent, W11
Thursday night (in bed) [14 July 1938]

Dearest David,

By return as ordered. Received your kind letter tonight after two on Tuesday. Lovely letters, almost as good as being with you, but why, oh why do you have to keep writing of double beds? I miss you enough as it is.

Thank you for thinking of me so constantly. I wanted you to have a lovely time so much, but was afraid that the incomparable freedom of rain and river, hills, trees, old castles and landlord's daughters, my lad, might dim the memory of Mary. But it seems my ghost stalks Normandy, and that is quite as it should be.

Your last letter sounds rather tipsy in parts. But still, you should be rather intoxicated at the moment – la belle France, jeunesse and BRANDY.

I am so sorry you haven't got the *Daily Worker* following you all over the place because on Wednesday I figured quite prominently on the book page. Did a review of the new batch of Penguins and it was branded 'by Mary Moss' in the centre of the page. Fame, success, cut . . .

Have just been to the flicks and seen the four Marx Brothers in 'Monkey Business' and the divine Hopkins in 'Trouble in

Paradise'.* Shades of Friday night, but no sequel . . . Deserted . . . jilted for la belle France and the landlord's lovely daughter.

This bed is about the same size as yours, but that is apropos of the conversation.

Eddie is terrifying me with stories of friends in Paris, and especially someone called Caroline who surpasses me as the sun does the glowworm and who is the sole justification for her sex. But I refuse to be outwardly impressed.

I am now going to [be] dramatic. David, forget the old days in Petrograd, have your fling, sow your wild oats, but remember, remember the fifth of November . . . etc . . . etc

Seeing you are not available, I have taken Auden to bed with me, T. S. Eliot is on the floor and Yeats is propping up Mrs Scribble. So I am not alone.

If you can read this you're a better man than I am Gunga Din. My hair keeps getting in my eyes. I think I'll shave it all off. I think I'll become a nun. Yes; on second thoughts, NO.

I can't rival 7 or 8 pages. You got me beat, pal, unless you would like a travelogue on London. But WAIT till I get to Ireland!

In three weeks' time we go hiking. And then, enfin seuls, I may be able to convey to you how much I love you; and how much, under this mundane and sometimes (often) crass exterior there beats a heart.

Goodnight my beloved David, and come back soon.

Mary

P.S. I hope I dream of you.
P.P.S. My second name is 'on the contrary'.
P.P.P.S. I love you inexhaustibly.

---

* A 1932 film by Ernst Lubitsch starring Miriam Hopkins and Herbert Marshall.

Thursday [21 July 1938]

Dear David,

I am writing to you today because there is not much more time left to write to you for no reason at all, except to establish a sort of makeshift contact.

I have had a change of heart about Sunday; of course I should love to come on a ramble, organised or otherwise as long as you go. I was in a most objectionable snooty mood last night. I even exaggerated my opinion of the Garden of Allah* (though it was a lousy film). You know though, the sort of mood in which the very word 'ramble' is a cue for affectionate contempt. Today I am not so cock-a-hoop, and should like very much to come with you if it is not too late to change my mind.

This sort of thing is why it would be so marvellous to be together, just so that when one (or both) of us is unbearable, the other needn't bear him (or her) just because it is Wednesday, and no more meetings until Saturday. And again, when that strange passion for each other comes over us, we need only reach out for the other, instead of biting the pillow case and being bad tempered (my symptoms). For instance, last night the bus tore me away from you, just when, for me anyway, it began to be terribly important to be with you. The feeling lasted, and this morning I am languid with desire for you, but no David until tomorrow lunch for a crowded, hungry hour, and then, maybe, Saturday.

Still nitchevo,† tomorrow we eat. Until 1.15, outside the Charing X.

Yours, very much yours,
Mary

---

* A David Selznick film from 1936 starring Marlene Dietrich and Charles Boyer.

† A Russian term with the approximate meaning 'it's too bad'.

[Kensington]
August 8

Dear David,

Am feeling miserable, so committing the unpardonable sin of piling it onto you.* Nothing has developed yet, and I hate NOTHING. On an impulse this afternoon I asked Jeff if there was anything in Paris and he said he would see what he can do, BUT I DON'T WANT TO GO TO PARIS. Please don't let me go to Paris. Use everything you have to stop me, if the chance comes, which it won't, I hope.

Hetty has lent her flat to Phil and Kate for the fortnight she is away, so I can't borrow it. That makes things difficult because I think it might be hellishly inconvenient for you to have me there such a long time. WHAT WILL THE NEIGHBOURS SAY! Apart from that, seriously I am worried about the next fortnight. Debating about whether to tell them at home or become one of Helen's lodgers for the time. Is this possible? Will Eddie be away? Oh don't bother to read this letter. It is all so much tripe. Stop being sorry for yourself, you spineless beetle (that's myself I'm talking to, not you).

With lots of love anyway,
Mary

---

* Mary has lost her job.

9

[Notting Hill]
Tuesday evening [9 August 1938]

Darling David,

Just a hurried note to thank you for your dear letter.
I will use it as a weapon to poke old man depression right in
the eye.

Anyway, why should I be depressed? You are in the world, so
it must be a lovely and sweet place.

I will call tomorrow about 8 and tell you a lurid tale of
sabotage in high places, of party discipline and other
developments.

Dorothy, dear woman, has also got the sack but doesn't know
it yet, mon frere,* mon semblable.

I am listening in to the Haydn–Mozart concert, and the cat
has got his tail on this letter.

Highly irrelevant to main subject, but typical of what?
Oh shut up.
Mary

P.S. Forgot to mention above, but I love you (oh so much)

72 Elgin Crescent, W.11.
[16 August 1938]

My darling beloved David,

Just received your wire and rung up Queenie. She's not
effusive, but hopeful.

---

* frere: properly 'frère', but readers will notice throughout that both Mary
and David tend to omit accents from foreign phrases.

Anyway, this cancelled my first letter to you. Decided under no circumstances to go to Paris. Something is sure to break for me in London, and I know now, by the relief I felt in getting the wire that I don't want to go. I feel it is too hole in the corner, rushed and not worth all that I would have to leave behind (meaning you). So I will try Unity* tomorrow, and if that fails, something else will turn up.

See you tomorrow at the Honey Dew and I will tell you all.

With love from Mary

P.S. Just in the thick of a violent row with my father and I think I will go out and post this letter to get out of it.

(Stratstone, Daimler agents
27 Pall Mall, SW1)
[22 August 1938]

Dearest David,

This day is nearly over, and thank god, thank god.† This afternoon I have been delivering Daimlers (by letter) and I feel like a gargantuan midwife, or something. It is still pretty bloody. The toothy female gets under my skin, and she is all I have to look at, or to talk to, and when she talks it is refained cockney, s'help me, so I don't talk much.

Thank god for you, and again I say amen.

---

* The Unity Theatre, a left-wing theatre club founded in 1936, based in King's Cross and aiming to bring social and political issues to the working classes using satire and agitprop theatrical techniques to highlight unemployment, hunger marches, and the perceived rise of fascism in Britain and Nazism in Germany.

† Mary has got a temporary typing job with Stratstone, a luxury car specialist in Pall Mall, and is hating it and her new workmates.

See you tomorrow at the Honeydew, appropriate name.

Darling, darling David, I love you very much, despatch case and all.

Mary

P.S. I have written to Jeff to say I am coming. Oh Christ!

[Thursday, autumn, 1938]

Dear David,

I must write to you this morning. I dreamt about primroses last night and when I woke up it was autumn. Bah. I am feeling very Celtic today, fey and foreboding and nostalgic for something or somebody. Sehnsucht or love, or maybe both. Perhaps I am hearing my cosmos call. Anyway I started knitting last night, so that's a bad sign.

I received a letter from Guinness enclosing a further form to be filled and saying that they would interview me early next week. Concentration-campish form threatening a medical exam, but I suppose I better send it in.

There is a wraithish mist hanging around the trees at the back of Pall Mall like a shroud. I have just been interrupted to type two purchase agreements and five letters, the spell is broken, the dream perished.

Anyway, as Mr Baldwin nearly said in 1936, 'The world is in a state of chassis'. I wish I were a Daimler, beautiful and expensive and respected. I wish I were a peasant in Connemara, living on seaweed and potatoes in a deep dank bog. I wish you were here looking at me with those disconcerting dappled eyes. Dear odd-eyes, cod eyes. No, sorry.

I wish sometimes that I might receive a letter in that so

distinguished handwriting, but that is beyond the dreams of avarice I suppose.

I love you very very much and am counting the minutes until I see you on Friday.

Till then dear David, goodbye.

Mary

52 Angel House, N.1
Monday evening [12 September 1938]

Mary darling,

Have you still got a voice after the Sunday night 'croon' session! Such a lovely day. Let's have days like that often – I've got the tickets for the Empress Stadium* on Sunday and Donald has consented to come, even though I did raise him from his bed this evening! I think he's quite eager to meet you after my lengthy descriptions and eulogies.

Tomorrow I'll go along to the Phoenix and getta da seats for the 'White Guard'.† Let's meet for lunch on Wednesday or Thursday at Tottenham Court Road 1.15? Saturday seems far far away, so do try to drag your wintered bones to the environs of St Giles Circus – I'm free after lunch on Saturday, so if you're not otherwise engaged, we could go for a walk somewhere.

Today I was paid – today I'm nearly broke! However, here's thirty shillings, which will buy you 2 and ⅔ bottles of whisky or

---

* The Empress Stadium at Earls Court was the venue for a rally in support of the 15th Congress of the Communist Party of Great Britain on 18 September 1938. The Congress itself was held in Birmingham.
† A play from 1926 by Mikhail Bulgakov about a group of ill-fated Tsarist sympathisers caught up in the Russian Civil War in Kiev in 1918. Produced at the Phoenix Theatre, Charing Cross Road, in the autumn of 1938.

that new hat you cast envious eyes on when you last passed Lafayette!* Thanks a lot.

Suddenly, without a word of warning, 11.55 so I must rush and catch the post, so that you can receive this inadequate missive in the morning, when you will be awakened by the dulcet tones of your brother's voice rising above the plaintive trill of a father-in-the-bath, which implies that you are scarcely the epitome of energy, and anyway, the legitimacy of your birth is severely to be questioned. Quick I must run –

Goodnight, dear Mary
please write
with all my love
David

---

* The French department store Galeries Lafayette had a branch in Regent Street. It closed in the 1970s.

CHAPTER 2

A Job in Whitehall

Thursday.

Dear David,

Just writing to say that you needn't wait until you
are 21 to be "tremendous!". You are now. Thank you very
much for being you, and don't ever change. Zee.

I hereby promise never again to be sullen about nothing,
to be unreasonable, unless I have to. And I will see you
on Friday night, and mend your supper and cook your
socks.

O.K.

Mary

Throughout the late summer and autumn of 1938 the couple's romance was becoming more intense and taking control of both their lives. A sexual candour exists between them which may come as a surprise to modern audiences brought up on the irritating nonsense that sex was invented in 1963. Mary was quickly spending weekends at Angel House. There is a pregnancy scare and a constant fencing over whether she should move in permanently with David without the benefit of marriage, despite the fact that, as modern young progressives, they like to give the impression of not caring much for the institution.

Mary claims she would love to move in, but uses her mother's distress at the prospect to dampen David's eagerness. David was under the age of twenty-one and therefore needed parental consent, which he obviously did not think he would get.

There was a delicious irony in Mary's new job. The Passport Control Office was at the heart of Britain's Secret Service and foreign-intelligence operations. In the 1920s the Secret Intelligence Service (SIS), which later became MI6, set up a close operational relationship with the Diplomat Service in order to provide its overseas agents with some sort of cover and diplomatic immunity. The post of Passport Control Officer was created at British embassies and at the centre of this web of international intelligence was the Passport Control Office, to which Mary had now been unwittingly recruited.

One of the major preoccupations of the SIS during the inter-war years had been the rise of Soviet communism. Many of the brightest and best young people were out of sympathy with their own society. But few followed Burgess, Maclean and Philby to the extent of betraying their country.

1938 ends with a long, idyllic weekend together at Angel House because Christmas Day fell on a Sunday.

★

Friday afternoon [24 September 1938]

Dear David,

I suppose you will be expecting a note from me, giving the latest bulletin. Unfortunately thumbs still point down. I have had a very strange day today. Last night I drank (in the depths of desperation) a colossal draught of quinine which this morning had completely taken away my sense of sound and space.

I have felt like Alice in Wonderland (but not quite so) all day, very muffled and remote, rather as if everybody I had ever known had died in the night. I could hear individual sounds, but the background of noise that is always present had completely gone. Weird! and very depressing. I have felt small and old – hundreds of years old – all day, revisiting a world I once had known and loved, but which now had no use for me, or I dream I have been on a demonstration with triumphal chariots and chained Gaulish giants, which suddenly turned itself into funeral carts trundling up Pentonville Rd, to be revealed with the dawn as the borough refuse vans. In short, I have had a nightmare all day, and living an ordinary working day on the surface.

(And still God gives no sign.)

Again, the demonstration, where you shout 'Chamberlain

must go' until you are hoarse and almost exultant. Surely he will go. Perhaps he has gone. Oh yeah! From which you will see what kind of a day I have had today. The suffocating effect (on my ears) has almost worn away, but the depression, thank God, is always with us.

Maybe tomorrow will be another day and not a drawn out nightmare. If so, I will send you a wire. If not – but if we can just hope, we need not then despair, as some blasted poet might once have said. Anyway, Sunday will still be Sunday, as we have arranged, if this is still O.K. by you, and I will meet you at Victoria at 10.15.

I will try not to blind, deafen or maim myself in any way by then, for both our sakes.

I hope this letter does not make you anxious. It's my very selfish and only way of expressing myself and getting myself out of my system (and if not to you, then to whom?).

And do not worry about anything else either, we'll fix the bastard!

I feel better already.

With all my love always, always, in a world of which I sometimes grow afraid and tired.

> Your extremely illogical, hysterical, fantastical, ungrammatical
> but ever loving
> Mary

P.T.O. I am going on writing.

N.B. This section completely off the point and needn't be read unless you feel like it.

It has been a beautiful day, but my favourite sonnet has always been

> 'Why dids't thou promise such a beauteous day
> And make me travel forth without my cloak

To let dull clouds o'ertake me on my way
And hide thy bravery in their rotten smoke"*

and I am afraid that the rotten smoke of fear and mistakes and other things might hide the bravery of the feeling I have for you. Because it is a lovely thing really, and I mean to concentrate on keeping it.

I disappoint you often, I know. I am not really the Mary who 'bounced' into your kitchen and borrowed your cups. That's me on holidays and birthdays, and also the Mary who irks you with her 'immaturity'.

But underneath there is a person who a long time ago wrote herself a Melancholy of Living (she was very young) and began with de la Mare's advice 'Look thy last on all things lovely every hour' (which is good advice)

quoted arrogantly

'Mistress of herself, though China fall'†

and ended with

'I have been long in coming, slow to move
I have been shabbiness, but I keep
Quick, quick the sharp eye
The heart's song and the clear cry.'

and that's Mary as she would like to be.

I shall despise myself for being 'soft' and writing this

---

* Shakespeare's love poem Sonnet 34 (slightly misquoted).
† A quotation from Alexander Pope's Epistle II, 'To a Lady: Of the Characters of Women'.

tomorrow, but tonight I am fey and feel perhaps I may never see you again, who I love more than anybody I have ever yet known.

I am crying large tears onto this letter, and I don't know why, except that this is the worst of possible worlds to be born into if you are young and sentimental, and if you are in love with somebody who might next week be given a gun and the death of a hero.

You have probably given up reading this a long time ago, but once I start really going with a pen (this is the first real pen and ink letter I have ever written to you) it is hard for me to stop the full spate and be impotent.

Oh David, why couldn't I have met you tonight. I might have been able to force you to see me as I want you to know me, not cynical and crass and over-occupied with trivialities as I must often seem, but honest and uncompromising. You once said that Brahms' Fourth was mine, but you took it away from me.

If something fierce and final happened and we didn't meet again, I wonder how you would remember me (because one thing I am certain, you wouldn't forget me easily). I remember you first standing on the hill on the last day of May, looking like a faun in a mackintosh. And then in the light of your gas fire with the L'Apres Midi [sic] d'un Faune weaving your own atmosphere around you.

And most of all, with your own drowned look, which I love most of all, being pagan and Celtic.

Have just received your letter. Can't bear to write any more. Oh David, I am so sorry that you are worrying about the psychological effect, because you are the one who is going to be affected. I love you enough to forget. But you . . .

[S.W.1]
Thursday [20 October 1938]

My beloved David,

This is to supplement and complement for the letter I didn't send yesterday. The theme of that letter was that I love you far too much. Je t'aime tant, je t'aime trop. Far too much anyway to be really happy or interested when you are not there, and far too much to be really bored or wretched while you are within thinking distance. And far, far too much to be free for a moment from your voice, your face and your touch. Pauvre singe. A poem has been following me about all day, like your shadow:-

> Oh westron wind, when wilt thou blow
> That the small rains down may rain,
> Christ! That my love were in my arms
> And I in my bed again.*

No wonder I can't type accurately today. Je t'aime trop. I hate fog. The fog that rubs its back against the window pane, ugh. I hate the winter altogether. The days are so short and the sun so rare, and there is something ominous and alien in the air, anywhere for me there is. I wish I could hibernate, be a dormouse or a squirrel, and sleep until the spring liberated me once more. I hate trees without any leaves, black against a sullen sky. They are stark and uncompromising and infinitely poignant, like people stripped of all fantasy and pretence, who though admirable, are nevertheless embarrassing. Anyway

---

* Old English song of anonymous provenance, whose first written appearance is in a Tudor manuscript probably owned by a musician in the court of Henry VIII.

November (horrors), December, January, February, March, and then the blessed April when the westron wind will blow again, and my love will be in my arms.

Writing letters to the beloved one at a moment of acute tenderness is a poor substitute for personal contact, but it has its own peculiar bliss. Anyway my treacherous fingertips keep curling, as if to stroke your hair.

Regarding Sunday, if there is no rain and no horrible menacing fog, please, please let us go out early and get the last of the summer, before everything turns to leaf mould and decay:-

Cue for song.

> Les sanglots longs
> Des violons
> De L'Automne,
> Blessent mon coeur
> D'un langeur*
> Monotone.†

Poor David, how boring to be afflicted with a frustrated poet, especially one stuffed with such indigestible quotations. I will go and live by myself on an Irish mountain, and add another wraith to the Celtic twilight. Goodbye, world and the light of the world. Today's too late. The wise died yesterday.

I think I had better stop this letter. I feel the old urge sweeping up, and YOU MUST NEVER DISCOVER HOW CRAZY I REALLY AM. I hope I find a letter from you this evening or tomorrow morning as a talisman against cold and damp and the creeping sinister fog.

---

* D'un langeur: properly 'D'une langueur'.
† From Paul Verlaine's 'Chanson d'automne' (1866).

Fare thee well, thou best and dearest,
Fare thee well thou first and rarest,
no more room on the paper.[*]

MARY

Heaven
Tuesday evening [October 1938]

Hullo darling,

Thanks a million for your much appreciated letter. Maybe when I'm as old as you are I shall be able to express myself adequately; somehow you have the ability to express yourself what I feel too, but am unable to convey to you – that's why I love your letters.

Tonight I have been working, playing the gramophone and thinking of you, so you see I've been busy! But thinking of you is such a poor substitute for being with you, being able to touch you and caress you: do you think parting such a sweet sorrow? I doubt it, because when you go you leave a sort of vacuum where Mary ought to be, but isn't. I hate being away from you too – darling, do come and live here soon so's we can see more of each other every day and all day. It seems so crazy that you should have to go miles away home on evenings when we could be happy together. It is the only solution to the problem as far as I can see.

Will you be able to manage the whole of the week-end? Do try. It would be lovely.

David

---

[*] From Robert Burns's 'Ae Fond Kiss', slightly misquoted and with Mary's own conclusion.

P.S. This isn't the letter I want to write to you, but I am feeling rather unexpressive at the moment. Please imagine the most comforting, loving letter that could be written in the place of this meagre little note, because that's what I would wish.

Monday [probably late on 24 October 1938]

My darling,

It is now 5.10 on Monday night – nearly the hour of release and one day nearer to seeing you again. I have been feeling very subdued and near-melancholy today, feeling that you were a long way away and everything was long ago and out of time. Probably a reaction to the exciting and lovely weekend. Do you remember in our darkest and most despairing moments we spoke of bringing our intercourse to a work of art? Well it progresses. I wish that we could have the same easy and intimate mental coition, entering into each other's minds and finding stimulation and ultimate peace, but I suppose this is the Utopia of personal relationships – the Soviet Union of love. I am not going to write any more today. I am going home to read – Milton, I think. I wish I could come and play your gramophone. Brahms and Bach and those monk things – graduals.

Tuesday morning

Good morning David, I hope you are well and not late for work. I wish we were meeting for lunch today. I have still got those old-man Hamlet blues and am missing you so much. Oh that this too too solid flesh might fade, melt and resolve itself into a dew, or that the Almighty had not fixed his canon against self-slaughter! Eheu fugaces, postume, postume labuntur anni[*] (now I'm showing off).

By the way, tomorrow on the Forum[†] is still Flashbacks but also Corinne Luchaire[‡] in 'Conflit'.[§] Let's go. I'll call for you about 6.30 p.m.?

I hope I hear from you today, but I suppose I will have to wait until the morning. Red letter day tomorrow – I receive your letter and I see you again. No more for the present.

Later in the day

Afternoon again, and soon to go home. I hate this beastly office. I am driven to marking off quarter hours on my blotting paper.

I went to the National Gallery this lunchtime. They have a special Spanish exhibition with some superb El Greco's: (Gethsemane, The Resurrection, Holy Family) and some Goyas, Velasquez and Murillos. What artists (barring the last, which I detest), what a country, what a fate. There is going to be an exhibition of French cartoons soon, which we must go and see.

Jill is coming over to see me tonight, and Mary Read I think, so we shall all gather in my bedroom and smoke cigarettes and I

---

[*] Alas, Postumas, Postumas, the fleeting years are slipping by'. Horace Ode 2, 14.

[†] Cinema in the Hungerford Arches under Charing Cross station. Victorian home of the Charing Cross Music Hall. Turned into a fire station at the outbreak of war and continued as the Players' Theatre after the war.

[‡] Star of French cinema on the eve of the Second World War described by Mary Pickford as 'the new Garbo'. Ironically, considering David and Mary's enthusiasm for her, she became closely linked to the occupying Nazis. Her father, a journalist and politician, supported the Vichy regime and was executed in 1946. She was sentenced to ten years' 'dégradation nationale' and died of tuberculosis in 1950, aged only twenty-eight.

[§] A French film from 1938 directed by Léonide Moguy.

will give them all my accumulated mending to do while we talk. A female paradise.

See you tomorrow David, alanna.

Slan leak, acushla*

Mary

Monday [November 1938]

My own darling David,

Hasn't it been a nice day today, between the rain and the miserable office hours. I woke up this morning with the feeling that you were there beside me and by exerting my imagination somewhat was able to keep up that dear delusion until rudely yanked out of bed. So the day began well.

I hope we always wake up wide-eyed and smiling at each other.

You looked so tired last night, and the weight of the branch on your shoulders. Please look after yourself and don't overwork. We'll have to fix something pretty quick so that we can look after each other – me after your diet, shirts, etc, and you after my education – political and moral, which seems to be going through a very sterile time.

Hurry up and be twenty-one.† Damn and blast you for not being born before I was. Hurry up Wednesday and then we can be together again. I will bring some food with me and then we can cook our supper. I feel very impatient today. I am feeling energetic and vital and bursting out of my shell, and nothing to express all this wonderful tireless feeling except by pounding a

---

* Irish endearments.

† At twenty-one David can marry without parental consent.

stupid and aimless typewriter, frowning at the ubiquitous and iniquitous Cotton and sticking pins in Paymaster (theoretical pins).

I like rain like today's. It makes me want to go to Brighton with you and dance naked on the downs.

Please write soon and love me always and forget that I am ever petulant and selfish, because really I would go to the ends of the earth for you; in sackcloth and on my knees (and my tongue in my cheek?) No.

    With all my love,
      Mary

9-11-38
Le Journal de David

BROKEN-HEARTS-CORNER
Scene: The Passport Office
    Pay occupying room off-stage.
    On stage, two typists, Cissie and Fatima.
    Time 2.55 p.m.

Pay (shouting): Is Moss back yet?
Typists (simultaneously): No, sir.

Scene: Same.
    Time 3.0 p.m.
Pay (shouting apprehensively): So, Moss back yet? Where's the girl got to?
Fatima: Don't know, sir.
Pay: Expectin' the chief down. Got to get some information from her. Where the hell's she got to?

Scene: Same.

    Time 3.5 p.m.

Pay (angrily): Ain't that girl back yet? Good God! What am I going to tell the chief? She's got that information. Can't do without her. (Paces up and down). What am I going to do? He's coming at quarter past.

Cissie: Never mind sir, she'll be here soon – (aside) the bitch.

Pay: Soon. Soon's no good. My whole career's at stake. What am I going to tell the chief? God, expect Halifax will kick up hell if I don't give the chief the stuff.

Scene: Same.

    Time 3.10 p.m.

Pay (tearfully): Isn't she back yet? Oh! Oh! I'll get the sack in 5 minutes. No more 160 ten shilling notes every month. Please God, send Moss back.

Scene: Same.

    Time 3.13 p.m.

Pay (convulsively): No more 160 ten shilling notes. Can't give him what he wanted all because there's no Moss. Can't do it. Can't do it.

    A step is heard outside the door. Enter Mary Moss apologetically.

Moss: I'm sorry, sir – the Lord Mayor's –

Pay: Quiet! (Another step is heard). Quick, before he comes – tell me, what does 'le chemin le plus court est souvent le plus long' mean?

    CURTAIN!

Le journal de David – 9-11-38

STOP PRESS   SPECIAL

    Hetty and Dick were married today ——

When interviewed by our Staff Reporter, Hetty appeared a little uneasy about future prospects and was inclined to regard the marriage as an expensive farce. 'Tell Mary,' she said wearily, 'that I remain a respectable woman.' When asked to explain the import of 'expensive farce', she revealed that it had been necessary to procure a certificate of divorce which 'knocked them back' £2-5-0. 'A bloody waste,' were the rather unorthodox but strangely apt words which this militant used to describe the affair. Nevertheless, despite the uneasiness on the part of Hetty, Dick seemed very happy.

STOP STOP PRESS: Hetty, Dick, Phil and Kate dining at the Indian restaurant Wednesday evening.

Hullo darling, just a note to say a million times that I love you dearly, and that I want to see you tomorrow, so do try and come. Hope you weren't late today. Do try and come for the whole week-end, it would be so lovely.

    Goodnight dear Mary and sleep well,

      Your David

Thursday [Autumn of 1938]

Dear David,

Just writing to say that you needn't wait until you are 21 to be 'tremendous'. You are <u>now</u>. Thank you very much for being you, and don't ever change. Zee.

I hereby promise never again to be sullen about nothing, to be unreasonable, unless I have to. And I will see you on Friday night, and mend your supper and cook your socks.

    O.K.

      Mary

72 Elgin Crescent
Ladbroke Grove W11
[Autumn of 1938]

My own darling,

I did not sleep very much last night thinking about us, and
the complications that arise out of simply being in love. When I
did sleep I had a nightmare – because I dreamt that you had
stopped loving me and left me. I woke up very, very much
relieved to find that it was just a dream; terribly much in love
with you and absolutely certain that if the dream had been true I
would die. It is not a question of being happy with you and
unhappy away, it's just not being able to live without you, which
simplifies matters I suppose and makes it sheer cowardice and
lack of conviction that stops me from coming to you. But I have
decided not to be such a craven, and on the first reasonable
opportunity I will talk to my mother about leaving home, etc.
Time's chariot is roaring pretty loudly at our backs and this
worries me about as much as it haunts you.

I know I let myself down with you sometimes pretty badly
and you must think that I am being fearfully petulant and
selfish, but honestly I do exaggerate my worst faults in front of
you, and am not quite so small and miserable as I may seem to
be. I was absolutely honest last night when I said that party work
could never make any difference in our relations and take no
notice when I become all Trotskyite and disruptive – it's only a
guilty conscience for a lazy party life, which I am anxious to
activise once again. I could not love you so much if you weren't
in the party (well, I am not quite sure about that, but I could not
admire you so much if you didn't work hard for the party). And
I do admire you tremendously compared with everyone else I
know, and some of them are wonderful in my opinion, and you
are the best and the grandest, and I tremble with strange dread

when I consider how much chance contributed to our meeting, and how colourless and uninspired life would be for the whole time I live if I had never met you. I love you so much that I would die without you, so living with you should be quite an easy step to take if you are quite sure that this would make you happy. I want to be happy myself, but it is far, far more important to me that you should be happy, and through me, so I must really love you very much. I hope that you get this letter by this evening so that you go to bed knowing that in spite of my contrariness, I do love you to the exclusion of everything and everyone. I am coming up to Angel House tomorrow with Jill, so that she can make official farewell to Hetty, so I may see you.

With that dear hope I say goodbye for the present, and I send you all my love.

Yours to a cinder
Mary

If you have time please write to me

[London S.W.1]
Monday morning [12 December 1938]

Darling beloved David,

This is to wish you all the luck in the world and the most reasonable and inoffensive questions.* I want you to pass so fervently, because I don't believe there is anything that you can't do, given a fair chance of course. So go in and win!

---

* David is obviously taking accountancy exams.

Tonight I am going to the Cecile Booysen Clinic* to have another try flashing my wedding ring in the face of all suspicion. So tomorrow we can compare notes, in triumph I hope, but if not at least together.

I enjoyed last night so much. That short walk from the cinema to the Corner House (outposts of romance) was ecstasy. I have never been so much in love before as at that moment, and never, never will ever love anyone so much. I am incapable at the moment of writing coherently so I will once again wish you success and I send you all my love.

Yours ever,
Mary

Wednesday [28 December 1938]

My darling,

It is now five o'clock, and Pay has just departed, or rather slunk home, leaving me the office to myself for one hour. I am just having a furtive cigarette, and afterwards am going to sleep until it's time to lock up. It hasn't been too bad today, plenty of fiddling little jobs to do, and a lazy Pay. I went home at lunch time and the place hasn't gone on fire or anything interesting. Tom has been here before me, but I have not seen him, or heard any news of the missing case. I hated the place, it looked so unfestive and drab, and alien to me. The only possible home for

---

* Cecile Booysen (1893–1937) was a South African-born doctor and birth-control pioneer who was keenly interested in women's welfare and social and political work. She founded the Medical Peace campaign. In 1936 she set up a voluntary birth-control clinic in Goswell Road, Finsbury, known as the Goswell Women's Welfare Centre. Only married women would be eligible for contraceptive advice and products, hence Mary evidently wearing a bogus wedding ring, although they were not to marry until several months later.

me is with you, wherever it may be. There were lots of cards and letters waiting for me, and a lovely book of poetry by Francois Villon (in French unfortunately).

It is quite bearable here without the obnoxious Cotton, and I have got the electric fire full on, and all the windows open. I hope you got up at a respectable hour this morning and that you are neither late for work, nor late for lunch with me tomorrow. How I miss you! I don't think I ought to see you again so that I can recover from this demoralising and un-self sufficient, but so pressing need. Please always love me, and be as 'gentle and firm' as you have been this wonderful weekend. I needn't tell you that I am just bats about you. *A une heure et quart demain, mon plus cher de tous cheris* (?)

votre genuflecting devotee

MARY

P.S. My dress has kept Christmas and your arms around me all day. I enclose a strand of silver just pulled neurotically from the belt.

1939

72 Elgin Crescent, W11

20.1.39

My dearest David,

I have had an impulse all day to ring you up and say 'Hello', but didn't know your Harlesden* number. Anyway, hello, now and how are you? I hope your cold has completely disappeared

---

* David at this stage in his accountancy training was probably being sent out from his City office to get experience in other offices around London.

and may all your troubles be little ones (as long as they are mine).

I went to Sadler's Wells last night and had an interesting, if mixed, evening. I felt quite all right until the first ballet – Harlequin in the Street – had started and was then attacked by the most violent toothache I have ever experienced. The pain was so intense that it was interesting; and I just sat through this rather pleasant comedy with my eyes shut tight, mouth wide open, drooling into my handkerchief and analysed the shades of agony that I was undergoing.

The first interval was distinguished by my standing in the bar with both eyes shut and a search by my companions for non-existing aspirin. Very effective, this latter. The second – Horoscope – was ready to commence and my tooth still vibrated like an overcharged electric wire. I decided that a tooth was a very small affair and that I was going to open my eyes during this piece. And I am awfully glad I did because I enjoyed it tremendously. Have you seen 'Horoscope'. It's tremendously vital and gymnastic, with a really masculine dancer in the main part. Really I think the sensualism of this was given a piquancy by the background of toothache. Maybe not. Anyway the male dancer reminded me so strongly of you that I actually felt the contacts between him and the woman dancer personally and delightfully. After that my toothache was very unimportant, and Les Patineurs came to delight an untortured Mary; to delight so much that I immediately agreed to go to the skating rink next week.

Today, I went for a walk in the lunch hour through the Green Park into Leicester Square, in a benificent mood, and bought you a present (only hypothetically I am afraid). You will never see your present as it is only on exhibition in this shop, but it really is lovely, and you are a very lucky man. It's a picture of people dancing, and when you really look into it, it is made of silk and thread instead of paint. But very, very lovely and exciting, and I give it to you, because it is the nicest thing I have seen today.

Play a good game of hockey tomorrow, and in the evening return to your loving and anticipating

Mary

P.S. I have missed you like HELL

12 Elgin Crescent
[12 February 1939]

Dear David,

Missing you a lot this morning, and hating the circumstances that make the continuity of life break up on Sunday evenings; I spoke to my mother this morning about your flat and the furniture etc, and she seems quite aware that the general idea of buying it was mutual. She seems to have accepted the fact that quite soon I will be leaving home, but she thinks it will be as a married and self-assured person.

This business is troubling me a bit. I know one direct consequence of my coming to live with you will be friction between my mother and father. He is as narrow as English Midland people can be, and anyway is prejudiced in my direction. Everything I do that isn't successful, or in his opinion correct, he attacks, and I can just imagine his attitude in this case. It will be my mother who will suffer, not I, and this seems very selfish and unnecessary – even stupid.

I wish that you were not so set against marriage. I agree with you that it is necessary to really live with a person before you really know them, but to all intents and purposes we have been living together (under difficulties I admit) for some weeks (or

weekends) and we do know now that we are physically suited.
Thank God.

To my mind, there is no reason at all why we shouldn't
marry if we are prepared to live together. It is economically
possible; we have a flat; we are very much in love and we have
tested ourselves in many ways for the ordeal. It could be, and
would be, no more binding or cramping than any other
relationship between us. I know the awful snag that it is so
bourgeois, and has such an atmosphere of irrecoverability about
it. This scares me as much as it must do you, but it is just as
cowardly to be influenced by people like Eddie, for example, as
by the staid and narrow principles of your parents. Even if we
had to wait much longer for you to overcome your prejudice
against marriage, I feel that it would be worth it, because
knowing myself, I am sure that I would be happier, if taking the
plunge, I got right into the deep end.

Please don't take this letter as a hard and fast statement of my
point of view, but it is an expression of an argument I have
wanted to put forward and haven't quite worked out yet. For
Christ's sake don't be put off, or influenced by it in any way, but
living together would be so lovely, no matter how we were
related, but I want it to happen quickly and with no stupid or
unnecessary repercussions. Let's meet for lunch as arranged
tomorrow 1.15 at the Temple.

Goodbye darling until then,
    Yours ever,
        Mary

CHAPTER 3

A Move to Bletchley Park

Tuesday.

My darling David,

        Just to let you know I am back in harness
Stands B--------- where it did? alas, poor country. Says
Macduff. I survived yesterday, which being the day after
my leave is the coldest, most all-hope-abandoned day of the
week. Now the back of the week is broken and Friday advances.
Brighton appears to be the promised land. Where are we
going to stay? At the "Glamourous" or "Amorous" or what?
How are you feeling. I hope well-fed at least.

        I am going to have my hair cut tomorrow,
and play badminton in the evening, so that is something to
look forward to. I hope your skill is incorporated in your
racket, and so I will shine as a champion. Rise and shine,
wakey, wakey, wakey, etc. I have tried it out to good effect
on some of the people here. Some have never been to sea, so
don't recognise "All hands to cocoa."

        Forgive the staccato quality of this letter.
I am feeling slightly mad today , by way of a change, and
so it shows. But if my sanity fluctuates, never my love for
you, my own Dave.

                        Your own Mary

The looming war makes its first big intrusion into their lives through Mary's new job. Shortly after she joins the Passport Control Office it is moved in early 1939 from Whitehall to the just opened Bletchley Park, in Buckinghamshire, the intelligence hub for the country's war effort and where the crucial Enigma code-cracking programme was developed. Mary, separated from the two things she loved most, David and London, went with it, but not happily.

★

[Undated, but February 1939]

My darling,

I'm very much here, surrounded by typewriters, ledgers and the other symbols of servitude, missing you like mad and positive that I cannot live through this.

It's a lovely old manor house, surrounded by park, with a maze and tennis and badminton courts. We certainly do ourselves proud, we Government officials. But it's all so terribly far way from anything that I consider important, and so overpopulated with quacking female and pompous male, that I can hardly breathe.

We were met by a car and given a very good lunch (oh boy,

did I need it – no supper – no breakfast). I have heard that baths are considered extras!

Please take care of yourself for my sake, and if you borrow any money, keep it for yourself. I probably will be able to manage. But write soon to me as I miss you, and am going to miss you most agonisingly.

Please write and tell me how you are and love me an awful lot. I am not sure about the weekend yet, but can probably manage Aylesbury on Saturday, if even for the day.

Love to the flat, and to the view and to Griselda,* and to you.

 With all my love,

  Mary

Thursday [February 1939]

My darling David,

You didn't write to me! I have been waiting ever since I arrived for the promised letter, but I was always an optimist. Anyway, write soon to Miss Mary Moss, Passport Control Dept., Foreign Office. S.W.1.

I have got the weekend off, circumstances permitting, and so if you can manage Aylesbury, we will meet there.

We are billeted in a superb hotel – marvellous service and such food – roast chicken, hams, grapefruit, coffee, cream galore, and all we do there is eat. I shall get as fat as a pig.

There is a most objectionable fly in the ointment – an intensely neo-Nazi young man, billeted in the same hotel, who is giving me a bad time, but more about him when I see you.

The weather is perfect and the most difficult thing to do is to

---

* David's beloved gramophone.

work. If only you were here I should think the Government was an excellent host.

It is difficult to write to you as these letters go,* so I will tell you everything when I see you. But please write to me before then.

If you come to Aylesbury will you please bring my tennis racket [sic] with you. I dreamt about you last night. For heaven's sake look after yourself and keep well and for Christsake write to me. You might be dead with diphtheria for all I know. Please, I'm worried because I love you very much, and am half dead without some point of contact with you.

With all my love, always

I have received a letter from home – money promised at the weekend.
Have you written to Hetty?

Friday [late February 1939]

My own darling,

I received your letter this morning so the world is liveable once more. I am longing so much to see you once again. It is said that absence makes the heart grow fonder, but this is more the case of 'comparisons are odious', seeing that living with you is so delightful and living with these freaks of nature such a strain. I will have so much to tell you about delightful conversations on the subject of Hitler, Hitler and more Hitler, until I have been on the verge of tears trying to control my temper. This Nazi Youth is rather interesting as a specimen of Fascist Britain. Anyway I can tell you so much better.

---

* Indicating she thought letters might be read by censors.

43

Come to Aylesbury on Saturday. I will go down in the morning, so come as quickly as possible. The address is: 59 Havelock Street and the name of my aunt is Wilder, in case you get lost.

       Hasta la vista

          With all my heart

              Mary   Salud – excuse this but I am
                      terribly repressed politically (and otherwise)

Sorry I can't write much but it is difficult here.

Thurs, March 2 [1939]

Dear Miss Lonelyhearts,

I am very lonely. My girl friends go out with the Toms, Dicks and Harries, and I stay at home with the willies. But seriously, isn't it a long time until Saturday. I miss you as if you were in Pondicherry, Ballyjamesduff or somewhere equally remote.

I composed you a beautiful letter this morning in my head, all about the fundamental sadness of things, the smiler with the dagger in his cloak, etc, etc, but fortunately, I was unable to take off to write to you. So you are reprieved for yet a little while. I was in the mood this morning to write – the old feeling of being able to use words as a chisel, cutting and shaping an idea. My ideas, however, belong to the linoleum media, rather than onyx.

This morning I would have offered you a humble and contrite hearty –

        For how do I have thee without thy granting
        And for these riches where is my deserving! –*

---

* An adaption from Sonnet 87, William Shakespeare.

This afternoon the expression of the mood has changed, but the affection that prompted it remains.

If this letter is incomprehensible, stop reading. But you once said you liked my meanderings, and oh boy, how I like to meander.

Pay has just gone home, and this office has the subtle, indefinable atmosphere of a funeral party, with Mrs Cotton as the life and soul of the above-mentioned event. Dear creature; how I shall miss her when she dies from the damage wrought (is that how you spell it) by a skilfully dropped typewriter.

Interval.

I have just been summoned by the watchman, who is an ally of mine and has been crawling around the call-box for me all afternoon, to the phone. It is Jill, she bawls louder than life on the phone and when I return my head is ringing.

Write soon to me, my darling David, a large, flat and almost empty envelope, that is yet more important than all the mail train's contents. I hope that Saturday falls earlier than usual this week.

Auf wiedersehn, mein liebe

Dein immer

Mary

Erst, o wunder! [sic]

Tuesday [March 1939]

My darling,

I think it's O.K. for Thursday, so expect me Wednesday night. It will be lovely seeing you again in so short a space, even though I will have to wait 9 (nine) whole days for the next break. But maybe you can manage to get down here, or something equally wonderful might happen.

I went to see my new billet last night. I live with a youngish woman rather sophisticated and intelligent, her mother and her absent husband, who is something on the L.M.S.* and only appears at weekends. I have a very small room, unfurnished except for a bed and chair, and the promise of a wardrobe and chest, ordered specially (under the Defence of the Realm Act I suspect) for me. I have to pay 6d every time I want a bath, so that will be my one extravagance. I mustn't expect an evening meal, only tea (thin bread and butter, cherry cake and the best china last night and I with an appetite like a horse) so your Mary will keep her sylph-like figure after all. I like my woman, however; she is hard and brittle and I think honest, so one knows where one is.

The others are in various houses all around me. We all live with different degrees of railway officials. Miss Hambly lives with the station master of L.B.†

Did Mammy return safely? I suppose she got entangled with friends and relations on Sunday and couldn't escape. I hope Tom is in the right mood for Portsmouth. Anyway, work on him fast before he goes, and we will have a naval cell.

Looking forward so much to being with you. Can't tell you again without being redundant how much I love you, and how beautiful it is to be with you. But nevertheless it is true, and I will be with you on Wednesday.

Au revoir, sweetheart, for the moment,

All my love

Your Mary

---

* L.M.S.: London, Midland and Scottish Railway, nationalised in 1948.
† L.B.: i.e. Leighton Buzzard.

Wednesday evening, 8.30 [probably 15 March 1939]
Leighton Buzzard

Mary sweetest,

I'm sitting forlornly in the saloon bar of the Bull and Bell or something and feeling more depressed and more lonely than I have ever been. All day I was looking forward to seeing you, being with you again and spending a gay and careless evening with you.

When I stepped out of the train at 7.45 and found no Mary I had a horrible premonition that you hadn't received the letter which I purposely posted early yesterday, telling you when I was arriving. And that horrible sickening feeling in my stomach jarred with frightening intensity when the Unicorn* announced that you had gone out for the evening 'with the other young ladies'.

I've spent a lonely evening locating the Unicorn and mooning hungrily around the cinema which probably houses your darling self. I'm feeling sick and deserted: and if only I had posted the letter at lunch-time, instead of at 8.0, you would be with me and we could be so happy.

I had intended to spend the night here, but a night without you and yet so near you would be the most agonising and relentless hell imaginable. A train goes at 10.24 and that must be my lot. Saturday seems an infinitude of time away. Come Saturday and we must atone for days of separation – days when the whole radiance of our interwoven lives is dulled – when one adorable sun shines elsewhere.

Oh Mary darling, I wish, I wish ten million times that I'd seen you this evening. I feel an inward rage that someone I love

---

* Pub in Leighton Buzzard where Mary was billeted at first when she moved to nearby Bletchley. It is still there.

47

so much, so completely and unalterably, is perhaps 50 yards away while I am unable to see or hear or feel her.

Please tonight, when you've laid your peerless head on some pillow think of me and love me. Think of me writing this and being so near you. Think of me aching to touch and caress and fondle you, to lay my cheek on your young yet matured breasts, to feel my whole body gathering yours to mine and my strength seeping into yours; think of me praying just to be close to you and hear your voice again; think of me wanting you – all of you – and before you've wafted away on the couch of Morpheus, shed a tear for a David that feels unutterably lonely.

I love you Mary – more than words can express. Be happy until Saturday –

    Goodnight dearest Mary
      with all my love
        David.

Thursday [probably 16 March 1939]

My darling,

My heart was broken in two by your letter. When I arrived back at the Unicorn (10.20 p.m.) I was told a Mr Francis had phoned. That was bad enough, but when I found your letter I too felt physically sick, because an opportunity to meet you is such a rare and lovely thing; to be wasted like that is a disaster.

It will have to be Sunday now, or Saturday night rather, and the meeting will be doubly beautiful because of this awful disappointment. And your letter was the most perfect of letters, and will be my most valued possession always, because it is the outward sign of the wonderful, unbelievable knowledge that you love me as I love you, completely, with all my mental and physical strength and for ever.

Till Saturday night, then, my darling
Your own
Mary

P.S. Your letter has just arrived Thursday 2 p.m. Post date Wednesday 9.15 a.m.

April 3, 1939[*]

Dear bastard,

Just to warn you that I am after your blood. You might have the common politeness to disguise the fact for two minutes that my voice bores you to death. I hate you, you snooty sod.

Yours to a cinder
MAIRE
(non equus, sed ego)[†]

4-4-39

Dear Sour-puss,

Thank you so much for your kind and sympathetic letter. Your considerate understanding of my condition, when tortured by a violent toothache and 20 steam hammers playing a

---

[*] Written on a piece of card with Mr B. F. Francis on one side and the message on the other, obviously after a spat over the telephone with an unwell David.
[†] Closest translation would be 'But I am not a horse.'

Stravinsky percussion piece in my forehead, I have to listen to a voice which whispers indistinctly to me from the furthest corners of eternity, has so overcome me that I feel unworthy of such attention.

Your expected letter from Hetty has not yet arrived: there is a possibility that Mrs Lewis has a message.

The tickets arrived quite safely and are in order.

Your very tired and haggard
David.

P.S. I see from your letter that you are after my blood. I wish I could return the compliment, but that would presuppose the existence of blood in your veins – something I am becoming more and more doubtful about.

CHAPTER 4

Marriage in Secret

Tuesday.

My darling David. Things look pretty bleak this morning both temporally and politically. What has happened to the S.U.? Is this non aggression pact with Germany true. Everyone here is very excited, I-told-you-not-to-trust-the-B. Bolshies sort of thing and I don't know what to think or say. Leave seems doubtful now so don't buy any tickets as I may not be allowed to leave England Oh David, I can't stay down here indefinitely as people seem to think we will. I will try to come up for the weekend anyway to talk the whole thing over with you.

Leave hasn't actually been cancelled, so don't give up all hope, but if the position today doesn't clear I'm afraid that I won't get it.

David turned twenty-one on 2 April 1939, thus being free to marry without his parents' consent. In early June, Mary, revealing an unexpected conventional streak and doubtless aware of the fact that he could be leaving shortly to go to war, applies subtle pressure designed to lead an obviously not totally willing David into the 'bourgeois institution' of matrimony.

They are married, secretly, without informing their parents, on 22 July 1939, at Finsbury Registry Office, just six weeks before the outbreak of war.

As the fateful year develops, the coming conflict starts to occupy more of their thoughts. David has to register in June under the new Military Training Act, anticipating conscription, as all twenty- and twenty-one-year-olds were required to do. The Non-Aggression Pact between Hitler and the Soviet Union in August causes consternation for both Mary and David.

Extraordinarily, only a fortnight before the outbreak of war they are planning a holiday in France. Their friends Dick and Hetty Goodman are living in Paris.

★

Friday night [9 June 1939]

My darling, darling Dave,

This is going to be the hardest letter I have ever written to you, and I have never loved you so much as at this moment. Oh my dear, I am so terribly afraid I am going to fail you. I have tried tonight to make my mother see our point of view and she has listened quietly and reasonably and given me her side of the question and I am at the moment utterly defeated.

She quite understands the fact that I am terribly in love with you and is reconciled to the idea of my marrying you and leaving home at once, but she cannot bear the thought of my being your 'trollop' as she described it, in the eyes of people she knows and who know me, and she implores me to marry you, secretly if necessary, so that she will feel secure about me. She also begs me to consider what her life would be with my father – he could and would make it hell, as I well know; and she knows we have been living together, and says if we are not sure of ourselves now we never will be. I cannot tell her that the only reason why we don't marry and take the risk is that you don't love me enough, but she made this point herself.

David, I know she isn't exaggerating one bit in what she has said tonight, and I simply cannot do this thing to her. If she became ill through worrying about me and through my father's swinishness, I would go out of my mind I think. But another thing I cannot bear is to see you growing less in love with me. That kills something vital in me, and I suppose now I have written this letter, relations between us will become impossible. Please believe me that I am not being cowardly. It is that I cannot be happy at the expense of my mother, especially when happiness for you and I could be won so easily. I would make you happy I know, in the right circumstances, but if my mother has to leave my father because of any action of mine, I would hate myself and grow to hate you also.

So my darling David, you have my full permission to say goodbye to me finally on Sunday. I can never be unhappier than I am at this moment, so don't be afraid to hurt me. This is something I have been dreading all these weeks. Oh God, darling, I love you so much, and yet I can't do what you ask me to, so perhaps I deserve to be unhappy.

Please forgive me, and be happy in your own way.

With all my love, always,

Mary

Tuesday. [22 August 1939]

My darling David,

Things look pretty bleak here this morning both temporally and politically. What has happened to the S.U.? Is this non-aggression pact with Germany true. Everyone here is very excited, I-told-you-not-to-trust-the-B. Bolshies sort of thing and I don't know what to think or say. Leave seems doubtful now so don't buy any tickets as I may not be allowed to leave England. Oh David, I can't stay down here indefinitely as people seem to think we will. I will try to come up for the weekend anyway to talk the whole thing over with you.

Leave hasn't actually been cancelled, so don't give up all hope, but if the position today doesn't clear I'm afraid that I won't get it.

Please write soon and tell me what you think, and what the D.W. thinks of the present situation, because I am so isolated here, and everybody is so unsound both mentally and morally that I only think war is inevitable, the S.U. has deserted us and life is over.

Please darling, write to your unhappy Mary, and soon. I hope everything at the flat is O.K. and that you have some money. I will be able to manage until Pay Day, which is Friday.

If only I can see you on Friday, I shall not ask for any greater joy in this world.

With all my love always,
Your
Mary

Angel House, N1
Tuesday evening [22 August 1939]

Darling Mary,

Don't be discouraged – this brilliant step taken by the Soviet Union has not only averted a war within the next few days but also made the possibilities of an Anglo-Soviet Pact more definite. Consider: firstly a deal of confusion exists over the nature of a non-aggression pact; so many seem to think it similar to a pact of mutual assistance. On this pact there will definitely be a clause to the effect that if one or both of the signatories commit an act of war on a third or other nations either by direct war or internal provocation, the pact will automatically be annulled. This clause exists in every non-aggression pact signed by the Soviet Union, eg with Poland, Afghanistan, China, Italy, Turkey etc. Secondly, the pact is similar to our own Munich agreement with Italy and Germany and France. Thus it is in line with the general foreign policy of the S.U., namely to conduct friendly relations with every nation in the world (a universal peace policy), provided such nations themselves are peaceful and non-aggressive towards their neighbours.

What are the effects of the pact? Most important is that it bears out Stalin's statement that Germany's territorial ambitions lie to the West and not to the East. Chamberlain can now no longer hope for a conflict between the Soviet Union and Germany. It is France and the British Empire which is now menaced. What to do about it? There must obviously be quickly an Anglo-Soviet military alliance against aggression. Now Chamberlain will not hinder and delay the talks in the hope of Germany turning East. It's now for the preservation of England (even from Chamberlain's point of view) that the Pact is needed. So we can expect a speed up in that direction probably as a direct result of public pressure.

Second effect excellent – Parliament has been recalled.

Third effect: the whole internal anti-Soviet propaganda together with the barrage inflicted on the German people on the subject of 'encirclement' collapses. How can there be encirclement with a non-aggression pact with the Soviet Union?

Fourth effect: within a day the rupture of the Tokyo branch of the axis.

Fifth effect: severe misgivings in Rome.

Sixth effect; end of Anti-Comintern Pact.*

Again it is an illustration of the military strength of the Soviet Union – Germany daren't attack her, so concludes a non-aggression agreement.

---

* Comintern: abbreviation of the Communist International, formed in Moscow in 1919 with the aim of spreading communism worldwide 'by all available means, including armed force, for the overthrow of the international bourgeoisie . . .' In 1936 Germany and Japan, later joined by other countries, signed the Anti-Comintern Pact to fight against 'Communist subversion'. Mary is obviously being despairingly ironic when she asks if the S.U. has joined this pact.

Personally I think it is also a demonstration by Hitler to Chamberlain that he can't go East against the S.U., therefore C. has got to give concessions in the West. Even C. (the arch Imperialist) will be forced to do the only thing possible to save the British Empire – namely conclude the Anglo-Soviet Pact.

Write and tell me when you're coming on Friday, darling. Won't being together at the weekend be lovely? Enclosed quid in case you need da dough –

All my love and look forward to the holiday,
David

P.S. What shall we do on Saturday evening?

Wednesday [23 August 1939]

Darling,

For God's sake write to me! I am sick of waiting in vain for a letter from you, especially as I don't know what to do about our holidays.

This morning I was told the situation is expected to worsen before the weekend, and my leave will be cancelled, but if it doesn't, then it can stand, at the risk of being recalled.

So if I don't arrive on Friday night on the 6.17 from B, getting into London at 7.5, then probably I won't be coming at all and you had better make arrangements for your own holidays.

What has happened to the S.U. Have they joined the Anti-Comintern pact or what?

I feel constantly sick, because all I can hear is attacks on Russia from everybody who forgets that it is Chamberlain's insulting treatment of Russia that has caused this.

If only I could see you and hear what you have to say about it I would then understand what is happening. Tom has written to me about my spectacles, the bill for which I hope will be met by the office.

How I wish you would write.

Yours anxiously.

Mary

Office,

Thursday [24 August 1939]

Mary darling,

So sorry you didn't get my last letter yesterday – it might have cheered you up a bit.

I enclose two letters from Hetty, and you will see from the note on the back that they in Paris realise that the Soviet Union's move has averted war. I'll meet your train on Friday evening at Euston – it will be lovely to see you and have you again.

I won't buy the tickets until Saturday, but I'll start gathering all the things we might need for the camping. If we go to the Ardennes the fares will be much cheaper than the South of France and we would probably spend 1 or 2 days at Varengeville for a change.

With regard to the political situation I can quite see why your office is wild. For months Chamberlain has delayed the signing of the Anglo-Soviet Pact in the hope that Germany could be persuaded to attack Russia i.e. expand Eastwards. Now it is quite apparent that Germany is afraid to go East and hopes to come West, thereby directly menacing France and the British Empire. If Chamberlain sincerely desires peace, he must sign the

Anglo-Soviet Pact now; – the next moves lie with him; if he sincerely wants to stop war he'll send Halifax and Hore Belisha to Moscow, not some goddam insignificant office boy like Strang. And it is now more than ever that Chamberlain must go because it is as a result of the inefficiencies and class prejudices of the National Gov. that England is placed in this humiliating position of being without a Mutual Assistance Pact after six months of negotiations while Germany, per Ribbentrop, gets a non-aggression pact after a week.

We found that on Tuesday and Wednesday it was we only who could correctly estimate the situation, as in September,* and it is as a result of an official statement that the general press lines have changed for the better. Today, the Chronicle has progressed by leaps and bounds and although she errs in thinking that Russia has to take the next step, the line is pretty good.

What is the next step? It lies with Chamberlain, or more correctly, with the Labour and Liberal opposition to force him to sign the pact immediately. If he doesn't then God help England.

(N.B. The Non-Aggression Pact holds good while Germany ceases to aggress – otherwise it is annulled.)

Anyway, cheer up. I think by the week, provided the opposition fulfil their obligations, the air will have been cleared.

See you Friday evening darling. Pop† came clean with £7 English, 160 French francs and a moratorium on the rent. Good eh?

What'll we do Saturday evening? Love, love and more love from

   your D

---

* A reference to Neville Chamberlain's claim in September 1938 to have achieved 'peace in our time' after talks with Hitler in Munich.
† David's father, who paid the rent on Angel House while David was articled. David was worried that he would stop when he learned they were married. Obviously he didn't.

Monday
52 Angel House, N1
[28 August 1939]

Darling girl,

It was a wrench to leave you this morning in such nerve-wracking times; the weekend was so lovely and I feel I love you more and more as each day passes. I never cease to thank God we are married.

Tonight the atmosphere is expectant. The Star carried an excellent editorial weighing up the debits and credits from the point of view of the Peace Front of the Soviet–German Pact and came to the conclusion that it was definitely advantageous to Peace. It felt, as we all feel, that Molotov's speech tonight may clarify the whole situation.

I just want to tell you that, if anything happens to me politically, you must at all costs stay where you are until further notice. You must not come back. Don't be scared at all. It's just taking the necessary precautions, as everyone seems to be doing . . . More later . . .

Malheureusement his speech is postponed until Thursday. We shall see what we shall see.

Cheer up, and don't forget me.

Yours with all my love.

David

Tuesday [29 August 1939]

My darling,

Have just received your letter and am very happy to know that you still love me. But I never doubted it.

Molotov not speaking is a blow, but it might be a deliberate action on the part of the S.U. to give time to all the deliberations now proceeding. I don't know, but I don't feel so panicky.

What I would like to know is what is all the mystery about not coming up if anything happens to you politically. Could you explain a little in your next letter as I will come up to see you at the first possible chance, maybe Thursday – is this off? Let me know if it would be a bad thing in any way and I will be patient, but oh my sweet David, how I long to be with you. If only we can be in bed on Sunday morning, drink tea and fight for the paper and know that next Sunday will come and be the same, I will never ask for anything more in this world.

I have had a letter from Mammy – still in Aylesbury. She is very worried about us all, so tonight I will try to get down there for a few hours.

Write as often as you have time. Your letters keep me alive.

With all my love for ever

Mary

P.S. As if I could forget you for one moment!

52 Angel House, N.1.
Tuesday, August 29, 1939

Mary dear,

Tonight Hetty and the kids arrived here and are staying the night. The kids are to be deposited in Cambridge with Dick's sister and then Hetty returns to Paris and from thence to Warsaw, where Dick has an assignment for an American paper! She's firmly convinced that there won't be a war.

The point I made yesterday was that if an attack is made on us and I am arrested, you know what to do, yes?

American opinion of the isolationist ilk is now decreasing and evidently the anti-Roosevelt section of the Democratic Party is now swinging into line – which is good. The general position is I think, clearer and I should imagine that Molotov postponed the speech in order that the maximum benefit could be gained by the original move of the German–Soviet Pact. The feeling that Molotov will make an offer of an all-embracing mutual assistance pact for all the major world powers is growing.

David (one of Hetty's children) is surrounding me with packets of chocolates, cigarettes and other gifts! He sends his love.

Unfortunately Hetty is out now, so she can't send you a message, but I'll get her to write you tomorrow. Hymie sends you his love (he is now one of 4 lodgers).

Please do come up on Thursday. Let me know what time you're coming and I'll meet you. Dinner and theatre yes? Remember it's pay day.

Love to you dearest girl. I'm thinking and dreaming of you nostalgically all day.

D.

Dear Marykins,*

I am at present moment in 52 Angel House, having brought over the kids. They are going to Cambridge to Dick's sister, not that we are afraid of war, but Dick is probably going to war as a correspondent. I am returning Friday so may see you. Love Hetty

---

* Added by Hetty.

Thursday [31 August 1939]

My darling,

I don't think I can possibly get to London tonight. We are not allowed to sleep away from this place and it isn't worth coming up for 1 hr. especially as I shall probably get either Saturday or Sunday.

Things look very much more like working out as you promised, and I am not in such a state of strain as I was last week. In fact I am quite ashamed of my jitters.

I cannot say what I feel about Hetty and the kids being in London. I don't know whether it is a good or a bad thing. I should love to see them, and try to persuade Hetty to stay over the weekend. If you ring up Tom, I shall probably be in London Saturday night, whether I get Saturday or Sunday off. A night out is decidedly indicated.

Your half-hints rather disturbed me. I hope you are not being TRAILED by flat-footed narks. But darling David, please look after yourself, and don't work too hard. But if you are nabbed, I think I know what to do. Write again to me and tell me how London is, and how the kids and Hetty are getting on.

Love to all in 52 Angel House (even Hymie), and forever, and most of all,

My love to you dear David

CHAPTER 5

'So it is war'

Sept 3 1939   Sunday afternoon.

My own heart's darling.
                    So it is war, and the
end of you and me as inseparables, for a
little while. But we are luckier than most
people in the fact that we have each other
really in our hearts, so never can be
alone. I am never without you, nor can
never be, so long as you continue to
love me, and if this helps, I shall love
you until I am dead, and beyond that
if it is possible.
          I must see you sometime next week.
If the trains are reasonable, I may come
sneaking up on Tuesday night, so don't be
surprised to see me; but I will say
more about this. If I can get a day
off I think it would be better for
you to come down here, but more
about this also, later.

On 3 September 1939, at 11.15 a.m., the Prime Minister, Neville Chamberlain, announced the outbreak of hostilities with Germany.

After six months at Bletchley Park, Mary is unhappy with the restraints which the top-secret establishment puts on her movements, restricting her visits to London and her new husband. She restlessly searches for suitable jobs elsewhere but then is overcome by a rush of remorse at her self-centredness.

Nonetheless, as her brother, Tom, is called up and David is advised by his father to apply for a commission in the navy, she decides to look for work back in London.

The war news grows more baffling and alarming. The USSR enters Poland, and the first British warship, the aircraft carrier *Courageous*, is sunk with the loss of 500 lives.

★

Sunday afternoon [3 September 1939]

My own heart's darling,

So it is war, and the end of you and me as inseparables, for a little while. But we are luckier than most people in the fact that we have each other really in our hearts, so never can be alone. I am never without you, nor can ever be, so long as you continue to love me, and if this helps, I shall love you until I am dead; and beyond that if it is possible.

I must see you sometime next week. If the trains are reasonable, I may come sneaking up on Tuesday night, so don't be surprised to see me; but I will say more about this. If I can get a day off I think it would be better for you to come down here, but more about this also, later.

I have been making tentative inquiries about the paymaster side of the navy, and will see what influence I can start working, if you really want to do this sort of work.

Another thing, I have also applied to change my billet from Leighton Buzzard to Aylesbury, which may be allowed, and then I would be far freer.

But, my darling David, where I want to be is in London with you, and if you really want it too, nothing will keep me away from you. I feel that if I am with you, I can protect you; because I love you so much, nothing shall harm you. This is a solemn vow, and I know one day we shall live, be happy, grow old and die together.

Write, my darling, to your own
Mary

52 Angel House
N.1
September 11th, 1939

Mary darling,

I've just been scanning the columns of the Telegraph and Manchester Guardian today to find a suitable job. There seem to be plenty of them generally but not so many of the right kind and none worth trying. However, I will look every day, yes?

I spent the evening at home yesterday, and collective love is sent to you from thence! Pera is very busy with the ambulance for which she does 12 hours duty every day. Daddy is very keen that I should apply for a commission in the Navy as I shall be the only one of his sons doing anything for the country!

It's a pity you couldn't have stayed for yesterday because we could have had a lovely day. I'm looking forward to Thursday. Somehow time seems to stand still while you're away: I can't remember anything that happened last week except Tuesday evening and Saturday – all the rest seems to have been merged in a mass of negligible and mechanical doings. Life is just a series of interrupted days together at the moment – what goes on between is just a kind of marking time.

What would you like to do on Friday? Let me know and we'll try and arrange something.

This week I'll be working out at Stevenage but will probably be able to get Friday off quite easily.

Tom spent Sunday morning trying out a lot of the records – he seems to like them.

I'll write again this evening during 'de patrol'.

> Be good, and polish the Admiral's buttons,
> Most care-ful-ly,
> Then you'll be the ruler of the
> King's Nav-ee

With all my love darling
    lil' old me

Tuesday [12 September 1939]

My own darling David,

It now is Tuesday, and in two more days I will be in your arms again. I come up on Thursday night, as early as possible, and would have the whole of Friday to spend with you. So try very hard to have the day off, so we can make the most of every minute.

You are quite right about the compensation of separation, Thursday (Friday) now seems to be the Golden Age, a lifetime of happiness captured in one short night and day.

Darling, I love you so much. On Sunday morning when we said goodbye at Euston among the fish smells and the train soot, I suddenly realised that this was as hard for you as it was for me; that you felt forlorn and lost too, and that I was so incredibly selfish to be so unhappy about B. We will discuss all this when I see you.

It would be lovely if we could go out to supper on Thursday night, and pretend that it was just an ordinary going-places Thursday; but perhaps this is impossible.

Train services to London have deteriorated, but not seriously, and I might catch an early train on Thursday night. But do not meet me as it is rather uncertain.

I have had a very matey letter from my father, who has been tamed very nicely by three weeks in a war camp. Now he knows there is a crisis on. It is still a funny war, and only time will tell, as the song goes. Write and say what you are doing and that you still love me, even more than your girl friends in Sainsbury's, and every other place where you show your ridiculously attractive face. My fingers are always aching to stroke your drowning hair. Friday will be beautiful. Life is like a phoenix. It burns itself out then rises from the ashes one day a week, which in these hungry days is something. We are exceedingly lucky we have each other and, ergo, life is rich and full.

This letter is most incoherent but is trying to tell you that I love you, and thank life for you and shall always be happy and regret nothing for having known you.

With all my heart and love for ever,

Your own

Mary

September 17, 1939

My dearest Dave,

Two interesting pieces of news have just reached me. One, that Stevenage is in this part of the world and quite accessible; and the other that Russia has just gone into Poland! The latter news fills me with trepidation, as I am completely unprepared, with my conception of the S.U., to understand it. Let me know the real meaning of this move by return of post please. The danger of finding ourselves at war with both Russia and Germany is fearful, however you look at it. We might have a chance against Germany, against the S.U. never and to fight a war against a Fascist/Socialist alliance is a ridiculous situation.

The Stevenage question now: perhaps instead of going back to town one night you could meet me somewhere and go to Stevenage in the morning! It would be so lovely to see you, even for an hour, and would make the long week which stretches before us until next Sunday more bearable.

I returned to the office on Saturday morning in good time, and survived the first day back, when the place seems more untenable than usual.

I am hoping with all my heart that we can meet. Will you try and think of a plan and so will I, and that Russia is still the Soviet Union and is still the Fatherland of every toiler, where peace and progress build their hope etc. etc.

I didn't go into Aylesbury last night as transport presents difficulties. No buses seem to be running these days.

I found your postcard waiting for me, and it was sweet. But what is the allusion to Ruth's husband. Very mystifying. I have had a letter from Jill. She too is working a 7-day week, with 12 hours leave and no nights off, so we are not the unluckiest ones on earth. There is a disturbing rumour around here that no-one is allowed to leave of their own free will, as it is war service, but this probably could be overcome. Anyway, I will wait for an answer from Mrs Hoster.

David, have I ever told you that I loved you madly, indescribably and that you made me ecstatically happy – I want to tell you now that all this is true and I just live to be with you again.

Write soon to your own
Mary

P.S. Love to Hetty and Dick.

Tuesday [19 September 1939]

My darling David,

I expected a letter from you today, but I suppose it has been held up, or censored, or is yet an embryo struggling for birth in the womb of your mind (!)

About the war, the reaction here is still puzzled and cross, childishly cross with Russia for being so independent, but of course, that is just the uninitiated reaction.

I will be up in town on Saturday night, as early as possible and have all day Sunday to stay with you; it will be lovely. The weather (actual) is so tantalisingly perfect, wind and sun and the atmosphere is September. I found some autumn crocuses this morning and a great bed of lavender in the woods around here at lunchtime today.

The sinking of the 'Courageous' is a serious reminder that someone is taking this war seriously. It makes the navy seem not so safe. For heaven's sake, darling, get a shore job, or develop a weak heart quickly, because I love you so much and you must not go into any danger at all.

Personally, I think I have got the Russian problem straightened out, and am not so worried about it. I have decided to wait and see.

I hope Dick and Hetty are still with you, because I want to see them at the weekend, but I also hope that things are working for them. I suppose Tom is still with you.

I went to the pictures on Monday with two airmen and saw 'They drive by night'.* It was very good. Last night I washed my hair, so that it will look nice for Sunday and you, my lover (or is mon amoureux less blatant?).

Write soon to me and tell me you also are counting the minutes to Saturday night.

With all my love, my lazy, indifferent, sweet darling

Your own

Mary

Tuesday 3pm [19 September 1939]

My darling,

I have just received your letters, both of them, together, and the promise of seeing you tomorrow (Wednesday) is marvellous.

---

* *They Drive by Night* (1938), British film directed by Arthur B. Woods, starring Emlyn Williams and Ernest Thesiger.

I do not doubt, but that my landlady will smile upon you, but whether she can put you up is a moot point. The house is small, and my bed is small, and I am not supposed to have told anyone of my whereabouts. But nichevo, we will put our combined heads together, and love will find out a way.

I have just read in the papers that you will not have to go abroad until March, 1940, so David, that gives us time, time for a miracle to happen, for Chamberlain to be ousted, for the Soviet Union to trick and outwit Hitler to the point of suicide, and for you and I to be together again. This might be the most futile wish fulfilment, but it keeps me alive, this hope that you may not be touched by the war, mentally, morally or physically.

I needn't write you a long letter, but tomorrow I meet you and talk to you, and become a human being again.

I arrive at my billet at about 6.30p.m. and the address is:

     39 Southcourt Avenue,
       Linslade

which is the road straight across the bridge, which crosses the Leighton Buzzard railway line.

    With all my love and I-hope-you-get-this-in-time
     Your own Mary

Monday [25 September 1939]

My own darling,

It seems ages since I last saw or heard from you, three whole days ago, and I haven't achieved sick leave. But I still hope and maybe I will get a week of my summer leave one of these days. I have been feeling pretty lousy since I came back, cough developing and general depression all round, but I hope this will be over by Friday when I see you again.

I heard on the wireless last night that your group is liable to be called up in the middle of November. That gives us time to have the war over before you actually go into action. But so little time, my darling, for me. When I remember how seeing you all week was not sufficient, how seeing you once a week is the most tantalising, beautiful torture, then I cannot bear the idea of your going away. Anyway, I still have you here for the present.

Coming down in the train on Friday morning 2 old men in my carriage were having a discussion on 'the war' and both came to the conclusion that the Poles were better off under the Russians anyway.

This fluctuating attitude to Russia is very interesting. It is a recurring graph.

Have you heard from Tom yet? I haven't, nor from Mammy. Make her write to me as I am anxious to know how she is and what she is doing. Anyway, I will write her a line myself today.

Let me know the D.W. line on the war every time you write, as I am rather left to the mercy of the capitalist press and my own, not always true, reactions.

David, I am not going to tell you how much I miss you, otherwise I might realise it myself and come rushing to you, or stop living, or something, and I musn't do that as there is still a chance that the war will be over before it touches you. Anyway, my love for you is strong and integral and that should keep you safe.

Write soon to me
your own,
Mary

Sunday,
52 Angel House N1
[Early October]

Darling,

Have you decided which day I can come down and see you? I
hope your gushing young wife act impressed your landlady
successfully, because I do so much want to spend all the available
time with you and not have to disappear to a hotel.

Today I applied for the much talked-of commission, and if it
is accepted it could be much better than being slung against the
Siegfried Line.* I have a feeling that my age group will be
called up very soon, anyway, so the application is the only thing
to do.

On Friday, while going through the audit papers of a job I've
just finished, my boss got talking about my salary. I thought that
he was going to give me a reduction 'because of the war', so
imagine my surprise and pleasure when he gave me a 10/- per
week rise, two months before any rise is due! It takes effect as
from the 1st October, so I won't get the extra £2-1-8 until the
31st. Nevertheless, it's very, very welcome. He also said that
when I go into the Army or Navy he'll give me half the
difference between my salary and army pay so that will be
an extra help for you. It'll probably work out at 23/- a week
or so.

Yesterday was the day of the Lewises' party. Unfortunately, as
I had to go to two meetings and a social on Saturday, I was too
tired to go. Nevertheless, it was from all reports an excellent
party!

Tom wrote to say he is at Skegness at Butlin's Holiday Camp

---

* The Siegfried Line: a defence system of tunnels, bunkers and tank traps
along the western border of Germany built by Hitler between 1938 and 1940.

with a chalet to himself !!* He gets all the amenities that are available for holiday makers, so there is reason for his evident pleasure at being there! Incidentally, there is a picture of him in the Evening Standard.

Dick would like to know where he should apply for a commission in the Intelligence Department (e.g. liaison officer and suchlike animals). Can you help him?

Your mother went down to Croydon today, so imagine our horror when your Pop arrived here looking for her! She must have got there just after he left.

Yesterday we won our first victory over the landlord. He painted most of the steps white, but only after Mrs Lewis had threatened to kick his plate glass window in unless it were done immediately. I'm sorry I can't enclose the 35/-, but I didn't get my cheque until Friday afternoon and the banks close now at 2 o'clock. However, I'll send it tomorrow.

Well my lil chickadee. Write to me and tell your hussiband when the coast is clear. Wednesday would be the best for me.

Remember the Navy is immensely superior to the Air Force! A bas les cochons de nuages!

Love and kisses, particularly kisses,
    LEFT TENANT
    Dave

---

* Mary's brother, Tom, on being called up at the beginning of September was undergoing basic training in the same converted Butlin's Holiday Camp where David would find himself a few months later. The Skegness camp, opened by Billy Butlin in 1936, was commandeered as a naval training base the day after war broke out on 3 September. The campers were sent home and the camp was renamed HMS *Royal Arthur*. It reopened in May 1946.

Monday [9 October 1939]

Darling honey,

This morning everything became O.K. on the home front after a very curious affair yesterday, when I took the full day's quota (6) and the only effect was to feel my blood pressure becoming very low and to be very cold and depressed. But this morning, pills or nature, n'importe, I am myself again.

So on Friday, you will have your own Mary, no frozen virgin or expectant mother, but ME.

Please write soon to me, because it is a very long wait until Thursday night. I have lived one day of it now, so maybe it can be endured.

Peace is in the news today, so my paper says. It is still 'wait and see' but my god, how I hope the miracle happens and we, good old you and I, can be together again. Look after yourself my David, because I love you tremendously.

Your own, always,
Mary

52 Angel House,
Pentonville Road, N.1
Monday, 9th October [1939]

Mary darling,

I hope by now that everything is O.K. on the heir front. Let – Hold everything! The post has just arrived with your letter and the tidings therein. I'm so glad you are alright now, and that on Friday you will be you again; but principally I'm glad because you no longer have to worry and be depressed about such things. I hope and pray that you haven't suffered any ill-effects from those damn 'window-sills'.*

Do you know that on Friday we were guilty of making one couple's cup of misery flow right over? Evidently Hymie and Mac are seriously confronted with the limitations and frustrations of their relationship; on Friday they had been trying to decide what to do about it all and were consequently feeling very depressed. The sight of us, who seemed so utterly happy when we met them, was enough to break them down. That was the reason they did not meet us after the show.

I enclose the letter from the bureau for the remittance.

Today I have been out at Stevenage in the most depressing weather imaginable. However, the compensation of short working days and free teas and lunches is summat.

Hurry and come home. What would you like to do on Thursday in the evening? Theatre, cinema, party, evening at home, ou quoi?

Sunday was fortunately quite a peaceful day and without incident likely to provoke hostilities. In fact all concerned seemed to have overlooked the incident except to refer to it in banter.

Well my darling, keep happy and on Thursday we'll make whoopee. Remember me to the landlady etc.

With all my love,
David

---

* Pills.

CHAPTER 6

David Joins Up;
Mary Returns to London

The early war days continue with snatched weekends in London and occasional visits by David to Leighton Buzzard, even talk of a holiday in Brighton. David signs on with the navy on 21 October.

Mary resigns and leaves Bletchley towards the end of the year and returns to London, where they live together briefly for the first time as man and wife. The letters cease for a couple of weeks and then David departs for basic training at HMS *Royal Arthur*, a former Butlin's holiday camp at Skegness, on the bleak East Coast.

★

52 Angel House, N1
Tuesday, October 17, 1939

Mary darling,

I hope you are not too depressed at being back at the old Buzzard hole after three days of freedom. It was wonderful to be together for so long; three days seems a period almost free from the bonds of time in these days. Saturday and the day of signing my body away to British Imperialism draws closer. However, who knows that I shall emerge the Voroshilov* of the Navy.

---

* Marshal Kliment Voroshilov, Soviet military commander and bureaucrat.

Tomorrow I journey to see your fair face again. I don't know what time the train will arrive . . . it may be possible to catch an earlier one than I anticipate.

Love, love and more love
David

Wednesday. [18 October 1939]

Darling Dave,

I arrived at here about 11.30 am and managed to evade, or ward off, too much annoyance by being rather vague, at which I am quite good, n'est ce pas? Anyway, being late for the office is too trivial to worry about. How are you all and please write every day to tell me.

Tom has written. He hasn't gone yet, but in his letter, says that when he fights it is fighting for the working class against Fascism, and not for England's honour, etc. He is going to try to see you before he goes.

I also received your letter my darling, and as well as adoring you I am very proud of you.

You have the supreme gift of personality and must, must, must be spared to use it for the right kind of work.

Nothing must happen to you:

> Do not die, for I shall hate
> All men so, when thou art gone
> That thee I shall not celebrate
> When I remember thou wast one.*

---

* From John Donne's 'A Fever', adapted by Mary.

84

Your point about meeting after being forcibly parted isn't true for me. I only live when you are there, and coming to life once a week is an unsatisfactory business. Never mind. On Friday night we shall meet; on Friday and Saturday I shall live.

Write so I receive the letter tomorrow.

With all my heart my darling,

Your own Mary

52 Angel House,
N.1
Tuesday October 24th [1939]

Mary darling,

The last frantic rush for the train on Monday prevented me from saying once again how wonderful the week end was. Sunday is one of those days that will remain in my memory as something very beautiful and complete; with lunch in the glare of bright lights and in the Reedian atmosphere of graduated poached egg-on-chips connoisseurs; with a lovely walk along the very placid riverside with a background of church bells; with a promenade overlooking a forestial and shimmering view of the Thames; with a bizarre tea of stale cakes and jazz; with an hour snatched from the realms of reality and placed for an all too short a space in the hectic regions of debunkable New York; with quiet minutes spent listening to you reading poetry by the light of an intimate and cheerful fire; and finally with ecstatic moments locked in your embrace, close to you and feeling every tremor, every movement, almost every thought that is yours. All combining to make a perfect, if slightly heterogeneous day. So lovely.

A weekend at Brighton would be very enjoyable, would it not?

The news has just come that Tom has been selected to play rugger for his Division, which comprises some 1,000 men. Pretty good work, eh?

The Badminton racquet has still failed to come to light, but I'll send it immediately it shows up.

I am working at Camden Town now; it's close enough to Regent's Park to be able to take a walk there during the lunch-hour. Today I went up to Primrose Hill, which is now desecrated by the establishment of anti-aircraft guns right on the top.

Hold hard. Special late news . . . Tom is coming home for two days on this Saturday and Sunday; he arrives early, at 3 o'clock in the morning. In that case we must postpone our weekend (in Brighton). It's very lucky that the leaves coincide.

Mind you write to me, my sweet.

Tell me when you arrive and I will get the lads to come and meet you.

All my love,
Dave.

52 Angel House,
N.1.
Wednesday Nov. 1st. 1939

Mary darling,

Many thanks for the letter. Friday seems very close now and two days by the sea sounds more and more attractive. I've had one recommendation for Hotel Chatsworth (on the sea front, stone's throw from the sea etc!) but am seeking further points of view. There is, of course, the Hotel Plaisirs d'amour to say nothing of the Hotel Nuits d'exercice, but that is by the by.

Hope you found the racquet sufficiently inundated with my inspired playing so that you were able to rout Mrs T.

Today I got my rise and celebrated with a mid-morning breakfast at the Honey Dew.

Summonses to court* are now prevalent in Angel House. Mick, Loewenstein and Minnie have all received a summons to appear on November 28th. The cases of course will all be fought.

Dick has got his book† accepted by Lawrence and Wishart and will get £15 advance on signing the contract. Everyone is very pleased about it!

Your Maw hasn't returned yet from her gallivanting, but a letter from Tom awaits her.

Come up by train on Friday and I will meet it (for the first time in fact, and the nth time in spirit) and we'll go to Victoria right away, dine and wine with the beaux of Brighton and spend Saturday on the windy reaches of the Downs – we can return either Sat night or very early Sun morning – preferably the former. What do you say, eh?

Dear Mary, I love you so much. I feel I should like to be at your side in bed in the early morning, just whispering in your ear – Dear Mary – Dear Mary – forever.

Yours and your

David

---

* After the outbreak of war, refugees of German nationality – mainly Jewish and many who had fled Austria after the German takeover – became 'enemy aliens' and had to appear before tribunals to assess the degree of risk they posed to Britain. There were several such refugees at Angel House, which is presumably what this is referring to.

† Richard Goodman, a great friend of Mary and David, published a book called *Britain's Greatest Ally* – a plea for a pact with the Soviet Union against Hitler.

52 Angel House
N.1
Tuesday [around November–December 1939]

Mary dear,

Have just got your letter – I'm sorry the final step has not
been taken, because I feel that putting it off is only going to
make the job harder. However, the moment will come: I'm
seeing Judith tonight about a job. I tackled Springie (who is still
here) but he knew of nothing at the moment. The papers this
evening announce the increase of wife's allowance for soldiers
on active service. They also announce the loss of yet another
boat.

I'm sure we'll be able to manage somehow even if the worst
happens and it's a number of weeks before you get a job.
Anyway it will be worth a little hardship a thousand times over.

Today I've been out at Stevenage, finishing up the job there.
Very cold and bleak now. I bought some frying steak this
evening and had steak and chips for supper. You must teach me
how to fry chips – mine are unquestionably grim.

Your Maw still hasn't turned up yet. A letter from Tom is
waiting for her.

Are you sure nothing ain't appened yet? I pray sumpin will!

Write again tomorrow. Are you coming Sat or Sunday this
week?

All my love darling,
me

CHAPTER 7

A Bitter Winter in Skegness

17 Jan 40   Skegness   (1)

Wednesday

Mary darling,

     Have arrived safely at this
utterly fantastic place. The train
arrived fairly punctually at 1.30
& we came on to the camp by bus
where accommodated, and dinner
was served. After being shewn
our chalets (there are only double
beds for the 1st night), we were
left entirely to ourselves, not
knowing what to do, where to go,
or what was what. In fact,
I'm sure if I had quietly slipped

David's entertaining letters from HMS *Royal Arthur*, the deceptively named Butlin's Holiday Camp in Skegness, which was rapidly converted into a training centre at the beginning of the war, pulse with sharp observation, droll humour and a generous good nature, despite the atrocious conditions. They begin on 17 January 1940, and flow copiously until the following June.

During their short time together in London after Mary left Bletchley, the couple had moved out of Angel House to nearby Myddelton Square, EC1, a square of fine Georgian houses on the Lloyd–Baker Estate subdivided into flats.

David arrives in Skegness as a trainee wireless telegraphist in the middle of the bitterly cold winter of 1939/40 to find chaos. Conditions are hard. Already there has been one death from exposure. Despite the privations and separation from Mary, his good humour and optimism never falter.

A few days after arriving at HMS *Royal Arthur*, he finally plucks up courage to tell his family that he and Mary have married – six months after the event. They must have had a shock, doubly so when they learned that Mary was pregnant with Rosheen (although at the time the couple assumed that 'Junior' was going to be a boy).

The opening months of the 'Phoney War', which ended with the German invasion of France in May 1940, were marked by disruption and irritation, but not yet desperation. Despite news of losses at sea, actual combat still seems a long way away.

★

1940

Wednesday, [17 January 1940]
Skegness

Mary darling,

Have arrived safely at this utterly fantastic place. The train arrived fairly punctually at 1.30 and we came onto the camp by bus, where a moderately good dinner was issued. After being shown our chalets (there are only double beds for the first night!) we were left entirely to ourselves, not knowing what to do, where to go, or what was what. In fact, I'm sure that if I had quietly slipped over the sea wall and come home, no one would have bothered.

Tea was at 4.30 and I am writing this before supper which is at 6.0. This chalet is bitterly cold and the bed is supplied with three blankets and no sheets, although the sea is only 25 yards away.

The impression one gets of the camp is of thousands of gaudily painted, shoddily built houses in long rows with hundreds of ratings, officers, marines and new arrivals just wandering about aimlessly among the rows and avenues.

Bugles keep on blowing at odd intervals for apparently no reason – at any rate if there is a reason no one seems to be very anxious to explain it to us.

In the carriage up to Peterborough were two more telegraphists from London with whom I have stuck so far. Quite likely lads.

I've found out about leaves from the notice board.
After two weeks' training you are entitled to one short
weekend per month (i.e. first train Saturday until Monday 8.45)
and during the 27 weeks' training you are entitled to 2 long
weekends (your own choice) from 4.0 Friday to 8.45
Monday. So I should be back between 5/6 weeks
from now.

I still find it difficult to realise that I shan't be back at
Myddelton Square this evening. Perhaps I shall be.

Take care of yourself my own darling and write to me
tomorrow.

I have no uniform, or number or division or anything. But I
will give them to you as soon as they arrive.

With all my love, Mary my sweet,
David

19th January
Class 219
Q/D Division,
HMS Royal Arthur,
Skegness

Dearest Mary,

Another day has passed. Today it was marriage allowances
and gas masks that were arranged. Your first allowance should
be payable on Thursday, January 25th at Islington High Street
and will be 24/-.

I was told to tell you that the Admiralty will be writing for
the marriage certificate very soon, so if they do it is in the
gramophone drawer.

The days seem very long indeed. I think it's due to

the endless waiting around we have. The day seems to be like this:

6.15	Up, wash, shave etc.
6.45	Fall in.
6.50	Fall out. Clean out chalets.
7.0	Wait for half hour.
7.30	Breakfast
8.0	Wait for half an hour.
8.30	Fall in. March to Pay Office.
8.30/10.30	Arranging for own allowance: 10 minutes. Waiting: 1 hour 5 minutes.
10.30	March to Gas Mask Office.
10.30/11.30	Learning how to fit masks.
11.30	Quarter-hour break.
11.45/1.0	Waiting in chalets.
1.0	Lunch.
1.30	Half hour's wait.
2.0/3.30	Lecture on conditions, pay, prospects, discipline etc.
3.30	Wait.
4.0	Tea.
4.30/7.0	Free.
7.0	Supper.
7.30/10.0	Free.

Evidently, for the first three weeks we don't so much as see or hear anything to do with Morse. We have no kit issued to us yet.

In my class there is one other Francis (out of 44) who has ship's number 8917 as opposed to my 8918 and who lives in Middleton One Row, South Shields! There'll probably be some mix-up soon.

There seems to be absolutely nothing to do here in the free

94

time. The chalets are too cold to sit in and the mess where I'm sitting now is a complete shambles. There is one billiards table and three darts boards between approximately 2,000 men in the division, so it's quite impossible to get near them.

A circulating library at the Post Office is provided at 2d a time, but the books are the worst trash imaginable. So that leaves only cards as an occupation. (Last night we played Solo and I won hands down until it was discovered there were only 48 cards in the pack!)

The weather is still very cold but shows signs of breaking up, but I tremble to think of what it will be like when the wind starts blowing hard. Last night it was much warmer in the new chalets, thank God.

Could you in addition to my pyjamas and socks send me another shirt and some handkerchiefs as it might be some days before the kit is issued. If you are sending me a parcel some time (as I hope you will my chickadee!) will you put in some fruit and cake as it is impossible to get them at the canteen.

I've spent all my money so far on cigarettes, tobacco and hot drinks and by Christ one needs them. Tobacco, duty free, is dished out once a month, maximum 1lb, price 2/2d, but unfortunately the last distribution was last month so we can't get any until next month. However, when it does come it should last a month and is considerably cheaper than 1/- an ounce.

We are allowed ashore for the first time on Sunday. It'll be welcome. We seem to be free every day at 4.0, at 2.0 on Saturdays and 11.30 on Sundays. Plenty of free time, but nowt to do wi'it.

Are you keeping warm these freezing days? Be sure you don't catch a chill. I hope the bed is not too lonely darling.

It would be lovely if, when the railway introduce the cheap excursion again, you could come up here for the day. Three days away from you seem like an eternity. Make enquiries at King's Cross will you.

Please write soon and tell me what you're doing, where you are and how you're feeling.

Goodnight my sweetest one. Look after yourself and J. too.

With all my love,

David

34, Myddelton Sq.
E.C.1
19.1.40

My darling David,

How are you my poor sweet darling? I hope that the cold is less vicious or you have acquired a few more blankets.

I received both your letters this morning when I returned home to No. 34 from staying a day and night with my mother. I could not bear to go back to the flat that is so full of you, and so empty! Putting your clothes away, I tried to pretend that you were coming back in the evening, but it was a poor attempt.

You sound so COLD in your letters, that I am knitting you a helmet which I will send with some socks and the cigarettes early next week.

With the letters from you there was one from Tom,* in which he compared the climate to that of Helsinki. You, I think, spoke of Petsamo,† showing a slight political difference – and also a magnificent wedding present from Joy – a series of casseroles, three dark blue with buttercup yellow linings, on a navy-blue

---

* Tom was undergoing training on the East Coast during the bitterly cold winter of that year.

† The Battle of Petsamo marked the beginning of the so-called Winter War between the USSR and Finland. Soviet troops invaded Finland in November 1939 and after fierce resistance a peace treaty was declared in March 1940.

wooden tray. Very nice, and I will look up her address in the telephone book and write her a thanking letter.

I also had a note about a job from Mrs Hoster, but the interview was Wednesday, so I did not attend. Still, it shows that such things as jobs exist.

You tell me not to be unhappy. Well come home again, for then and only then can I be happy. But I have learnt a lot from you my David, more than I knew, and one thing I have learned is that happiness and unhappiness are just states of mind, and while I can still think of you, write to you and read your letters I cannot be entirely without joy. So write often and think often of me and then I have a talisman against despair.

I have no more news except the ancient history – I love you more than anyone, anything in the world – much more than the world, and that I am thinking of you constantly, wishing happiness and warmth to compass you around.

Be happy my darling and keep yourself safe and well

With all my love always

Your Mary

P.S. Keep away from the ex-Paxton PT ogre!
P.P.S. Junior is behaving very well, not advertising his presence so much.

January 22nd [1940]
Skegness.

Mary, my darling,

It was so lovely getting a letter from you to hear that all was well, and that this temporary separation was not making you too unhappy. I'm glad junior is behaving himself, the little bastard!

Very little else has happened here. On Saturday, the sum total of our work, after deducting time wasted in hanging about, amounted to being issued with two pairs of boots, which were very welcome in the snow. Today, all we have done is to have our gas masks marked! It seems such an incredible place, this, completely lacking in system or in imaginative organisation, with the result that squads are kept hours hanging about in the snow for one article of clothing and drafts for naval bases get the majority of their kit some three days before completion of their five weeks' training.

The toll of the weather has been very heavy. Already this year there has been one death from exposure and the gymnasium, sick bay, local hospital and local miners' rest home are filled to overflowing with ratings suffering from various degrees of bronchitis, pneumonia and chills. So far our class has only lost two from bronchitis, but if the cold winds come, I'm afraid more are going to go down.

Saturday there was an excellent concert, part of which was broadcast, given by the ratings themselves. It included one really excellent Max Miller type comedian, who made some lovely cracks about the camp in general and certain petty officers in particular, that went down very well. After each bitter thrust he leered at the officers sitting in front and said, 'I'll give them squad drill. I'll give them class instruction.'!

In addition there were a couple of first class swing pianists and some good vocalists. On the whole a remarkably enjoyable concert.

The audience at these affairs seem to be a mixture of hooliganism and university rags (or is that a mixture?). Thus when the commodore and his daughters arrived, he was cheered while the girls heard 3,000 voices shouting 'Oooohh'. Similarly, when some army officers and NCO's arrived from a nearby depot, some 3,000 voices gave them a hearty Boo. The Senior Service, what!

Every night, either the Port or Starboard watch gets shore leave, and regularly whichever gets the leave cheers lustily at the announcement, the accompaniment of boos from the unfortunate stay-at-homes.

Our class had its first shore leave yesterday. A gang of us spent quite a good time by first of all having a good look at Skegness (which seems a prime example of a one-horse town), following which we visited the local cinema and saw 'The Spy in Black' and got warm for the first time since arriving. We then had tea and a game of cards at the local YMCA, which was surprisingly pleasant, with warm fires, plenty of tables for writing, playing cards, reading, etc, billiard room, dart boards and canteen. They have dances there twice a week, with specially imported, YMCA-censored partners! After cards, we adjourned to Charlie's joint for supper and then returned home.

Tonight we go to the camp cinema (price 2d) to see 'The Saint in New York'. Money seems to go very quickly here in buying cigarettes, hot drinks, fares etc. The food is quite good, but invariably cold and therefore not at all satisfying, so it has to be supported by buns, fruit, chocolate.

It was very kind of Joy to send some casseroles. They'll be mighty useful for stewing giant chickens when I come on my first leave.

Have you cleared the flat yet? I hope it's been done by now.

My darling, all my waking hours contain some thought, some reflection back to you, wondering what you're doing, where you are, whether you're feeling happy or not.

It's really miraculous how much one can be in love and it's even more wonderful to think we found each other so early and so young, so that the rest of our lives will be spent together in

complete understanding and in the knowledge that we love each
other dearly.

When this bleeding war's over we'll finish with separation
and be together. How I wish we were together now, that you
and I could spend just this evening together – it would be
happiness enough. Write to me quickly, because the receiving of
letters is a thrilling thing, and when it's from you it's ecstasy.

Goodnight, my sweet darling Mary.

Your own,

David

72 Elgin Crescent,
Ladbroke Grove W11.
Jan 21, 1940

My darling David,

The first weekend without you has almost passed and I still
live, mirabile dictu. The weekends will be the greatest ordeals,
and also the greatest joys because they will sometimes bring you
back to me. But why 5 or 6 weeks to wait? I cannot understand
the workings of this calculation.

I have spent the weekend with mother, who is being very
kind and sympathetic and over here there are no poignant
reminders of you at every step. I am breaking myself in gently to
living alone.

On the wireless last night there was a naval concert from 'a
training camp in the north'. Could this have been Skegness, and
I wonder if you were there. Handel's Largo and an imitation of
the Western Brothers featured on the programme. It was quite a
good concert and I hope you were there.

The cold here is intense and there is no water in any house, so I cannot bear to think what it must be like with your Arctic circles. I have the finishing stitches to put in a Balaclava I have knitted for you, which I will send as soon as completed.

Let me know all the details of your life in camp, the people you know and like, and those you don't like, so I can have a background for you and feel that I know where you are, instead of this lost-you feeling that I now have. The letters you sent have kept life in me up till now, so write often.

Personally I feel much better physically after the early morning spasms, so I think the worst is over. I am going to visit Mary Read this afternoon and compare notes.

I will write again tomorrow, my own David, but keep well and happy, and think often of me.

> With all my love, always
> Your Mary

> Tuesday 23/1/40
> Ord. Tel. Francis
> Class 219,
> Q/D Division
> HMS Royal Arthur
> Skegness.

My darling,

Just after I finished the letter to you yesterday the class leader came up with a letter from you. How lovely. Yes, that was our concert all right on Saturday. Didn't you hear me singing 'Roll out the barrel'. Actually the best part of the concert came later, but the Western Bros. impersonation was pretty good, especially the local allusions.

Last night we saw a pretty lousy film, the Saint in New York.

Most of the audience left before the end, although they remained to give the first kiss a rousing cheer!

Today we have been issued with a greater part of our outfit, everything except the essentials. There are no naval coats here at all, everyone wears specially issued civilian coats, but our class has been lucky in getting new coats that are cut in a very similar style to the naval ones. In addition we have vests, socks, oilskin, stockings, suitcase, shoe brushes, tooth brush, blue jean collars, silk scarf, gym shoes, hair brush, lanyard, caps and ribbons. There is still piles to come, though, as the Admiralty issues everything down to the last article of personal equipment, which is very satisfactory. All these things are issued free, but we are expected to replace them if lost, stolen, or worn out, for which we get an allowance of 2d a day from the date of joining up. I still have no cap as they had no more of my size.

Today has been quite energetic, as we also, as a class, had the job of clearing all the snow and ice away from the roadway through the camp. Warm work, however.

I'm so glad your mother is rallying round so that you won't be lonely. Write to me often though and let me know all you're doing. We'll have a wonderful weekend when I come home on leave. I don't know for sure when the next leave date will be but according to the rota it should either be three weeks from Saturday last, that is the 10th February, or five weeks, which would be the 24th February. I'll know soon though.

Yesterday I wrote to Mother and Father and informed them in the choicest manner that we were married. I expect I'll get an answer tomorrow some time.

Would you get my address to the local lads and lassies as I'm very anxious to get a lot of letters. It's amazing how exciting letter arrival time is! And as for parcels!! How's about it baby? Don't forget the socks and pyjamas, will you.

Our class is composed of a good lot of lads on the whole.

There are exactly 50 in the class, including the four visual signallers who have been transferred on account of bad eyesight. Of the remaining 46, some 11 are volunteers and of a greater age than the 35 conscripts. About 20 of these come from London and the rest from the environs thereof, and from the North. They are for the most part a well-educated lot, as opposed to the seamen, who are tough babies!

My chalet mate is married (in July) and is a good mate as he doesn't go out very much and invariably turns in early and warms the bed for me! Our solo playing four consists of one Patrick McMahon, who comes from London, works in the Pearl Assurance, is fond of music and a very likeable fellow and my constant companion; secondly, Len Lelew, a rowdy but very amusing telegraphist from Exchange Telegraph, completely obsessed with sex (he's only 20!!) but is full of life. Another boon companion. Thirdly, Maurice Francis, a volunteer from the North, much older and more staid but exceptionally easy to get on with. The class leaders are two picked at random by name, Ayton and Mackintosh. Ayton is very tall and stately and has been christened Jeeves unanimously; is very quiet and keeps to himself. Mackinosh is a volunteer, just the type for a leader. Had a guards moustache until forced to shave it off. Is very witty and doesn't retain much seriousness on parade unlike his co-leader, who even looked dignified when a snowball, thrown with unerring aim from the far rear rank, hit him bang on the napper!

There is one Roman Catholic, who looks every bit one. An audit clerk, who is a shit and looks one. The rest are a good type, none very enthusiastic about the war, all straightforwardly blunt in their opinion of HMS Royal A. But to use everyone's words about everyone else in the class, 'It's a good crowd.'!!

Well don't forget a parcel, will you, and let me know how the flat is at Angel House.

Love to Hetty, your mother and anyone else who feels entitled to it.

Write please dearest one. With all my love and may it keep you happy.

David

34 Myddelton Sq
Finsbury E.C.1
Jan 23, 1940

My own darling,

Thank you so much for writing such frequent and wonderful letters. This morning's was peach. I can imagine you now in all the vicissitudes of your new world, standing at ease, standing at attention and drinking tea in the Y.M.C.A. Quelle vie!

As for the other Francis, it is the most remarkable coincidence. Don't let him get any of my letters to you.

I have been quite busy these last two days. Yesterday visited agencies job-hunting, and I don't think it is going to be too difficult. Today, with the aid of a man-with-a-barrow, I removed the divan, ottoman and carpet from La Maison des Anges plus various tiddly bits and have had a busy afternoon cutting good spots (very rare) out of the red carpet and pushing the divan around hoping to find a place where it will be invisible.

I am now sitting by a big fire, very tired, surrounded by:

      item – 1 pr wet pyjamas (yours)

      item – 4 prs wet socks (yours)

have also been washing clothes and will send these to you when dry and ironed. I have posted a small parcel to you with this letter. But you will probably receive the letter first.

You say that money goes very quickly. Do you need any

now? Let me know in your next letter and I will send you all I can.

The cold here is so intense and there doesn't seem to be any water in the whole of London. People are breaking ice and boiling it. The conditions in Skegness sound terrifying – 1 dead already this year – for God's sake David don't die, or get ill or let anything harm you, will you. This is a most desperate request because now I know, if I didn't before, how empty, flat and unprofitable life is without you.

Junior was naughty this morning but is good now and sends you all his love.

Everyone asks after you and wishes you well. Have you heard from your Bushey home yet? I should encourage the bold Bertha to make you a cake, because I warn you, I am going to make you one and it is just as well to have an alternative.

I am going to a GY meeting on Thursday and will try to be a good little comrade in an attempt to fill the breach.

I have bought a yellow crocus in a pot which is growing and which I weep upon regularly, for it is so springlike and therefore reminds me of you.

Tom wrote me a most sympathetic letter regarding your departure. He is thrilled at the prospect of becoming an uncle, and offers financial assistance if needed. Coming from Tom this is something.

Everyone is very nice to me. Joan Paterson is taking me out to lunch tomorrow. When I am working I must reply.

I will go and see our fairy godmother from Euston tomorrow and report back to you. David, my sweet darling, I miss you like hell. I can't sleep at night and I want you all day. I thought it would be bad but it is much worse. I must come for a day before the first five weeks are over, because I need you very much.

I will write again tomorrow and look anxiously for your letter to me.

Be happy, darling, and love me always as I love you.
Forever and ever
Your Mary

Class 219
HMS Royal Arthur
Skegness
Thursday 25/1/40

My darling,

Tonight it is only a hurried note as it is now after 6.0 and the last post goes out in a ½ hour. Usually the time between 4.30 and 7.0 is free but on Thursday here is an instructional lecture which was replaced by a film of the same category this evening.

This afternoon we got paid – the singles £1 and the 3 marrieds 10/-. I still don't know how the pay is arrived at, except that it will have to last until today fortnight, the next pay day.

I don't know how the announcement of our marriage has gone down at home as I have had no letter. But today two parcels arrived, one containing warm stockings and the other chocolate, cheese, humbugs, barley sugar, raisins and biscuits, all sent from Watford tradesmen! By the way your parcel hasn't arrived yet. When did you post it? I'm very anxious to get my clean shirt as we haven't been issued yet with our uniforms.

We get our next shore leave on Saturday and I am going into Skeggy, either to the pictures, or the YMCA or both.

I and my friends have decided to spend an hour every evening between 5 and 6, learning how to fence, since there is still one piece of the gymnasium which is not a sick bay.

Today also I was issued with my cap and look quite ducky in it! If you have any time to spare, and if anyone else has any time to spare, would you knit some pairs of blue (navy) gloves, as my present pair are soaked. Several pairs would be very welcome, as they get wet so quickly. A scarf wouldn't be sneezed at either.

Well my darling, write soon won't you. I look forward every post for a letter from you – your letters are my very lifeblood. Can you get a photograph of yourself, a good one, so I can have it up here to keep me happy.

With all my love to you, my darling wife. I'll write again tomorrow, so until then goodbye.

Dearest Mary I love you so much. This separation is every day a greater strain and more unbearable.

David

Sunday 28/1/40
4.0pm
HMS Royal Arthur
Skegness

My darling Mary,

When I come home for the weekend on Feb 17th or 24th, I want to spend every moment of the leave with you and with no one else. This maddening separation is only serving to intensify my love for you so that I feel from the moment I arrive at King's Cross to the time I depart, I must not let you out of my sight, but must have you always at my side. Let's make a weekend of doing all those delightful domestic things we used to do. Out on Saturday night, long lie in together on Sunday morning, a walk over the Heath at lunch, the Times crossword, and tea by a big fire. That seems paradise to me now, especially with you there.

I'm writing now lying on my bed wrapped up in blankets as the weather is bitterly cold. A strong NE wind is blowing off the sea and I have a bit of a cold. I've just been playing solo with Pat, Len and Ken, who have been similarly wrapped up. They have now gone over for tea, which consists of 2 pieces of bread and butter, 1 cake and tea, which resembles a hell-brew, but I decided it wasn't worth leaving my extremely warm position. Now I'm alone with my thoughts and they are naturally straying to you.

Yesterday was a leave day, so we went in to Skegness and saw Gordon Harker in 'Inspector Hornleigh' at the local cinema. After that we had a high tea and adjourned to the YMCA where we played cards and table tennis and listened to a concert which had been arranged there.

Thank you very much for the big parcel which came yesterday. I haven't started the cake yet, so I'll give you any opinion the next letter, but it looks mighty good. The laundry was all present and correct, the balaclava fits perfectly and I like to think of your hands around my head when I put it on.

Thank Hymie very much for the cigarettes and tell him that I'm using my present and that I'm pleasantly surprised at the sentiment about the war here. What's this about him getting married?

Tom wrote yesterday – a very nice letter.

I'll write again tomorrow. Write soon dearest Mary.

 With all my love,
 David

 1/2/1940
 QD Division
 HMS Royal Arthur

Well, my darling Angel,

I've finally succumbed and am resting my weary body in the sick bay! Yesterday I felt very bad indeed and after seeing the doctor in the evening was shipped off to the sick bay with a temp of 101. However, after a night in the warm and better food to eat, I'm feeling much better and only feel bad about the throat. By a stroke of good fortune I'm in a bed next to Harry, who went on Sunday. I am the 14th from the class.

On Tuesday evening a miracle occurred – two letters arrived from you, a quite unanticipated joy. I'm sorry to hear your Pop is, shall we say, slightly apprehensive about becoming a grandfather! Yes your observation about a father's aversion to any manifestation of his daughter's physical intimacy is only too correct. Still he'll change his mind when he sees junior!!

It's too bad that the latter has been giving you trouble recently. Just wait till I come home and I'll put everything right.

That last night together seemed to be a culmination of our sexual experience and was wonderfully satisfying from every point of view. May my first leave come quickly so that you and I can come together again. You cannot conceive of how much I long to be in your arms again, to feel, with mine, the luxurious exciting softness of the whole of your lovely body. Just to be able to caress your breasts would be worth spending a month in jail for. We must make the weekend every bit as memorable as our last coming together.

I'm feeling sure the leave will be on Feb 10th. It's now only a matter of whether I can get better in time, which shouldn't be too difficult. Please write again to comfort my sick bay days. Keep happy and look after yourself and junior.

May my love keep you warm and protected,

Yours forever,

David

34 Myddelton Sq.
Finsbury E.C.1.
Feb 4th 1940

My darling David,

I hope by now that your temperature has abated and that your throat is better. What can I send you to make you feel well?

I also hope by now you have received the letters I have written since last Tuesday.

Will you be well enough to come home next weekend? I shall die of disappointment if you don't come, so you have got to be well.

I have been feeling so much better these last three days that I am daring to hope that junior has reformed. I have just washed my hair and it is all spread out to dry like wet grass, and great drops of water keep dripping on this letter.

It is Sunday, and I am going to lunch with Jill and Arthur – the first time I have seen them since you went away. I will give Arthur the usual raspberry from you.

The thaw seems to have arrived at last, and London, which has been the home of the Great Unwashed for the last month is now becoming uniced and instead great rivers of slush are racing down the streets. Nice going out into the blackout when you suddenly find yourself up to your waist in cold, cold water.

Tom has written to say that he is getting a recommendation from his captain for a commission this weekend. Darling, I'm afraid that you <u>will</u> have to salute him first. I am torn between the two of you. Perhaps Tom will pretend not to notice you on the streets as you cock your snook at him.

Hymie was knocked down by a taxi the other day, sustaining bruises and, most unfortunate, the loss of his spectacles. His hush-hush girlfriend was with him so they had to hush-hush the

accident and therefore cannot claim for damages done. He's
barmy.

Have you heard from 'Les Parents'. I feel the Arctic gloom
prevailing is the direct result of their displeasure, so I wish that
they would hurry up and thaw as it is still bloody cold.

Daisy and I are going to spring clean the flat next week
against your return, my ancient mariner, so don't let me scrub
the floor in vain. Send me a programme of events next weekend
so that I can arrange beforehand and no time will be wasted.

Write constantly and remember I love you to distraction.

Goodbye sweetheart

Yours ever

Mary

February 7 1940
HMS Royal Arthur

Dearest Mary,

A thousand thanks for your letter, which arrived today. I'm so
glad that the allowance book has arrived and that you now have
a little more cash in hand. You should be able to draw another
24/- tomorrow as well, shouldn't you?

I've been up all day and my temperature remained normal,
which means I shall sleep in my chalet tomorrow night and
will be discharged on Friday – just in time for the uniform
and pay.

Mother wrote again today – a pleasant letter about nothing in
particular. She asks what you are doing and suggests that you go
out one day. Could you manage a visit all by your little self or
will the presence of awe-inspiring in-laws have a revolutionary
effect on junior? She also sent a Men Only, a Wide World, a

Strand, Punch and Picture Post – all of which were welcomed with open arms by the ward.

Did you see the film or play of 'Golden Boy'? I'd heard the former was very disappointing. The letter from Sagalov is a little worrying. However, I'll have to see what the form says.

The constitution of the wards is rapidly changing. Now all the old contemptibles have gone and only I and 2 others are left. However, Friday will see the last of us. Well, my sweet, the post goes in a few moments and my messenger boy is restive. I write again tomorrow and Saturday I'll be in your arms again.

Take care of yourself and meet me on Saturday for sure, won't you. I'll let you know the time of the train.

With all my love irrevocably, David

8/2/40
HMS Royal Arthur

My darling,

Each day brings us closer together and Saturday ceases to be a figment of the imagination and becomes an ever-increasing reality. Today I was discharged and sleep at my chalet tonight for the first time for several days. I tried to get paid today but the news of my discharge had not reached the ears of the Paymaster, with the result that I have to wait until tomorrow. However, I shall get £1, which will be sufficient for the fare.

About the allowance. My chalet mate tells me that his wife is getting 27/6 a week, which is the ordinary allowance plus the special rent allowance for London, which is 6d a day. We must get that rectified.

I feel much happier mentally today and have even sung and whistled a bit, in an aimless, tuneless way.

After the ravages of influenza a lad in the next ward has caught measles, and that being what it is I expect the whole camp will catch it within three weeks!

I see the situation in Finland, according to the press, 'is beginning to change and it is necessary to realise that the Russian advance, although slow, has been methodically steady.' How lovely. I prophesy complete victory by the end of March, or at latest, in very early April. Perhaps even on my birthday.

I still don't know the time of the train arrival so I'll drop you a line tomorrow and let you know what it is.

I'm getting my overcoat altered by the admiralty tailor tomorrow in time for the leave. The barber has also done his damnedest.

Well my sweetest angel, come Saturday and life will begin again for a few precious hours.

Remember the wine!

With all my love, dearest sweetest Mary. Keep well and happy. David

CHAPTER 8

'Every day is St Valentine's Day'

NG–A345

MARY FRANCIS   34 MYDDLETON SQUARE LONDON EC1

WILL YOU BE MINE

DAVID

Greetings Telegram
G.P.O.

David gets his first leave after a month and the couple are re-united in London for an ecstatic weekend. David then begins to get to grips with Morse code, as a basic part of his wireless telegraphist (W/T) training. The harsh conditions facing the young recruits in the freezing Skegness winter are again underlined when he reports that one of their number has died after sitting too close to a brazier to keep warm and inhaling carbon monoxide gas.

News arrives of the progress of Mary's much-loved younger brother, Tom, aged eighteen, who is based for the moment on anti-submarine duties in Yarmouth.

★

February 12th 1940
HMS Royal Arthur
Skegness

My darling,

The precious hours yesterday passed all too quickly, and now I'm back in this God forsaken hole, miles away from you and home, feeling a complete stranger. The weekend was lovely from the very moment I saw you, smart and gay, at the station until the damnably wretched hour of parting. Life will consist now of passing the days mechanically, just waiting for the next leave. The whole of my thoughts will be concentrated on the ever-decreasing number of days before I see you again.

It was so completely satisfying to be able to spend a weekend together doing so little, and yet enjoying ourselves so much. A Saturday night super supper, a walk on the Heath, hot Sunday lunch and the Times crossword, together with our patent gymnastic lovemaking when the spirit moved one. Try and keep happy until the next leave. 25 days can pass like lightning and I'm going to see that mine do.

The journey home from King's Cross was not too bad although I had to sit in the corridor all the way. I got to the station about 3 minutes to eleven.

The gramophone has gone down very well and several of the boys have promised to procure records from various points of the globe.

This afternoon we had a lecture on Morse procedure and practically the whole class fell asleep. We only had four hours' sleep this morning and just after lunch the strain began to tell.

There was one thing I forgot to mention and that is if you have any spare cash (ONLY if it's spare) could you buy me a Thermos flask. It would be immensely useful up here.

I had a letter from the Income Tax Inspector today and have filled in a return for his benefit, which allows me the income free of tax for a married man with no mention of your earnings! I hope it goes down all right.

Well regrettably I must rush away and get my evening medicine (I still have to attend for the throat medicine and rentalising tablets!). I'll write again tomorrow and I hope there will be a letter from you before then.

Thinking of you constantly and living for March 8th. With all my love my dearest Mary.

Think of me sometimes,
David

Class 219
Feb 13th 1940
HMS Royal Arthur

My darling Mary,

Yet another day has passed with the rapidity of full routine. It's been rather tiring having 3 sessions of Morse with headphones like loudspeakers, but bit by bit it's becoming clearer. The class is beginning to be weeded out now and many are finding it very difficult to understand Morse procedure and transmission. In a couple of weeks there will be an examination and those gaining below a set percentage will be placed in a class by themselves. That will simplify matters.

There has been one more death up here under rather tragic circumstances. A lad in the adjoining row of chalets had felt the cold very acutely and had acquired the dangerous habit of sitting in the wash house over a brazier which is there to keep the pipes from freezing. On Sunday the snow came back again so he spent a long time by the fire, probably until bed time. When his mate returned from leave early on Monday morning, he found him dead in bed – he had died from carbon monoxide poisoning. The brazier gives off a gas like the exhaust of a car, and if it's inhaled too long the bloodstream becomes poisoned.

Terribly tragic to die from such a trivial cause in such a useless way. As a result strict rules have been made about the brazier.

The weather now is comparatively warm although snow is still on the ground. I'm feeling much better except for a slight cough, and that is already on its way.

Well my sweet. Please write soon – sleep well, and don't let junior trouble you too much.

Thinking of you and loving you always,
David

34 Myddelton Sq
Finsbury E.C.1
Feb 15th 1940

My own sweet darling,

Your lovely letter received this morning has made me feel all warm and happy inside. And as for the Valentine, it will be my most constant companion until your return. Now we are engaged officially.

At last the Angel flat is evacuated. After much promising from Hymie and other people, this morning I took the bull by the horns and with the help of the Italiano greengrocer's boy, moved the lino myself and stacked it in one of Myddelton's subterranean passages. Hymie has just called and I have sent him away with a flea in his ear, because I am tired of his incompetence and colossal impudence (by way of a change).

This morning I received a P.O. from the Admiralty for 17/6d and a promise of an extra 3/6d pw. This has come in the nick of time, for I am pretty poor this week owing to arrears of rent paid and other little bills. So if I receive a surprise packet like this every week (last week it was the Marston 12/6d) I shall soon be rich.

I am going for an interview this afternoon regarding a job, so pray for me. If I get it all our troubles regarding junior's coming into the world will be over.

I haven't seen Reg since to ask him about the extra allowance, but can't you ask for the form that Sagalov mentions at your end? I think I have to make a claim from the P.A.C. at this end.

A whole week has gone since you were home and in 3 weeks more, I will have you again. That is the thought that keeps me alive and the knowledge that you love me as I love you, and that our love is unique, perfect and everlasting.

Yours for ever
Mary

February 15th 1940
HMS Royal Arthur

My darling,

Thanks so much for the letters and delightful telegram which arrived today. For me, every day is St Valentine's Day – a day of remembering the woman I love with all the feeling and understanding of my body and mind.

I'm so sorry to hear that you're not feeling well again. This production of junior is a process not entirely enjoyable and I often feel very guilty to have caused you so much pain and discomfort, even though at the same time I'm happy that a child of you and me, a child that is part of you and me – a synthesis of us – is to be born into the world. I'm quite confident that the pleasure and happiness which a child will eventually bring to us will more than compensate for the pain it causes you now. My only regret is that I am unable to share in or at least alleviate the pain that you feel . . .

So Angel House is finally evacuated. Thank the Lord for that. Did Reg construct the shelves, or didn't he have time for that?

Yesterday we went into Skegness for the evening and had a pleasant time. Ken and I decided to walk so that we would know exactly how long it would take us, but by a stroke of good fortune, a thumb cocked in the appropriate Clark Gable style brought us a lift on a lorry when we had gone about half a mile. After supper at Charley's Joint, we went to see 'The Man in the Iron Mask',* which is a pretty good film. Quite an exciting story with good acting from Louis Hayward and Joseph Schildkraut. What did you go to see with Elsie and Joan?

---

* *The Man in the Iron Mask* (1939), directed by James Whale, starring Louis Hayward and Joan Bennett.

Yes, the gramophone may be borrowed provided the usual care is taken with it.

I hope Tom comes home this weekend. Give him my regards and tell him I'll write again soon.

I clean forgot that the 1/- calls operate only after 7.0. I'll make a point of ringing between 7.0 and 7.30 in case you want to go out. These calls will be a blessing in disguise – it will be so lovely to hear your voice again so soon.

Good for the Branch! A pretty good collection for war time.

The class has just got another instructor, who takes the latter half of the class for Morse. He is a dour Scot, with a very whimsical sense of humour and seems preferable as teacher to our instructor (1st half class). Today, just after we had been issued with our second pair of suits plus two pairs of ducks, we had to parade for divisions. The instructor comes up, eyes us and says: 'Now then, where's the chap whose trousers don't fit him under the armpits' in such an indifferent, dour way that it almost caused a riot on the parade ground!

I had another parcel from Mother yesterday containing some shortbread, chocolates, biscuits and cake.

The sea today was very calm; in fact it looked quite pleasant from the sea wall. Four or five ships were out, plus the inevitable armed trawler and a destroyer far out to sea. The weather is much milder and although the snow is still on the ground, the horrible biting wind has at last dropped.

Write to me as soon as you can, just to keep me alive.

This brings you all my love in the hope that it will make you happy.

Thinking of you always my dearest wife.

David

29/2/40
HMS Royal Arthur

My darling,

The hearing of your voice last night has provided an inspiration for days to come and imbued me with fortitude to face the remaining 18 days before I see you again – I'm terribly glad to hear you have the prospects of a job and the fact that it is with the Mond Nickel will assure that you put another link in the chain of incredible occupations that you have had (including looking after me!). I did not quite catch one remark which you made over the telephone. Put it in your next letter if it is important.

So Tom came home for the weekend. Is he well or has the rigour of the Yarmouth climate told on him?

I'm filling in that form for extra allowances this evening so will include it in tomorrow's letter. It seems to be the thing to do for a temporary extra allowance.

The weather today is very depressing – sleet outside and cold inside and it's such a horrible change from yesterday when we had a very pleasant three-mile walk along the beach to Skegness. I saw Stanley and Livingstone again and enjoyed it just as much.

Have there been any developments regarding the flat at Myddelton? I hope Winifred has decided to take the house over.

Darling, to jog your memory – please have a good photograph of yourself taken and send it to me. I do so much want one. It would bring an added brightness to life here and in the chalet would provide a warmth and cheerfulness that no amount of dampness and cold could dispel.

A parcel arrived today from Pera containing some fruit and magazines – a welcome combination.

Our march past yesterday produced a word of praise from the officers – not bad for the first time of leading Q/D.

Tonight we are duty class and I have to spend an hour in the galley cleaning up supper dishes. I hope the hell it's a clean supper.

Please write again soon. It's Saturday since I had a letter.

With all my love darling
David

20/2/40
HMS Royal Arthur

My darling,

Many thanks for the letter received today and the very welcome enclosure. The news of the flat is most depressing and serves to increase my feeling of complete impotence where our affairs are concerned, being so far away and unable to see to things myself. It needs a lot of thinking about and I'll write a proper letter tomorrow about it.

Tonight I'm going onshore for a whist drive, a thing I've never been to before. However, it should prove most interesting.

I'll certainly write to Tom and wish him many happy returns. Is he still on the yacht?

When compiling that form I'll make the rent figure 19/- a week, e.g. including 2/- for cleaning and 2/- for coal.

Curse and blast Winifred. But more of that tomorrow.

There was one painfully depressing note in your letter – the making of junior the butt of your depression and unhappiness. Please don't do that, it hurts. There can be nothing more tragically useless than a woman bearing a child she resents.

Goodbye darling. Tomorrow I'll write a long and satisfying letter.

With all my love
David

21/2/40
HMS Royal Arthur

My darling Mary,

I've been thinking a lot about your letter and the complications caused by bloody Winifred. It's very difficult to say what's to be done, but here are some suggestions. Firstly what do you say to packing up the flat on 25th March, storing the furniture and coming up to live in Skegness? I've been talking to one or two people up here in the town and have established the fact that it is quite easy to get full board and lodging for 30/- per week up to May at least, and slightly extra after that.

The weather is becoming distinctly milder and by the end of March should be considerably better. We could then see each other every other evening, which seems at first thought a thing too dear to be hoped for, but on second thoughts quite feasible. Could you manage to live if you were by yourself all day in a place where you knew no one? And would it be financially possible if you had 24/- plus 15/- to live on (discounting anything I get from the office which I can't include until I hear from them), see my suggestion?

Alternatively, Pat MacMahon is contemplating marriage and suggesting that we should combine and both bring our wives up to Skegness and get them a furnished flat, if such things are available for a reasonable price (we are investigating that on Saturday when we go into Skeggy).

On the other hand you could move into Roddy's part of Myddelton, but whether or not that is financially possible depends entirely on the office. An advantage of coming to Skegness would be that the heavy railway fare would be avoided and my part of the naval pay we could spend together.

Personally I should now favour either the first or second suggestions. Now that the weather is clearing one can feel the mildness of the weather and provided that you would not be bored to death through living by yourself in Skegness, it should be lovely. Think about it, darling, then we can discuss it fully when I come home in 16 days time. By that time the office question will be finally settled.

Perhaps by a stroke of superb good fortune you might be able to get a temporary secretarial job up here.

The news that Cyril Mann* is to paint you is excellent. We must buy the painting, by hook or by crook. But don't let it make you forget the photograph I want so much.

Talking about photographs, today some press photographers came up and took pictures of Q/D Division at eating time (219 in foreground) and running round the mess (219 well to front).

Today we had some Morse sending practice and I find I do very well at it because my sending is 'rhythmical' and my spacing is OK. A lot of the class find it very difficult indeed.

Last night in Skegness was great fun – I spent two hours in the whist drive (not doing too badly in the scoring) and then had two hours dancing. We had special leave until 12.30 for it. The dancing was quite fun, although I had a heart-rending feeling of loneliness for you, I was wishing the whole time you were there to dance with. The total cost of the evening was 1/-, which was certainly excellent value.

Another parcel came from home today containing some foodstuffs and a pair of gigantic stockings and gloves (both white) which had been knitted by an old lady belonging to mother's C.S. church! You should see the size. Big enough for an ox at least.

Today I sent off the UAB† form, spinning a long and heart-rending story which should extract an extra allowance.

Well, my sweetest heart, I must close now as the post draws

---

* Cyril Mann (1911–80) was at this time a promising London-born artist and a good friend of Mary and David.

† U.A.B.: Unemployment Assistance Board – the Dole – set up in 1934.

nearer. Think a lot about Skegness and I hope you will want to come and I'm praying that the office will make it possible for you to live as comfortably as you deserve to live. Write to me quickly, as it seems an age since your last letter.

With all my love, and may it guard you and keep you well. Goodbye, my darling. David

34 Myddelton Sq
Finsbury E.C.1
Feb. 22 1940

My dear David,

I received two letters from you this morning, both of which contained statements that annoyed me intensely. item: the crap about the tragedy of a woman bearing a baby which she resents – you should be intelligent enough to realise that no woman can be exhilarated by something amounting to physical upheaval which makes her sick and tired for the best part of the day and also to know that I could never resent your baby but I do resent the possibility that I may degenerate into a shapeless, toothless wreck because I cannot afford a real maternity corset or get the right amount of calcium in my diet. That, and not 'the comfort you deserve' – your other dirty crack, is what is troubling me. Though I have the honour to be that worthy creature 'a wife and mother' I still wish to retain some recognisable features of my less worthy days, among which my teeth are important. But this is not your concern, so don't make futile remarks.

I have been today to the Labour Exchange about this myth of 'temporary government work', and filled in numerous forms and interviewed horrible cowlike women, with, I suppose, the same minimum result. Anyway if I don't get a job soon I shall become a Nippy* or start mantling radio sets in some wireless factory.

I am glad you enjoyed your whist drive and dance. It sounds fun. I am also glad that Keith† sends me his regards. He probably hasn't been told about your misalliance, a continuation of the same hush-hush plan.

A man has threatened, by letter received today from the U.A.B., to come and check up on me. That will be nice. What with insulting Labour Exchange bitches and U.A.B. spies, life is one long round of excitement.

Enough of this moaning, I grow old and bitter before my time you are probably thinking in that oh-so-subtle psycho-analysing mind of yours.

Goodbye for now,
Mary

Class 219
23/2/40

My darling,

Your letter today caused some acute bewilderment and depression. When I said you should have the comfort you deserve it was not said with one iota of maliciousness, but rather with the fully conscious realisation that at present you were not well, not eating enough, and generally not happy – and your reading into it made me rather sad.

Believe you me, I want you to have this baby in the best possible circumstances and my constant regret is that I am placed

---

* Nippy: Lyons Corner House waitress.
† One of David's three brothers.

in a position in which it's impossible for me to provide them. It's always worrying me and your references to lack of calcium in your diet and your inability to buy a maternity corset only serve to intensify that worry and increase this damned feeling of impotence I get up here.

Please, dearest darling Mary, don't misunderstand me and think that your poverty is something that I don't consider my concern. It is and always will be until I'm able to see that you are living properly and comfortably. How can I cease to be conscious that it is I who put you in the condition you are and that it is I who have prevented you from being a well-placed secretary at Bletchley? I cannot, and I fully realise that any bitterness you feel about your life now must necessarily be directed against me. That I can bear by now, but darling please don't misconstrue my attempts to make plans to try and make you happier. That hurts to the point of being unbearable.

I'm glad that the UAB have replied quickly. I don't think that they will exactly spy on you. We may be fortunate in getting a substantial allowance from them. By the way, for information purposes, I put our joint income as £8. 5. 0 (3/10/- plus 3/15/- and £1 from father), rent as 19/-.

I had another letter from mother today. She again asks after you and asks whether you would like to come out for the weekend sometime. I gather from the letter that Poppa is sore, but fuck him.

Today has been a miraculous day, warm and sunny and a definite tang of spring in the air again. Is it like that in London?

I'm going into Skegness tomorrow, so I'll give you a ring between 7.0 and 7.30, provided the trunk line is disengaged. It should be quieter from Skegness.

Yesterday evening when just about to settle down for letter writing we were suddenly whisked off to endure 1½ hours of crude film propaganda about life in the Navy, as if we didn't know. Blasted nuisance.

Yesterday was pay day, so I'm enclosing 7/- to help. Actually I think it would not be a bad idea to sell the gramophone and records and try and raise enough cash thereby to ensure that you have everything you need. Because darling, you must have everything, and the sooner the better.

To think, 14 days from now (5.45) I shall be arriving in London seeing you again and then I'll try and erase this bitterness from your heart. Darling, however angry and annoyed you are feeling with me, please don't cease to love me lest the light go out of my life. I love you unceasingly and treasure every moment's happiness with you – it's that what keeps me alive in this nest of drifting morons.

Tomorrow I shall be speaking to you again, a great event to look forward to.

Please write quickly and tell me how you feel.

    Yours for eternity
      David

34 Myddelton Sq.
Finsbury E.C.1.
Feb 25th, 1940

My darling David,

First I want to say how sorry I am that my letters were so miserable last week and worried you so much. I was a little under the influence of the full moon and therefore not quite as gallant as England expects, perhaps, or else I am not great enough or generous enough to keep my bad temper to myself . . . Anyway, my darling, forgive me for my vindictive outburst and please believe me that I am really very happy about the baby, and very grateful to you, not resentful in the least. The beginnings of spring always depress me in normal circumstances, so last week the sight of grass, pale sun and early flowers had the most unusual effect.

The U.A.B. called and I stuck to your story, through thick and thin, though I didn't know we were still hiring fittings from the Gas Co. Anyway I told him about my dole and made myself very pleasant to the funereal creature (complete with bowler hat and umbrella), so we may hear something to our advantage. BUT I couldn't produce any Sagalov evidence – where have you hidden the agreement and receipt in case they want to inspect them?

I had another most unpleasant interview with Madame Collier – she blew into my room on Saturday morning before I was up and sitting with girlish friendliness on the end of the bed told me on second thoughts she wanted Roddy's room for herself, and I could move to the top of the house, reason being that George Curtiss sometimes works nights and our gramophone would disturb his diurnal rest. She then smiled sweetly and waited for my customary mild acquiescence. Instead of which I sat up in bed and proceeded to tell her what I thought of her sordid excuse and the general buggering about and that it was Roddy's rooms or nothing as far as I was concerned. She was very surprised and said we would discuss it further on Monday. I really am livid with rage at the way in which these so-called progressives behave – worse than any Tory landlord dare do.

Still, I think I have got Winifred's manoeuvres straight now and, as I am so angry, quite look forward to battle with her. But if I'm evicted on March 10th, lock stock and barrel, it wouldn't surprise me, as she is an unscrupulous bastard.

As for the 7/- you sent me – I was outraged. I have changed it and spent some of it this weekend as the milkman became a little insistent, but I will return it tomorrow. Don't you dare supplement my income out of your navy pay again. It is bad enough having to allot 7/- a week already.

Well tonight, you will speak to me and drive away some of the clouds that hover around my head. But I am beginning to overcome some of my neurosis, and to quite enjoy being on my own in the flat – in fact it is preferable to many visitors who insist on calling and eating all my week's rations. Blast their souls.

There's a west wind blowing today and a lightness in the air that makes me remember

> 'Oh sweet west wind, when wilt though blow
> That the small rains down can rain.
> Christ that my love was in my arms
> And I in my bed again.'*

And on this poignant note of 14th century yearning, I say goodbye to my love until tonight, when you will speak to
    Your Mary

February 26th 1940
HMS Royal Arthur

Darling Mary,

It was lovely to hear your voice last night and to know that you are feeling happier and physically better. What a blessing the phone is – it lets one anticipate and look forward to a conversation for a week and at the same time provides something to remember for the same time.

---

* Early sixteenth century song.

Tonight I'm writing this from the YMCA as I'm going to follow up the question of lodging from here and Mrs Jones is just up the road. I hope something constructive comes of the evening.

I'm glad the UAB man has called so promptly and I've a feeling they'll be more considerate towards a sailor's wife than towards the ordinary unemployed man.

You should be able to find the agreement in the left-hand side of the gramophone draw, in case you didn't hear over the phone. On Saturday Mac, the class leader, Pat and S combined to buy a super Thermos flask which now provides us with a nightcap of hot tea – very useful indeed.

The weather today has been just perfect and the sun has been shining like a June day. Our class has suddenly found itself the 'darling' of the P.O.'s as a result of its organisation, marching and table behaviour, so we are cashing in on our popularity by making a request for our chalets to be changed to a row which catches the sun. It will be marvellous if the request is granted. Actually this partiality of Petty Officers to 219 is affecting the senior W/T and signal classes who feel that their position of seniority is being threatened. It's really rather amusing this inter-class rivalry and will probably develop into a pitched battled sooner or later as the RNVR classes regard us as annoying upstarts definitely of a lower social order, being conscripts! In such a battle I'd lay 10–1 on our class against two RNVRS!!

I was rather disappointed not to receive a letter from you this morning, but expect that it will be waiting for me when I get back this evening. I hope so.

Could you possibly send me some of the handkerchiefs that were washed and a pair of pyjamas. I want them rather badly.

Keep well my darling Mary, and write as often as possible. Think of it. In 11 days I'll be with you again.

With all my love, dearest Mary,
David

Class 219
February 27 1940
Q/D Division
HMS Royal Arthur

My dearest darling,

Today there are two big items of news. Last evening I went round to see the woman whom the YMCA recommended and she explained she had found just the place for me nearby. We accordingly went round to see a woman by the name of Mrs Chester who keeps a house just a few minutes' walk from the sea. I explained again just what we wanted and how we were placed financially, and she seemed throughout the conversation a very pleasant and sympathetic woman (I learned later that her husband is partially paralysed as a result of the last war), and expressed her willingness to help.

The final result of the talk is that she is prepared to let you have a bed-sitting room with full board for 27/6 a week, or alternatively a bedroom and a sitting room for 32/6 full board. This seems a very reasonable price but I haven't yet had the opportunity of seeing the rooms in question since she is moving to another house on Friday, but I have arranged to go on Sunday and have a look at them.

From what I could see of the present house it was very nice indeed. In addition she would allow me to stay with you whenever I got the opportunity free of charge and would feed me at small cost.

This seems an extraordinary piece of luck lighting on such a good place for the first time for not only are the terms good but I like the woman too. I told her that I would give a definite answer on March 11 when I returned from seeing you. Think it over darling, it seems a good prospect.

The second item of news is that leaves will be one short and one long weekend a month. (This has yet to be officially confirmed.) It would mean that at the end of a fortnight a short weekend would be due and at the end of a month a long weekend, which would be really marvellous, particularly if you are up here, and those precious hours of travelling would be far better spent.

This afternoon since our plea for a change of chalets produced the necessary result, we moved from SY to SZ and are now confronted by a vista of tennis courts instead of another row of chalets and in addition the sun will shine on us all day.

Your letter today was lovely and I humbly apologise if my written words were at all ill-chosen. My thoughts are constantly dwelling on you and planning a better life for you and the possibility of an unkind word is as remote from my thoughts as East is from West.

The UAB man sounds most amusing, far more so than does Winifred. Her attitude has been most outrageous.

But as for the 7/-, phooey to you madam! You keep it or I'll be angry!!

And now it's only 10 days more until I'm with you again. Lovely.

Write again soon and I'll phone you again on Sunday after seeing Mrs Chester again.

With all my love my dearest Mary and with innumerable kisses

David

34 Myddelton Square,
Finsbury E.C.1.

My darling David,

Today I started working in a temporary job in Hanover Square. £3 per week and should last three weeks or a month, so it really is very suitable as I don't want a job much after that. I have to pay the agency that got me the job my first week's salary, but apres, je suis riche. It is rather a vague place, but I think it is a sort of superior surveyor's office. My immediate boss is far more interested in juvenile crime, however, and most of the office seems to be devoted to visiting childrens' courts and prisons. Very nice influence for the wretched junior, who was predestined anyway. I only applied this morning and was so distinguished and charming that they asked me to start right away. They will now proceed to check up with Monsieur Sykes, but for a temporary job I shouldn't think it mattered about being married. I will be able to buy some necessary articles so quit worrying about me.

It was lovely speaking to you last night. I am so desolate about Saturday, but I honestly thought that you only operated on Sundays. Still, next week any time and day very clearly.

I must write to the Labour Exchange tonight and let them know that I am no longer one of their ranks. My boss has just come in and said the letters I did were 'Lovely'. Oh boy. Wait till he sees Sykes' reference. I will be out.

It is now Thursday darling, and I didn't have time to finish or post this last night. I am now in my new office, thinking of you with great longing and wishing so much that we could meet for lunch as in the old days of mutual employment. It is quite a strain rising at 8am after so long a holiday, but I think it is worth it and I can save madly during the next few weeks, if it lasts, and then relax a little.

Oh darling I miss you so much and love you so much and please write to me soon.

 With love always dear David
  your
   Mary

P.S. I enclose the 7/- you lent me.
P.P.S. The laundry is in two parts – hanks and pyjamas not yet returned but will forward them as soon as they are ready.

CHAPTER 9

Behind the Barbed Wire

16, Prideaux House
Prideaux Place
W.C.1.
March 31, 1940.

My own darling David,

At last I am writing to you about the hospital & junior. I have definitely been given a bed – & the confinement should be August 22nd or thereabouts. Free ambulance ride provided by courtesy of Finsbury Borough Council. The cost of the confinement is £5.17.6 for 10 days, which is the normal stay & £7.00 odd for 12 days, which is if the birth is difficult or overlong. I did not have a very profound examination – the fact of my pregnancy is without doubt & the doctor said I was normal in every way & shouldn't have a bad time. He advised Halibut oil capsules for the cough, which

To be paid at the end of the hospital period and not officially allowed

March arrives. The weather gets warmer. David gets the chance to play hockey and the letters are full of anticipation of the next weekend leave, with David trying hard to persuade an obviously reluctant Mary to go out to Bushey with him and meet his parents as his new wife. Then a bombshell – an outbreak of scarlet fever results in the camp being put in quarantine and leave is cancelled.

The Myddelton Square flat finally falls through and Mary has to move again, but just around the corner to Prideaux Place, WC1. David's normal good humour is beginning to be tested by events at Skegness – overcrowding, damp chalets, cancelled leave.

★

Class 219
Q/D Division
HMS Royal Arthur
Skegness
29/2/40
8 more days

Hullo my darling,

Probably when you receive this you will just be starting forth for Hanover Square to deal with the day's juvenile delinquents – and I hope you have a happy day. I'll be thinking of you all day in the heart of Mayfair and loving you continually and wishing not only could I meet you for lunch but that the evening would be ours again without interference and without interruption. That is the very Eldorado of my dreams.

Today has been a lovely day again and we were actually able to sunbathe after lunch. The daily routine has been changed somewhat owing to the switch over to summertime but even now we parade by moonlight!

I enjoyed 'This Man in Paris'* a lot. Both this and the previous one, although a bit weak in story, have had a pleasantly witty dialogue which is refreshing in a British picture.

The rumour about two weekend leaves a month has turned out to be for ship's company only, which is a pity, but one new innovation is that instead of 4 short and 2 long weekends in the six months we shall have three of each, and the P.O.'s are trying to get four long and two short for us.

It's just struck me. Surely Hymie has to register with the 25's? Tell him to join the Navy as a telegraphist and so ensure the maximum training possible!

The RNVR class (advanced section) are taking their exams this weekend and will probably go on draft if they are successful. That will mean four months more at Chatham and Portsmouth signal schools learning how to keep watches. If they do pass I think they rise from Ord. Tel. to Trained Operator or summat.

What news of your Pop these days? Has he definitely decided to stay in the Army?

By the way, don't forget to ask Kay to check Rose of Hornsey for Poutney or Jones . . .

We get a Morse exam at 8 words a minute next week, the first

---

* *This Man in Paris* (1939), directed by David MacDonald, starring Barry K. Barnes, Valerie Hobson and Alastair Sim.

of a series. It will consist of 40 words of plain language followed immediately by 30 groups of code, and 30 groups of cypher. Those getting over 90% will be placed in Y class and those under in X class. Today we had a test and I managed to get 96% – counting 1% off for each error in a word, code or cypher group.

Well my darling Mary, let's have a line from you to hear how you are getting on in Hanover Square. I'm terribly glad you have a job because it must make a terrific difference to your comfort, both physical and mental. Think – in a few weeks we'll have known each other two years – did we ever imagine when we were up on Hampstead Heath that memorable morning that we would be husband and wife and at the same time separated by all the boundaries the R.N. could conceive of? I doubt it!

Write, please, my darling heart. Think always of your very own.

David

3/3/40
HMS Royal Arthur

My darling,

This weather is truly magnificent. Just now I'm sitting out on the Skegness sea-front and feeling as warm as toast. Yesterday was just as lovely and I spent a most energetic day by going first of all for a six-mile route march in the morning, playing a fast and furious game of hockey on the hard tennis courts in the afternoon and table tennis all the evening.

I'm damned stiff as a result. The hockey was very good but too fast owing to the hard surface. There were some officers playing too, one of them a Cambridge blue. The final score was 6-6, I having scored four for our side. Unfortunately I injured myself by crashing full speed into the wire netting round the courts. and cutting my ear, bruising my side, grazing my wrist and, worst of all, breaking the catch of my watch, which will have to be put right.

The letter from Bertha is a bloody insult. Roddy made it quite clear to us when we first came in that even if he did give up the tenancy in March we should have no difficulty in arranging with the New River Company to continue in our flat. It was only for that reason that we vacated Angel House, although rent was going to be paid till Feb 28 there. Now we find ourselves in the position of being asked to vacate Myddelton Square just 25 days after the Angel House lease expired. Actually it is not really Winifred who is to blame – Roddy is the one at fault and I am writing today to tell him so as to make it quite clear to him that his obligations to us will continue until such time as you are in a position to move and that no amount of compulsion will cause you to move until you have found another flat.

It's bloody sauce enticing us in for three months on the strength of us believing the tenancy to be for the duration of the war and then asking us to leave just like that.

I enclose a very nice letter I've just had from Keith, who by the way has just risen to lieutenant. The prospect of a cash wedding present is a pleasant surprise, and I have just written to the said Mrs Verley giving her your address. You should be hearing soon.

I suggest that on the Saturday (next in fact) I pop into the office and see them there and at the N.O.W. and then we both go out and have lunch at Bushey. I know they'll be very pleased to see us. We can come back after tea and spend the evening together in town.

The proximity of Friday seems almost incredible – just five days – and we must make it, if it's possible, even more enjoyable than last time.

Tonight I shall be speaking to you once again and the sound of your voice will lighten the load of five days which separates you from me.

Interlude – the Skegness Boys' Brigade are just marching past playing that infernal tune that used to waken us every Sunday morning.

Write back to me again as soon as possible. There's another photograph on the way taken by one of the Marines. I haven't seen it yet.

Look after yourself, and remember that I love you interminably.

Place your hand across your lips, close your eyes and think that it's me – and kiss yourself for me just enough to last until I come back. Then I'll kiss you enough for ten years. Oh my darling you can never know just how much I miss you.

    With all my love, my dearest darling Mary,
      David

March 5, 1940
Naval Message

Darling one,

Many, many thanks for your letter. I was most surprised to see the letter headings. Claude Leigh* is the firm I tried to rent those premises from on the Angel corner from last year on behalf of the branch!

Roddy should get his letter at the same time as this. I enclose Bertha's letter and suggest that in the reply to her you point out that we paid rent at Angel House up till 28th Feb on the assumption that

---

* Mary has found a new job in Hanover Square working for Claude Leigh, a pioneer of quality housing for working-class people in London.

our stay in No. 34 would be a long one, and yet 25 days after that lease had expired we are requested, in no uncertain terms, to vacate the said premises. And if I were you I wouldn't pay any more rent until the whole business is cleared up satisfactorily.

I do hope you will come out to Bushey on Saturday. I know just how you feel about my family, but at the same time I feel it is rather my fault in not telling them sooner, not their own.

Up to the present I can only count on arriving at King's Cross at 9.45, so I think the best thing for that evening is supper and bed, unless some of the people like Kay, Hymie, Joan, Alec etc would like to come round after the meeting to have tea. That would mean I could see them all and have the rest of the time with you undisturbed. If we go to Bushey let's come back after tea and have a tete-a-tete supper like old times. Then on Sunday a walk over the Heath and lunch in would be ideal. Forgive me if I'm a trifle unimaginative over the weekend but doing all those things we used to do seems delightful and unsurpassed in my eyes! And perhaps someone pleasant to tea – Mary and Cyril, or your mother, or who? Then the last hours definitely and decidedly to ourselves.

Today has been a bit colder, but it has passed very quietly. Only three more days now and my love will be in my arms again. Write once again before I come and speed the remaining days.

With all my love darling, your very own David

Thursday 7th 1940
Naval Message

Mary my darling,

The finger of fate has intervened to stop what was destined to be a lovely week-end. Today we were all very excited about the

146

prospective leave. The sun was shining and everyone was gay, really gay.

After lunch an order was broadcast for our class to fall in outside our chalets; a commander then came along and politely told us that one of our number had got scarlet fever and therefore our leave was cancelled and in addition we would be in quarantine until Monday in case any more broke out. The class gave one long heart-rending groan of despair, as though a long week-end was too much to hope for anyway. We are now isolated from the rest of the camp in the officers' building, not allowed to mix with other ratings and generally feeling sorry for ourselves.

The prospect of not seeing you has made my heart sink to depths of despair. And I'll have to start counting the days again until the next leave. Your letter today was so lovely it made me feel very happy and excited and then this blasted bleeding scarlet fever comes along.

There is only one compensation. We get the leave again in a fortnight – Easter week-end – and will be allowed an extra day to cheer us up. So I'll be seeing you on March 22nd, 14 long days.

I sent you a telegram just in case by some mishap this letter did not arrive in the morning. I had thought of phoning you up, but was feeling so full of resentment and disappointment that I just hadn't the heart to.

Darling I love you boundlessly and the disappointment of not seeing you is overwhelming. Tomorrow, when I'm feeling a bit better, I'll write a longer letter.

    Yours, with all my love,
    David

PS I've had scarlet fever by the way.
PPS I love you so much.

March 10, 1939
11 more days
HMS Royal Arthur

My darling Mary,

Being able to speak to you on Friday was a definite consolation for not seeing you, but I wish to hell that everything had gone well and that I was with you now and not simply writing to you. There is good news about the prospective leave, however. No one else has contracted scarlet fever with the result that we are now free from quarantine and in compensation for the lost week-end we shall definitely leave at 2.00 on Thursday (which gives us an extra day) and at the moment the CPO and the doctor who examined us are trying to arrange that we travel back on the Monday night instead of Sunday night which would give us two extra days. That would be marvellous if the request succeeds.

The CPO has been really marvellous during the last few days and has been doing all he can to make us a bit happier and a bit more comfortable. He is a peculiar character. He swears at us like hell, calls us all the fucking bastards under the sun and jeers in his dry, comical way about our marching, but at the same time would decapitate any other CPO or officer who dared to criticise us!

We've just had a whip round for him . . .

Hymie could come round and help you move to Prideaux Place and the balance to North Ken could be done by removal van.

I'm glad you'll be living with Kay. There's no one better I could wish for.

Did you ring up Bushey and tell them I wasn't coming? What did they say?

Tonight I shall be talking to you again, which will be lovely, and there's no reason why I shouldn't ring you on Wednesday as well. If you'll be in circa 7 o'clock.

How goes the job? Are you still enjoying working again?

We had our first test on Thursday. I got 98% but came 13th in the class: there were only 3 out of 26 who got less than 90, a remarkably good average.

Well my darling, in a few hours I'll be speaking to you again.

Until then with all my love,

David

March, 1940
HMS Royal Arthur

My darling,

In answer to the tirade of vituperation and malignity which was delivered today in the form of a letter may I at once offer my humblest apologies for being so optimistic about the possibility of a cheap move – it's an old failing of mine as you know – but please please don't accuse me, in so many words, of being responsible for you having to carry the lino and oddments from Angel House to Myddelton, and thereby forming the deep-rooted opinion that my sole object in life is to see you moving 'beds and wardrobes in 5 minutes and with one hand'. How often did I have to endure the tearing of my heartstrings when those beautiful eyes of yours pleaded with me and you said in such appealing tones, 'David, please don't make any more journeys tonight.' Mary, sometimes you are a treacherous female, straight you are, but I love you with an unmitigated fervour for all that.

Quite seriously I'm sorry that you had this second moving forced upon you. I know what a complete mess-up of your life it makes for days on end. I'm working on a plan to make it easier, about which later.

Today I've got a horrible cold and sore throat again. I think it must be the move from dry chalets to damp ones which we made on Monday, much to our annoyance! I hope the cold has gone by Easter.

The class has been transferred from 1st Port Watch to Second Starboard to act as a steadying influence therein, which is a bloody nuisance. 1st Port was an excellent watch with good officers and PO's but 2nd Starboard is full of snoopers and bumboys both among the officers and PO's. The change is marked, and today I had my card taken for being in bed ¼ an hour after the PO had wakened us. (That'll probably mean three days in the galley!) In 1st Port when the PO's wakened us they just buggered off and so long as one was on parade in time everything was OK. Fortunately the instructors remain with us and seem to dislike 2nd Std as much as we do.

The dance last night was moderately enjoyable. I did much better at whist being only seven points behind a prizewinner. There seems to be only one dance band in Skegness, which plays at every dance in the town, so I can imagine myself becoming quite familiar with it.

Tonight, in fact in an hour, I'll be talking to you again. Lovely. Write again quickly. There only eight more days now.

    With all my love,
        David

March 19th 1940
HMS Royal Arthur

My Dearest darling Mary (if sometimes a trifle bitter/sweet),

I was glad to receive your letter this morning and to hear you are still well. In less than two days now we shall be together again and shall be able to hammer out a number of burning questions still outstanding. My darling, I know how easy it is for you to jeer, even playfully, at my insane desire to do nothing in particular over the weekend, but if you had been incarcerated in this place for weeks on end with a chain of fixed routines which completely abolish any normality in life and which completely get you down to a level of drifting along aimlessly, the prospect of spending just a few hours together with someone you love very dearly and someone you crave to be with is in fact a veritable paradise.

However, to satisfy you, I would suggest the following outline: Thursday evening, definitely supper at home. Friday, perhaps seeing a person or two and supper at home again. Saturday, lunch at Bushey, show in the evening (finances permitting). Sunday a walk in the morning, lunch at home and someone for tea. You plan the rest. Anything you think of is bound to be perfect; so long as I'm with you I'll be quite happy.

The train time is still indefinite, but I'm pretty certain we're catching the 4.30 train, which is destined to arrive at 7.39. However, I'll confirm that tomorrow when I get the liberty ticket. Tonight I purchase my railway ticket – nothing now can happen to stop the leave.

The memory of Paris last year almost hurts. So far removed from war and separation. Do you remember that incredibly lovely evening up at Sacre [sic] Coeur with all the lights of Paris beneath us?

You know, thinking of moments like that, I think that I could go on my knees and beg forgiveness for every moment we've wasted quarrelling and bickering. But perhaps I'm only being my foolishly sentimental self.

The cost of moving and Kay's request for a month's rent in advance is rather a blow. However, we must cash in on Keith's wedding present to replenish your coffers. You'd better keep the good Mrs V's letters until I come now.

Still nothing from the U.A.B.?

Yesterday I went to see Dodge City,* the companion film to Union Pacific. Very good indeed, Errol Flynn doing very well.

Well my sweet one, I have to rush away both to post this and to get the ticket that musn't be missed.

So goodbye until Thursday, angel.

With all my love,

David

March 20, 1940
HMS Royal Arthur

My lovely darling,

In 24 hours from now I shall be in your arms again, that is if you consent to having me in your arms again after all the worldly misfortunes I've heaped upon your proud head!

The train leaves at 5.3 and arrives at King's Cross at 8.20pm Thursday; you will be there, won't you?

There is a great air of excitement prevailing, and everyone is spending this evening bathing, polishing boots, brushing clothes and generally making themselves smart for the few hours of freedom that are allotted us.

You will be getting the whole of the weekend off from work, won't you? It would be a tragedy if any moment should be lost in separation. I'm feeling terrifically excited and look forward to being with you like nothing else on earth. It's pleasing to know the flat will be empty over the holiday – it certainly gives us more room to move around in and we'll probably need it! How

---

* *Dodge City* (1939), directed by Michael Curtiz, starring Errol Flynn and Olivia de Havilland.

about going to see 'Ninotchka'?* It sounds very amusing, if a little heretical!

Well, my darling angel, I must away and have a bath. Keep loving me until I see you and I'll repay everything a hundredfold.

Goodnight dearest Mary, with all my love

lil' ole Dave

March 25, 1940
HMS Royal Arthur

My darling Mary,

It's so difficult to write after spending such a wonderful weekend together and then returning to a further period of isolation from each other. Everything about leave was so perfect, and although we did nothing momentous, the return to each other and the doing of things we had grown to look on as ordinary, was in itself perfection. I've come back here refreshed mentally and happy in the knowledge that we love each other more than ever, and I'll be counting the days until Saturday or Friday week.

The journey back was quite comfortable and I was able to get a little sleep in the train, which arrived just 2 minutes late on a 3¼ hour run! Today has been an odd day, with everyone a little glum and subdued despite the almost perfect weather. We had a procedure lesson for first period followed by a cash issue of extra kit for those who wanted it (I got two lanyards, price 4d!) and then morse with everyone falling asleep. This afternoon we got a villainous PT lesson which has made us all as tired as hell and I know everyone will be in bed by 7.30 tonight.

---

* *Ninotchka* (1939), directed by Ernst Lubitsch, starring Greta Garbo and Melvyn Douglas.

Enclosed is the photo which the Marine took. I think that it's delightful and laugh every time I look at it. Six angelic youths, eh? Looks more like Hughesie's entourage than a group of sailors! I must certainly send that one home. Somebody remarked that that it looked as though we were about to repel a fierce attack by fists, guns and broken bottles!

There has been a continual stream of cars, bicycles, pedestrians and what you will going along the road past the camp to the sea today – the tail end of the Easter weekend holiday makers. And all day long people have been staring through the barbed wire at us, watching us marching, eating, having divisions and doing nothing. Quite an object of local interest.

What have you been doing today! It would have been perfect to have gone to Kew or Richmond to take advantage of the fine weather, had we been able to have the extra day together. You must get rid of that horrible cough quickly, otherwise it will make life wretched.

Well, my angel, I've just heard that the post goes at 6.15, being Easter Monday, so I'll have to rush and post it.

Thanks a million for the lovely weekend and please write quickly.

    With all my love,
        from David

P.S. You know, I love you far, far too much!

March 26th 1940
HMS Royal Arthur

My darling,

Today has been rather depressing and dull, with everyone realising once again that they have definitely left home and are back again in vinculis. There was no letter from you today, which is probably due to the erratic Easter post, but I hope and pray there'll be one tomorrow.

Have you been to the hospital yet? Let me know with what result because I might be going to be a second Mr Dionne,* for all I know.

Tonight we have all come out en bloc and are going to escape the hateful camp atmosphere by going to see Deanna Durbin in First Love. Isn't that the picture in which your heart throb appears for someone's delectation?†

How did you like the photograph? You won't forget to send me the promised boitday present will you.

I am liking the Isherwood book very much. He writes in a very lucid and interesting way, and succeeds in avoiding the detracting feature of most autobiographical writers, namely the presenting of 'I' as someone who forced himself on the reader in every other line leaving an impression of strident egotism. He seems to draw his characters easily and naturally as life-like creatures, and one gets a similar impression of the 'I' without the 'I' having to go through paragraphs of psychoanalysing himself in order for the reader to understand the relative importance of the 'I' and the character concerned.

Let me have a word from you quickly. Is there anywhere I can ring you up on Sunday? Perhaps Ralph would let you use his phone and I could ring you up circa 7.0. Let me know though.

Loving you always my darling,
with all my love
David

---

* The Dionne quins, born in Canada in 1934, were the first quintuplets known to have survived their infancy.
† *First Love*: 1939 musical directed by Henry Koster, starring Robert Stack and Deanna Durbin.

March 29th 1940
HMS Royal Arthur

My darling,

It's only just over seven more days now, and as each hour passes so my anticipation of seeing you increases in strength. What will we do this time with our precious hours together? This time I think it's your turn to map out the programme.

I should like to go to the office on Saturday if it's possible, as a visit might have more productive results than letters.

I was disappointed not to receive a letter from you today giving the results of your visit to U.C.H., but perhaps you were very tired after the examination, which must have been pretty grim. Write soon, or better still, telephone. Look, if you can't manage to take a call anywhere could you ring me at 7.30 sharp on Sunday and I will make a point of being outside the camp phone box at that time. Should I get a letter from you tomorrow giving me a number to ring, then of course I'll ring you there. The Skegness number is 692.

Yesterday an immense parcel arrived from mother containing everything conceivable in the form of food! Very welcome, as the food recently has been atrocious; the kitchens are coping with far too many ratings with the result that helpings are small and sometimes we wait as much as half an hour before our class's food arrives. In these cases the noise is terrific.

Incidentally mother included the remains of a tin of Balkan Sobranie in the parcel. The comments at table when I commenced smoking one after breakfast were quite unprintable.

The second RNVR classes had their final exams yesterday and everyone failed! It caused quite a sensation among the W/T instructors, who felt, probably unjustly. that it reflected on them. It doesn't augur very well for us!

Last night I had a bath and today I have a sore throat. I seem quite unable to get rid of the cold completely so I suppose I'll just have to wait until the summer comes and lose it naturally.

I think one of your ambitions is about to be realised. A fellow in the class has a copy of 'Cold Comfort Farm' which he's promised to lend me when he's finished! He also likes it very much.

Well, my darling angel let me hear from you soon . . .

    With all my love and thinking of you constantly

    David

Just seven more days when you read this.

16, Prideaux House
Prideaux Place
W.C.1
March 31, 1940.

My own darling David,

At last I am writing to you about the hospital and junior. I have definitely been given a bed and the confinement should be August 22nd or thereabouts. Free ambulance ride provided by courtesy of Finsbury Borough Council. The cost of the confinement is £5.17.6 for 10 days, which is the normal stay, and £7.0.0 odd for 12 days, which is if the birth is difficult or overlong (to be paid at the <u>end</u> of the hospital period and not officially cut and dried). I did not have a very profound examination – the fact of my pregnancy is without doubt and the doctor said I was normal in every way and shouldn't have a bad time. He advised Halibut oil capsules for the cough, which didn't disturb him at all. I had a most amusing time in the hospital, waiting around in the usual way of hospitals from 9am to 1pm and listening to other women's comments and reactions to their 'certain condition'. It was very enjoyable and educative.

I have to attend next on April 25th and afterwards on May 30th, so if we can fit Skegness between those dates it would be very good. I am stricken with remorse at the lack of preparation for junior's wardrobe, and this weekend am knitting like one possessed and have bought him a frock, size 0.

Tom is home this weekend and having a good time beating up his old comrades and going with them 'to town'. He looks very well and is a full-blown sig. now. Inevitably he is very sore at missing you once again, but had to take his leave when it was given.

I saw Mary and Cyril yesterday, Cyril weeping and tearing his hair over his latest masterpiece, which is intended for the Academy and upon which the paint refuses to dry – in spite of the fact that tomorrow is Selection Day. He has entered three – divine optimism. His Midnight Sun bee is still in his bonnet.

They both send you their love and best wishes for your birthday. Their baby will be born only one month before ours. But Mary already begins to look the infanticipating one. Incidentally the slight pulse I have felt beating when in the cinema is junior, and therefore with one there, there will be no spectacular quickening as he started to be alive very early in his career which the wiseacres say rather denotes male sex.

I saw 'The Proud Valley' with Paul Robeson and a lovely film with Leslie Howard and a Swedish girl by the name of Ingrid Bergman who is utterly beautiful and charming and has my vote every time for a really nice piece of work. See this, it's called 'Escape to Happiness'. 'The Proud Valley' is extremely good. Paul sings Welsh songs and some Mendelssohn oratorio with his lovely organ voice.

The room and flat have not changed. The boiler does not work yet – and our room is still delightfully fantastic, but hurry home and fill it again with your personality and untidy clothes.

Oh darling David, how I wish I could be with you on 2nd April for your birthday, but we will have to celebrate it on

Saturday – which is only 6 days away. Let me know what you are going to do – about going home or going to the office etc.

Write to me soon and love me always.

Yours ever with all my love,

Your Mary

16 Prideaux House,
Prideaux Place,
W.C.1
April 3, 1940.
Only 3 more days

My own darling David,

I am so worried about your last two unhappy letters – you will have to take something for that cold – how about Halibut liver oil capsules, ugh! But you sound so depressed and I feel so miserable when I think of you waiting for the telephone call that never came. But I didn't get your letter until Monday morning – hours too late. Still, this weekend isn't too far away and we will make your cold better and talk, and talk and talk much more satisfactorily than we could on the phone. I have a lot to tell you on the subject of babies so be prepared to be bored to death with catalogues and patterns, etc. It is a horribly complicated business, and an expensive one, this having a baby; the brat had better be worth it. Did my fotos [sic] arrive safely and did you like them? I thought they were quite a good representative pair – the rare wistful expression, and the frequent jeering laugh – but I am so anxious to hear what you think. Alas, I am no Vogue beauty.

I will try very hard to get Saturday morning but if this is not possible perhaps you can meet me after you visit your office. But it would be so much nicer if I could meet you. That is a thrill I don't want to miss, seeing your train come in and then finding you.

Tom took me to see 'Haw Haw' at the Holborn Empire on his last night – which has got Max Miller in it, and which is typically Holbornishly low and funny. I think he enjoyed his leave, but he was very sorry not to have been able to coincide with yours.

This morning I received a very matey letter from Clare – one sister-in-law to the other – I will save it for you to read at the weekend. How did your birthday go darling? I was thinking of you even a little extra all day, and wishing I could be with you. We are such sticklers for celebrations that being away from each other on these grand occasions is harder than ever. But I will see you soon, hurrah, and don't forget to write and tell me when and what we'll do, etc.

Get rid of that horrid cold and remember I love you madly
    Yours ever
      Mary

                        April 4th 1940
                     HMS Royal Arthur

My darling Mary,

Your letter today was lovely and cheering and made me feel much happier and the photos are being looked at during every spare moment to try and come closer to you. The sore throat that troubled me so much is at last under weigh [sic] and there only remains an inevitable remnant of cold.

Yesterday I went into town to do three things. First I went to the gramophone shop to get the handle which, after spending about an hour in the shop while they fiddled, I decided didn't fit after all, so that meant another six days wait. Then I went along to see the good Mrs Jones, the prospective landlady, who was very pleased to see me. We had quite a long talk and she says it will be quite OK if you come for a month between about 1st and 31st May – in fact she's quite looking forward to it. In addition, if the weather is warm and does not necessitate having a coal fire continually in your room, she will drop the charge to 25/- a week, which is eminently reasonable.

After seeing her, I popped off to the cinema to see 'Rulers of the Sea',* which I liked very much indeed. Quite a nice evening and after the cinema I went for a long walk along the front (it was such a lovely starlit night) and thought a lot about you and I and what we had done together and what we could do in the future, and wondered a lot about what would happen to the child and how you must be well looked after both before and after the birth. Dozens of fantastic plans shot through my head. One or two of them may even come to fruition – it depends very much on what happens during the next few days . . .

I do hope you will be able to meet the train on Saturday – it's far more exciting that way. If you can't, however, I'll go straight on to the office and come back home for lunch. That's all the visiting I'm going to do for this weekend! Except I think we should go and see your Ma this time – I had a very nice telegram from her on Tuesday.

Had a nice letter from home for my birthday; my present is some cash which they have kept at home in anticipation of my visiting them over the weekend, but I'm writing to ask Mother to send it on to me at Prideaux Place in time for 'ze weekend'! There should be some left, I guess, to store away against a showery day!

---

* *Rulers of the Sea* (1939), directed by Frank Lloyd, starring Douglas Fairbanks Jr and Margaret Lockwood.

Any news from the Verley front? I'm glad you've had a letter from Clare – I certainly must read it when I get home.

By the way, I've drawn McMoffat in the class sweep on the Grand National. I wonder if there's any chance of winning it?

The definite train arrival time has not been given to us as yet so I'll probably have to send you a telegram on Friday night to make sure you get it in time. This time my darling I'll leave the programme to you.

Did you notice in the papers that your boss Claude Leigh is divorcing his wife, who is an ex-Ziegfeld Follies girl!

Well my snickersee, this is the last time I'll write to you before I see you – only 1½ more days now and then together again.

I love you and will love you until the end of my days. You're such a lovely person to have for a wife, a piece of good fortune for which I never cease to be grateful.

With all my love my darling Mary.

David

CHAPTER 10

'The kit bags are all packed'

Skegness

Thursday evening,

My darling,

At last everything is definite. The kit
bags are all packed, the hammocks slung and
safely stowed away on a lorry and all is
prepared for tomorrow's departure. I'm off to
Portsmouth proper, and not to Shotley after all, so the
first thing I shall do will be to apply for leave.
I hope there's a kind commander there!

Sorry not to hear from you today, but I
heard from Ken that Tom was there to meet you, so
I guess you had a celebration. It must have been
a very pleasant surprise.

The train arrives tomorrow at King's Cross
at 1.10 so try and be there to meet it — bring
Tom along too. I may not be able to have
lunch with you, but at least I shall be able to
see you for a few moments.

Yesterday we had a very pleasant
evening at Addlethorpe & Ingoldmells. Pat got very
tight, so Ken and I had to "do" him on our return
to camp.

Until tomorrow then, my darling —
with all my love

Dave

Germany invaded Denmark and Norway on 9 April 1940. The Norwegian situation awakens Mary's fears for the safety of her brother, Tom; fears which eventually are tragically justified.

A final weekend leave at the end of April is rapturously recalled afterwards by David, and another fortnight is to pass before their next meeting, on 10 May, when Mary arrives in Skegness for a month's 'holiday'. On 14 June, David leaves Skegness for Portsmouth and his next posting at the drafting office of the Royal Naval Establishment Barracks.

★

16 Prideaux House,
Prideaux Place, W.C.1.
April 9th, 1940.

My darling,

The Skegness problem is resolved completely and utterly. This morning I received our wedding cheque from Keith and Clare – TEN POUNDS! Isn't it miraculous. Write and tell me what I am to do with it, how you would like your share etc. But it means I can surely come to Skegness whether I can let the room or not, doesn't it? It is the most generous gesture imaginable and they are absolutely splendid, both of them. Would you like me to send you the cheque so that you can see it, and then believe it? It's made out in my name though, so you'd better send it back again.

The whole town here is in a state of flap because of the Scandinavian situation – what did they expect Germany to do once the minefields were laid? It's just the situation the B.G.* have been working for. Anyway, London is quite panicky today. What do you think about it? Thank God your training isn't finished yet, because the navy is now going to get a packet it seems.

I received your very lovely and dear letter this morning, and I agree with everything you have said. I think that love must be infinite to be mutual, and mutual to be infinite. I am looking forward so much to coming to Skegness and to seeing you as much as every week, or more. It will be so good for the baby also, because if I am near you I will be happy, and I suppose pre-natal influences are important. The existence of our child is another blessing in the most fortunate of partnerships, you-and-me.

Goodbye until tomorrow my dearest David,.

with all my love
Your own
Mary

---

* B.G.: i.e. the British Government. In April, 1940, the British navy mined the channel between Norway and her offshore islands aiming to block the passage of Swedish iron ore through neutral Norwegian waters. On April 8 the operation was partially carried out but the Germans invaded Norway and Denmark the following day, sparking the start of the Norwegian Campaign and the first direct land contact between the Allies and Nazi Germany.

10/4/40
HMS Royal Arthur

My darling Mary,

What really marvellous news! 10 whole pounds! It's really great of Keith and Clare to give us such a large present, particularly as we didn't tell them at the time. Well, that certainly solves the Skegness problem once and for all, even if you can't let the room. You can buy yourself a real maternity frock now with a vengeance!

I think we should split it in the ratio of 9 to 1. You have the £9 and get a frock etc etc and keep the rest in reserve, just in case the room cannot be let, and send me £1 so that I can get my boots and watch mended. Oh boy! What a gift. And I have a premonition we ain't seen nothin' yet. I must certainly write and thank them very much, and this time by Air Mail.

The Fleet Air Arm is definitely out. A total of 200 people volunteered for 20 places and every one of them was given to the advanced classes doing in excess of 20 per minute, so that's that.

Last night we saw a good American film '5 Came Back'* and an absolutely atrocious English film 'Discoveries' with Carroll Levis. A painful film. Tonight we are going to see 'Slave Ship' in the camp cinema.

The invasion of Norway is something that the British Government welcomes, in the same way that it would welcome a German invasion of Belgium and Holland – it makes it easier to fight Germany in the open. However, the line-up is still not complete; I feel sure there's more to come yet.

Yesterday the CPO's were all in the receiving room listening to the naval battle near Norway; it seems that at least two British destroyers were sunk inter alia.

---

* *Five Came Back* (1939), directed by John Farrow, starring Lucille Ball and Chester Morris.

Well my honeybunch write again quickly and give me some more exciting news.

 With all my love,
  Dave

          April 11th 1940
          HMS Royal Arthur

My darling Mary,

 Just a few lines tonight. I [am] still thunderstruck over the amount of Keith's present – ain't it grand? I've told the landlady that you'll be coming on May 3rd (Friday) for a month, so that you will be able to return in time for the hospital visit. Actually if you are able to get the dole up here AND let the room there's no reason why you shouldn't stay during June as well. However, we'll have to see about that.

 The film last night was rather a disappointment, but worth 2d I guess.

 Had a test today – c12 per minute. Result 93%.

 Be good, my honeybunch and write quickly.

  Your Dave

          16, Prideaux House,
          Prideaux Place, W.C.1
          12.4.40.

My dear David,

 Your letter was disappointingly short this morning, shorter even than the previous ones this week, which seem to have degenerated into film reviews. It didn't do much to lift my depression, which in spite of having won a chocolate raffle at the office today, deepens hourly. It seems to me that I am perpetually on the brink of giving up jobs to come to you – I have told them here that I am going to have a baby and will be leaving shortly. They are all very sorry, surprisingly enough, and so am I.

You ask me to let you know how I am – if it really interests you, lousy, thanks; I am worried about Tom, who might be concerned in this horrible North Sea massacre, and several other things are narking, causing sleepless nights and tired days.

Your indiscreet friend Hymie informs me that fresh supplies of ergot* will reach you as soon as he can get them. Really, David, you should be more careful. Isn't one poor little bastard enough for you. Anyway I hope the bloody stuff will be more effective this time than the last. I <u>might</u> ring you on Sunday at 7p.m. to tell you what I think of you.

    Yours, not so madly in love as usual
      Mary Lump

                                Skegness
           Monday [probably 15 April 1940]

My darling,

Speaking to you on Sunday ended three days of acute depression caused by your last two letters and the pain of this damned wrist. I'm sorry if you got the impression that I was unfaithful to you; you should know by now that I love you far too much to ever want to be unfaithful to you, my honey.

---

* Ergot: used for inducing abortions. Hymie, a friend with a quirky sense of humour and a fancy for Mary, was indulging in a bit of mischief-making.

Parting happily over the phone made me feel much better and has made my wrist feel better too. Shall I definitely write to your landlady and postpone the visit by a week? Can you get your hospital date changed, because as it stands it comes in the middle of the stay at Skegness, doesn't it? I'll apply for my leave to come on April 26th but could you by return give me a reason for the application, actually in the course of the letter. Something like this eg: 'The hospital want me to come for a complete examination on May 4th and I shall probably have to stay 36 hours. Isn't that your weekend date? It would be tragic if I had to spend all that time in hospital while you're at home. Can you alter your weekend or is that quite impossible. Do try.'

Something like that, see, and if the commander asks any questions I can produce that as evidence; he's the kind of a bastard that demands proof of everything.

If it's OK I shall see you again in 11 days. Oh Boy!

Saw Love Affair* on Saturday and liked it very much; there was also an excellent March of Time† on with it.

My watch is costing 7/- to repair. Would you believe it? Just for cleaning, new strap and ratchet.

I took your photo in on Saturday to be framed and have to collect it on Wednesday when I go in. It will look nice in the frame and then I shall have your mischievous face to greet me every morning with that naughty smile.

It's good to hear that the 8/- allowance is retrospective. You do as you like with it, considering that you're the best judge of the financial situation. Old's Discount address is in the gramophone drawer if you need it.

---

* *Love Affair* (1939), directed by Leo McCarey, starring Irene Dunne and Charles Boyer.
† 'March of Time': U.S short newsreel series shown as preliminaries to main features in cinemas from 1935 to 1951.

Well my darling angel, my wrist is beginning to hurt badly.
Please write quickly and confirm that you can still love me in
spite of what I've done for you! And remember, Comandante
Volente, it's only 11 more days until we meet again.

    With all my love my darling and hoping you're happier now.

      Your very own,

        David

P.S. I believe Mrs Engering has suddenly become reconciled to
the idea of being a mother. Ken isn't!

                16, Prideaux House,

            Prideaux Place W.C.1.

               April 17th, 1940

My darling David,

Your letter received this morning was a very good start to the
day, even though it was addressed to 'Mrs David'. Anyway,
thank the misguided Peter for me.

I hope your hand is recovering and that your back hasn't felt
any ill effects. Was my letter yesterday sufficient 'evidence' to
persuade il comandante to let you come home a weekend from
next? If not, I'll give birth to quins and send a telegram. Do you
remember the romantic pair of children I told you about who
eloped from Oxford and were arrested on the delightful charge
of 'carnal knowledge'? Well their baby has arrived, and the
verdict of the charitable probation officer who has been acting as
angel of mercy is that the child is 'mental', despite the fact that it
is only 3 days old. If this is true then I think the court, who
have placed the expectant mother in a heavy atmosphere of sin
since the child's conception, is entirely to blame. It is awfully

tragic and depresses me unutterably, as I have grown very fond of this girl (she is not yet 16) through her letters, supposed to be strictly private, which circulate freely round this and probably other offices.

Yes please, learn to knit, then we can swap patterns, and be all girls together.

My 'maternity gown' has been created by Madame Loewenstein, and isn't at all bad. In front I have enough natural arrogance to bludgeon people into 'keeping my secret' but at the back – Mary der lump herself. Anyway, it's comfortable and doesn't split a seam every time I bend down.

I will ring you up on Sunday at about the same time if you can be near a phone, but let me know about this. I have made inquiries regarding the dole but everyone thinks it is a bit of a gamble, and I surely cannot ask them here to fix things for me as baldly as that. I shall have to try it on when I get to Skegness and I might approach the L. Ex* here before I come down and see what they think. Has your mother been approached about the gramophone yet? When I come to Skegness we will have time (the most rare of our possessions, it seems) to decide what to do when the baby is born, where to live, etc.

I am living in hope that I will see you the weekend after next. Will it be a long weekend? Perhaps you had better go home and see les parents as it will be a long time before you come home on leave again, as I will be with you. Eh?

Write constantly, my own darling, and remember I love you ad infinitum (and then some).

Look after yourself very carefully my dear David.

With all my love Mary

P.S. Comment on Ken's baby . . . These bloody amateurs!

---

* L. Ex: i.e. Labour Exchange.

Skegness Thursday [18 April 1940]

My darling,

It never rains but it pours. Today I had a short and cheery letter from Basil,* who came home for only 12 hours, in which he wished us the best of luck and saying that he wanted to present us with a wedding gift of £5. Lovely eh?

It is to be collected either by my going home, or by my writing and giving instructions where it is to be sent. There's another wad to add to the baby fund.

I saw the Divisional Officer today about the forwarding of the leave and he was very sympathetic. He endorsed the request and I have to see the Training Commander tomorrow at 7.30, complete with documentary evidence AND envelope! (evidently ratings have been trying to get extra leave by writing entreating letters then presenting them to the Commander!). If the leave IS granted I'm going to see you enjoy every moment of it.

I collected my watch on Friday, but since then it hasn't gone for more than 2 consecutive hours. The bastards must have done something wrong to it.

Skegness was beautiful on that evening. The sun was still very warm while the wind had dropped completely. The sea looked a picture with the dying sun casting long fingers of light across it to the shore. Saturday morning was extremely hot, especially while we were on our mile route march, but after lunch it began to drizzle quite suddenly and never stopped the whole evening.

It's good to know the records have not been sold by Uncle S.S. I can pop along and collect them on the Saturday morning.

---

* Basil, one of David's three brothers.

Well my honey bunch there's little else. Write to me again tomorrow. This with all my love and innumerable kisses because it's nearly your birthday. On your birthday I'll double them because you'll be up here then.

Keep very well and remember it's only five more days now.

Bye

David

Skegness
Sunday [21 April 1940]

My darling,

How I longed to be with you yesterday. After spending a dreary afternoon up here, speaking to you was damnably tantalising to my spirit of nostalgia. How was (or were) Les Neufs Celibataires?* It would have been lovely if I could have come back into the cinema with you and gone home together afterwards. But that seems a dream of past pleasures. However, Friday seems very close now, only five days away, and we can then be together with a vengeance.

It must be getting pretty tiring for you to work now, and I'm glad for your sake that the financial questions have worked themselves out nicely; otherwise you would have been worrying all the time you were up here. Now you can relax and enjoy the climate with an easy mind. It's going to be lovely.

Love, David

---

* *Ils Ètaient Neuf Célibataires* (1939), French film written and directed by Sacha Guitry.

Skegness
Monday [probably 22 April 1940]
4 more days

My darling,

Thanks a lot for your letter which came today. Yes, by all means have Jill and Art over to tea. I should think Sunday would be the best day as we shall probably be out at Bushey for tea on Saturday. Try and have 'Chagrin d'Amour'* by the weekend. I'm looking forward to hearing it after your enthusiastic description of it.

The gramophone handle for the portable is OK now and we play it a hell of a lot: the dance records are certainly popular, particularly Ella Fitzgerald!

Yesterday we had quite a pleasant day out of camp. Saw Jimmy Cagney's 'Each Dawn I Die' in the afternoon (sounds funny) and after tea at the YMCA had one or two rides on the Dodgem cars where HM forces ride half-price. The rides last well over five minutes and it reminded me of our marche solitaire at Brighton. Remember? This time however I got as much jolting as I gave from our gang of lugs!! Later on Mac and Len rashly went on a diabolical machine which hurled you up into the air, hung you there upside down and then came crashing down to earth only to repeat the process again. Mac came off feeling very sick while Len had a bad attack of neuralgia! The evening we spent doing the Skegness stroll, and so to bed. The days ashore are getting somewhat monotonous but I suppose being out of the camp is pleasant.

Oh – could you send me some cash to pay for fare home. The weekend comes before pay day instead of after it, so it finds me low. 18/- will do.

When does Tom get his next leave? Perhaps we might arrange a

---

* Reference to classic French love song: 'The pleasure of love lasts only a moment. The grief of love lasts a lifetime.'

weekend together while you're up in Skegness. Yarmouth isn't very far away as the crow flies. I hope he doesn't get drafted again and land up on a capital ship. On Wednesday we will have completed 14 weeks of our course. It's frightening to think that in 13 weeks we shall leave here as telegraphists bound for the open sea! Brrr!

How's your Maw these days?

Write quickly my dear Mary – and in four more days I'll be in your arms again, to lose my cares in the depths of your embrace.

With all my love as always,

David

16, Prideaux House,
Prideaux Place, W.C.1
April 23, 1940.

My darling Dave,

I enclose herewith £1 for your fare. It won't be long now – three days only, and we will be together again. I was extraordinarily unwell yesterday – thought I had German measles or something, and although I still feel a bit measly, I am so much better that I know I will be quite well on Thursday for the hospital interview; I spent Sunday with Jill and Arthur, and probably it was the poisonous Arthur who produced the ill effects. He really is a bastard! Such an uxorious attitude towards Jill, after 5 months of married life, that I shudder to think what he will be like after 5 years. Thank God for you, my darling David, who manages to be kind without being patronising and passionate without being furtive. Anyway they are coming to tea next Thursday, so squash him hard, politically I mean.

The weather is incredibly warm and lovely, like Paris last Easter, and the office is stifling. I shall be so relieved to leave

London. It is terrifying, isn't it, to think how shortly you will be transferred to active service. It makes my blood run cold to think of it. At least I know where you are now and that you are moderately safe, but when you actually go to sea I shall become a nervous wreck. Will this horrible war ever end?

The Nine Bachelors on Saturday night were very much a la Francis and very amusing. Still, I have seen better films. Perhaps we shall go and see 'La Marseillaise' or 'La Tragedie Imperiale' (Harry Baur as Rasputin – oh boy) on Saturday night? I presume we are definitely going to Bushey for lunch Saturday, so I will shop accordingly.

    Hurry up Friday and hurry up David
      With all my love
        Mary

Skegness,
April 23, 1940 [probably]

My dearest darling,

The time is passing quickly and in two days' time I'll be home. Thanks very much for the £1 which will fix the fare. I've just realised that next week (being after May 1st) the fare will be 18/11 instead of 17/4, so we've saved a bit by having this weekend together!

My honey, you mustn't get ill, especially with measles of all things. On the other hand, I can well imagine Art producing an exactly similar feeling. However, wait until Friday. I'll soon put you right.

The film last night was atrocious – a terrible example of British handling of a very incredible fairy story with the result that it became more incredible still. Merle Oberon looked more like a Piccadilly whore in technicolour than a young and presumably simple country girl suddenly the heiress to untold millions.* However.

We have now fixed up buzzer communication between our three chalets, so that in addition to extra sending practice we can flash warnings of approaching officers or PO's when we're skulking or smoking at illicit hours.

What do you think of the budget? If there's any doubt in anybody's mind as to who is going to pay for this war, there certainly shouldn't be now. The postage increase is scandalous and it seems to me that it's bound to defeat its object in that the volume of mail will decrease on account of the price. We'd better get a lot of letters written before May 1! The only redeeming feature is the ban on the issue of bonus shares, which has always been an easy means of avoiding income tax. However, I suppose there are a thousand other ways of avoiding taxes.

Our class by the way is gradually becoming smaller. We started with 53 in January and since then 10 have gone – 2 demoted to seamen, 5 transferred to less advanced classes on account of so much time lost at and in the sick bay and three transferred to signal classes on account of the ill effects of wireless transmissions and conditions on their health. I expect some others will soon be joining them.

Roll along Friday. The train time is still unknown, and I may have to send you a telegram, but anyway you'll know in time all right.

Write to me once more before I come home.

    With all my love as always my precious wife

      'bye

        Dave

---

* The film is *Over the Moon* (1939), directed by Thornton Freeland and starring Rex Harrison.

Skegness
Monday [29 April 1940]

My darling,

The weekend was nothing short of heavenly and it seems that each time we come together we love each other to a greater degree than before. Going back this time wasn't so difficult, as I keep reminding myself that it's only 11 more days until the time you arrive in Skegness and then we shall be together delightfully often.

The journey back was excellent. The compartment remained empty the whole way, so I was able to have a good sleep.

A pleasant surprise today was the removal of our mess table to a different part of the dining hall – much quieter and definitely less crowded, a change which is going to have a good effect on the class I think.

Tonight when I go to bed I shall surely dream of all the lovely moments of the weekend. Supper a deux in our charming room; the delightfully amorous feeling in the Brasserie and the hilarious journey home by taxi; waking up on both mornings to find you and me together again; being together all day and lastly you on the station waving a goodbye that is to be so short. And if I do dream of these things, I shall surely wake up feeling very happy.

Write to me quickly,
With all my love
David

Skegness
Sunday [5 May 1940]

My darling,

I'm sitting in the sun on the grass outside my chalet, listening to the BBC orchestra playing a Haydn symphony and writing to you. (Me I mean, not the BBC orch.) It's an incredibly lovely day with nary a cloud in sight, and a brisk breeze to stop the sun from scorching. And it's only a few more days before you will be enjoying the same weather. Wunderbar.

It was good to hear you again last night, and such a kind operator, too! Congratulate your Maw and Paw on their 26th anniversary for me will you.

I spent a very enjoyable day yesterday at Skeggy. I rode in early and went for a long walk along the front, wandered around the pier and environs, then had tea at a private joint where I relaxed and read for a bit. Then I cycled home, spoke to you and spent the evening listening to the radio in my chalet. I did nothing after breakfast except read and smoke. In fact it seems generally desirable to have one's weekend out of turn!

Cycling into Skeggy is very pleasant but coming back is a real battle against the elements, and the last stretch from one end of the camp to the other is the worst. One travels slower than walking!

The newspaper comment on Norway and the debacle seem to confirm everything the Daily said. What a bloody scandal sending half-trained territorials coming from Nottingham and Lincoln to fight against a fully-trained and highly mechanised German army plus a large bombing and fighting air force in a country the exact opposite in terrain to the one they have been accustomed to. There's going to be a hell of an outcry when the losses are published, but as always it comes too late.

There have been several bursts of machine gun fire out to sea.

I don't know whether there's a battle in progress, or merely target practice. Anyway, half the camp is up on the sea bank.

Well my sweet, write again and tell me about the trains.

Yours eternally with all my love,

David

Naval message
Skegness
Wednesday May 8

My darling one,

There are one or two developments about the weekend. Ken is bringing his wife up here for the weekend only, and she will be staying also chez Mrs Chester. In addition she will be travelling up on Saturday morning (1.15 train) so you'll both be able to come up together. I'm very glad actually because it's a long and tiring journey and having someone to travel with makes a great difference. Could you meet her at 1pm Saturday outside the gate at Platform 4?

In addition the request for the travelling voucher has been granted and I should get issued with it tomorrow, so I'll send it off tomorrow evening so that you'll have it in plenty of time for Saturday morning.

I have also passed two hurdles in the fight for extra leave – the regulating officer and the divisional officer – and the main hurdle is tomorrow when I battle with the Commander! Pray for me again!

Apart from the extra leave which I'm fighting for I'm definitely entitled to one night ashore with my lil' wife. Anyway I will write tomorrow and let you know exactly what's what about the amount of extra leave I can get.

There will also be some news about finances, god being willing, but that has to be verified before publication!

Tonight I'm having my first game of tennis as the courts are repaired and prepared after the ravages of handball.

It really looks as if Chamberlain might at last be shaken from his pedestal. For the first time the Chronicle really seriously attacked him and made the somewhat belated suggestion that C. should go! His only hope is in the evil genius Margesson* whose iron hand rules the government supporters insofar as voting is concerned. However, it will be very, very interesting indeed to see what sort of majority he gets, if any.

Weather's a bit uncertain at the minute but it still remains warm. According to the landladies the town should be very full over the Whit weekend. Ken's wife has got the last room available at Mansfield Villa. Her name, by the way, is Peggy for when you meet her Saturday. Think of it – only three more days now and that will go very quickly. We'll both be at the station at 5.3 Sat and then we can all have tea at Mansfield V before we go our respective ways.

Please write again before you come up. Could you manage to bring your tennis racquet up as the stuff they give out here is pretty mediocre. Don't bring it up if it's going to overload you and don't on any account lift or carry your suitcase by yourself, my lil' babe, otherwise you'll injure yourself.

Thinking of you constantly and am I looking forward to Saturday!

　　　With all my love,
　　　　Dave

---

* David Margesson, Secretary of State for War.

16 Prideaux House,
Prideaux Place, W.C.1.
May 6 1940
ONLY THREE MORE DAYS!

My darling,

I have just found out there is a train on Saturday morning at
8.15 which catches the same connection at Peterborough as the
7.20, so I think I will try and catch that one and therefore arrive
at Skegness at 1.22 pm. This will give us so much more time
together on Saturday than if I wait for the late train, which doesn't
get in until 5.30, and there is only one hour longer travelling, so
I think it is definitely worth it. If I miss the earlier train or decide
at the last minute not to catch it I will send you a telegram on
Saturday morning but I think I should be able to manage it. I
am very busy this week getting ready to come and soon we will
be together again. I do hope that you will be successful in your
petitioning for extra leave, and also the voucher for my ticket.
I will not buy my ticket until I hear from you on that point.

The weather here is wretched, dull and raining and I do hope
it is better with you. I am looking forward so much to a
combination of sun and sea and have made a firm resolve to do
absolutely <u>nothing</u> but it for most of my holiday. To hell with
artichoke's wardrobe – let him go naked. He's done nothing for
me, why should I spend all my life knitting for him?

I went to the cinema and saw 'Drums along the Mohawk'* –
injuns and then some more injuns. Also Laurel and Hardy in 'A
Chump at Oxford' and what a pair of chumps. Very soon we
will be able to picture-go together, and I shall probably have seen
all the films months ago, says she with town-bred superiority.

---

* *Drums Along the Mohawk* (1939), directed by John Ford, starring Henry
Fonda and Claudette Colbert.

I haven't heard from Tom since, and he would probably find it very difficult as well as expensive to come to Skegness for a day – it's bad enough to get to town for three or two days. My mother sends you her love, and wishes she could come to Skegness – misguided female.

Please let me know what my future address will be so that I can leave it with her, and also in case you are not able to meet or something horrible like that, and I am stranded on Skegness station, far from home and not knowing where I live.

Write and give me all the information I have asked for, and confirm that you still love me.

    With all my love as ever
      your
        Mary

Skegness
Thursday [probably 9 May 1940]

My darling,

Thanks for your letter which came today. I'm at present waiting for the travelling warrant which will be issued to me this evening. So if it comes before 6.15 I'll put it in the letter.

I think on the whole it would be better for you to travel on the 1.15 train, as it will give you plenty of time to catch the train without having to get up at an early hour, and in addition it's much faster than the 8.15.

All day I've been annoying the lieut-commanders and cmdrs re leave. I put in a request for 2 days extra leave out of watch per week (which means I could see you five times a week) and in addition a request for 1 night ashore per week. The latter has been granted in principle and it's up to me to name the day each week. The former caused obstacles, as the Training Commander is away on leave (he being the only one able to grant it), so I have to make the request again when he returns. But in the meantime the other Cdr granted me Sunday provided I can get a substitute from the watch ashore, which will be fairly simple. Thus by buying a dance ticket on Friday I can be with you from your arrival until about 11.15pm, on Sunday from 12 o'clock until 9.45 pm and on Monday from 4.30am, until 7.0 Tuesday morning. Not bad for a start, eh? Then I see the Commander on Tuesday about further extra leave.

The travelling warrant has at last arrived. Here it is. You'd better get to King's Cross well before 1.15 so as to get the ticket in time. And dinna forget to meet the good Mrs L at 1.0, top of platform 4. Actually there may also be a girlfriend of another lad in the class waiting there but that is uncertain.

We had the marks of our half-course test today. I did very well on procedure getting 88% and coming fifth in the whole class, but did very badly in Morse getting 65%. Something will have to be done in the latter!

It's wonderful to think that in less than 2 days you will be up here and we'll be together again. We must celebrate on Saturday night. Guess what's on? 'French Without Tears'!*

Your room at Mansfield Villa, 5 Algitha Rd., Skegness, is on the ground floor until Tuesday when you move to first floor room which is very light and airy. A meal has been arranged for 5.30 Saturday evening.

Oh, it's so lovely and I'm looking forward to it like hell. Come quickly my dearest darling and love me always as I love you.

> Your own
> David

---

* *French Without Tears* (1939), film version of Terence Rattigan play, directed by Anthony Asquith, starring Ray Milland.

Skegness
Thursday evening

My darling,

At last everything is definite. The kit bags are all packed, the hammocks slung and safely stowed away on a lorry, and all is prepared for tomorrow's departure. I'm off to Portsmouth proper, and not to Shotley after all, so the first thing I do will be to apply for leave. I hope there's a kind commander there!

Sorry not to hear from you today, but I heard from Ken that Tom was there to meet you, so I guess you had a celebration. It must have been a very pleasant surprise.

The train arrives tomorrow at King's Cross at 1.10 so try and be there to meet it – bring Tom along too. I may not be able to have lunch with you, but at least I shall be able to see you for a few moments.

Yesterday we had a very pleasant evening at Addlethorpe and Ingoldmells. Pat got very tight, so Ken and I had to 'do' him on our return to camp!

Until tomorrow then, my darling,
with all my love
Dave

CHAPTER 11

Portsmouth and a Commission

(3 MP)

16, Prideaux House
Prideaux Place
W.C.1.
July 11th, 1940

My darling David,

Thank you so much for your letter this morning. I was terribly sorry that you had to camp out on Sunday night but I hope you had a chance to make up your sleep. I bet you did. What a lovely story about the man from hough - I hope Admiralty London ask for you.

I am sending you 5/- to help out with the collar problem, and I hope that it will do some good. The pyjama situation sounds bad, and I don't think I can do anything about the wasp-patterned model, but the blue ones will come from the laundry on Saturday and I

David left Skegness on 14 June 1940, and after a weekend with Mary in London arrives at his next posting, in Portsmouth, as a Writer in the drafting office of the Royal Naval Barracks on 17 June. Writers are ship administrators looking after pay, welfare and personnel issues.

The military situation was looking grim. France had collapsed and the British Expeditionary Force had been evacuated from Dunkirk.

★

Prideaux House
Prideaux Place
June 19, 1940

David, my dear love,

My head is very heavy because I have not received any news from you since you returned on Sunday, and it seems an unbearably long time until the next post when there might be a letter from you. I am full of dread that you have been sent away and so cannot get any letter posted to me. Please hurry up and explain.

I am very perplexed at the moment as to what my future arrangements should be. I went to Finsbury Clinic this morning and they advised evacuation as soon as they could arrange it. The good Sarah has got the jitters and is deserting this flat tomorrow, and Kay is anxious to move away from London. So an earlier move than I anticipated is indicated. But to where – that is the question. If you can't get leave indefinitely may I come down to Portsmouth to discuss this with you! I wish you would write and ask your Mother to look after the gramophone while I am in exile as it is a great problem at the moment. Ask if she could take it at once as I haven't much time to arrange this move.

Oh David, life grows more complicated every hour. If only the baby were born safely already and not in this precarious position of nine weeks to go, and the devil knows what is going to happen. I am trying not to be too worried for the child's sake and I have just read a book which says there is no nervous connection between the mother and baby so that war scares cannot injure the unborn child. The only danger is premature and unexpected delivery. Don't forget to write at once to your Mother about the gramophone, or shall I do it? But first of all please write to me.

With all my love as always,
Mary

Writer DHF.
Mess 8AA
R.N. Barracks
Portsmouth
Tuesday 18/6/40

My darling Mary,

So sorry not to have written yesterday, but I was enveloped in the writers' watch org: and was not off until after 9pm, and tonight am on full duty which includes sleeping in the office all night, and being ready for any work which might suddenly affect the Drafting Office as a whole! Just now there's a lull, so I'm seizing the opportunity to write to you.

All went well on Sunday night. I arrived at Waterloo with ten minutes to spare, travelled down first class and managed to get into barracks on arrival. I've been allocated to a very pleasant job in the 'advancement office', the section that deals with the promotion of all ratings attached to the Portsmouth division. There are only a Chief Writer and a Wren P.O. in the office besides myself, and both are very pleasant to work with. The Chief wants me to stay at least <u>6</u> months as there is a hell of a lot work to do and at the same time it's specialised. However, one can't take that as being definite, as nothing ain't definite down here!

Working hours are from 8.15 to 11.45 and 1.15–3.45, quite congenial, except one day in five full watch which means in addition duty from 4.15 to 7.15 the following morning, and one day in five stand-by watch, which entails extra work from 4.15 to 6.30. The bitter pill of all-night duty is coated by the fact that work finishes at 12.00 the day after, which is very nice. There's no work on Sunday, unless one is on duty or on stand by. Malheureusement I am on duty again this Sunday, which cancels the possibility of weekend leave this w/end, but the following weekend is quite free, so heigh ho the holly, we'll be <u>ever so jolly</u> – when <u>that</u> time comes.

This afternoon I noticed a familiar face protruding from underneath a P.O.'s hat, and suddenly noticed the little caretaker from Angel House! Not the one wid a choiman wife – the man before that. Needless to say, he did not recognise me!

Our week-end passed far too quickly. It's incredible really, that we've been able have the last few week-ends together. Some of the writers back from Narvik only got three days' leave and were then drafted off to bases all over the bloody place. Actually I'm already quite an old hand in the mess, so many having already been drafted.

It's 10.30 and the office may close now and let us get to bed upstairs soon.

The capitulation or attempted same, wasn't so very surprising after the onslaught of the Germans on the French army. Churchill's speech was quite a sane one this evening (we even have a radio in the office!) or seemed to sum up the military position fairly well.

Its a great problem whether you should be evacuated or not:– there seems to be a choice between safety and medical attention.

How do you feel about having a flat under Cyril and Mary? The size seems excellent and there is the advantage that 1) the furniture is nearby, 2) the flat is convenient, 3) you will be in a house with someone you know, and 4) most important, you would be close to someone (either the menage Mann or your mother) who could be invaluable when the time for the birth draws near. Against that, there is the very important point that Ladbroke Grove, for all its advantages, is just as vulnerable to air attack as Finsbury is. I wish there was some acknowledged hospital in the country you could go to . . . it's a hell of a problem.

<u>Wednesday</u>. Have just got your letter which has been waiting since this morning under heading N instead of F – you careless girl! Don't be too depressed about the war. Lots can happen yet.

I spent last night sleeping on two desks, which can, in certain circumstances, be comfortable! This afternoon I'm going out to see the sea and the town, and also to express this letter to you, as you will not yet have heard from me. Please write to me again quickly. With all love and living in expectation of seeing you on Saturday week.

Goodbye my darling, David

Mess 8AA
RN Barracks
Portsmouth
Tuesday, [probably 25 June 1940]

My lovely darling,

Many thanks for your two letters, which were lovely to read. Well, under threat of one flat iron well directed at my esteemed cranium, I will leave everything to you to decide. It would be all the better if the furniture minus bed could be stored at Elgin Crescent, and as you say there is not much else when the gramophone has been dealt with.

We shall have to hammer everything out over the weekend, especially what shall happen after la naissance of Julian David, or Patrick Gordon, or Michael D., or Lucifer Nick etc etc etc . . . (Sorry and/or!). I'm all in favour of you staying in the country once there. But that will depend entirely on what sort of billet you get. However far you go makes no difference to weekend or long leave, as I can always come back first train on Monday morning, even if it means arriving at 9pm on Monday here!

Air raids are now occurring with monotonous regularity and last night we were down in the shelters for four hours. The destination of the planes seems to be Southampton every time so far and quite a lot of damage has been done to the docks area, although the docks themselves have been untouched so far.

Last night I saw Ninotchka and enjoyed it very much. I wish we had seen it together though. There were some lovely bits in it and produced in me, at least, 'earty larter! Just the sort of film to go with a good dinner, some wine and you and a taxi-to-bed; but principally you.

I was talking last night in a haunt known as Aggie Weston's, to a Maltese steward who was a survivor of the Afridi (sunk by bombing attack off Norway). The story of the sinking was pretty grim, as it was not generally disclosed that although only 35 naval men lost their lives, there were some 400 troops on board being evacuated from Namsos. Over half of these were killed. He expresses the definite opinion that Britain will lose the war! Peculiarly now, he has visited the S.U. off his own bat.

Work is going along very well and the days pass very quickly. I've heard nothing else about the commission yet, so, for all I know, I may have been forgotten. I've discovered an ally in the Padre (tst tst), who, making his weekly rounds of the office to administer spiritual comfort, asked me all about myself and hearing about the commission told me to come and see him if nothing was said after two or three months. Strange ally! He says he will drop a hint in the right place.

Well, my honey bunch, keep as happy as is possible under the circs. <u>AND</u> don't forget to keep loving me.

With all my love,
your very own
Dave

Mess 8AA
RN Barracks
Portsmouth
Thursday, June 27th, 1940

My darling,

Thanks very much for your letter, which brightened an otherwise dull day. Well I shall be with you tomorrow, but unfortunately later than I expected. The commodore has taken the opportunity of completely altering all schedules as from tomorrow, by putting everything forward by one hour. (This is on account of the loss of sleep caused by the air raids. We will get one hour extra sleep as a result, since the raids occur at the same time every night). It means also that the liberty boat, instead of leaving at 4, leaves at 5 o'clock; there was a special train at 4.50 which arrived at 6.30 so I presume there will be a putting forward of this time to 5.30 so that I will arrive at Waterloo at 7.30 pm. and will be home about 20 minutes later.

I had a letter from my mother who says it is quite OK about Griselda and records. She also advises evacuation for you as, according to her, 'you are young and healthy' and she says it would be far preferable for you to have a peaceful atmosphere with plenty of fresh air, than to worry about medical service, which is possible only in an atmosphere of air raids etc etc . . .

I also hear that my uncle-who-keeps-a-pub has joined the Navy, was up at Skeggy last week and has since been transferred to Liverpool, the home of les francois.

Well my lovely one, have you thought of 'what to do' over the weekend? Have a good supper for me tomorrer, and look as lovely as usual when you greet me.

> Yer old hussiband,
> Dave

> Mess IDD
> RN Barracks
> Portsmouth
> Tuesday July 2nd

My darling,

Everything was perfectly all right yesterday. I arrived about 20 minutes late and by good chance the P.O. on the gate did not look at my liberty ticket and when I reached the precincts of the leave hut I was able to make the right sort of appeal to the Regulatory Officer in charge, and got away with it. Peculiarly enough, I had another stroke of good fortune. After stand by duty I came across to find there was no supper left. So my pal and I decided to make use of our stand by privilege and go ashore at 9 o'clock. We went out to a very pleasant restaurant-cum-roadhouse at Cosham, three miles away, and the time passed so quickly that by the time we emerged it was nearly midnight. A bus came along which we caught and we arrived at Portsmouth at 12.15, and by the time we reached barracks it was 12.25. I looked piteously through the gate at the armed P.O. behind and explained that the last bus back from Cosham always arrived at ten to twelve but tonight it was very late, and heigh ho, we were inside (much to my pal's amazement!). We had prospects of walking the streets as all the hostels are full after 7.0.

Surprisingly enough there were no air raids yesterday, but today (which is supposed to be Hitler's blitzkrieg on Britain) no leave was granted until now (7.30), so that all the seamen could be formed into emergency defence parties in case an invasion materialised.

I enquired about trains on Friday and found there is one at 10.24 which arrives at 12.1 – the fare is unchanged at 10/9d. So I'll be with you at about 12.30 or thereabouts.

The weekend was really a lovely one and is in fact the longest leave we've had together so far. Sunday isn't so far off now though.

Write to me quickly my love, and keep happy

with all my love David

16, Prideaux House,
Prideaux Place,
W.C.1.
July 5th, 1940.

My darling David,

I have just returned from N. Kensington and found your letter waiting for me. I was too sick to come home last night and my mother was getting quite agitated and was going to take me to the U.C. Hospital this morning, but luckily I felt much better and was able to come home. Just a temporary lapse, but horrid while it lasted. The news of the French fleet* is absolutely horrible, but I'm glad to know that it can't be manned by the Fascist bastards against you. But the idea of French sailors being killed by British sailors is the most unthought thing in this crazy war.

It will be lovely to see you on Sunday and I have sent Peggy a postcard to let Ken know you are in town. I haven't yet decided on the menu for lunch but I will try to feed the brute (you). I am glad you have heard from Seth and his offer of birthday gift is very nice too. I inspected the bassinet (safety pins and bassinets await the gal that fascinates) this morning and it is O.K. More good money saved in that way, although it will be a poor little second hand junior. Teach the little snob the right attitude to life. Esther Hambly bore the gift of one knitted frock, the pansy, when she came. She was highly impressed by the flat, but as I expected, is living under orders of immediate evacuation. Geoff has lost his stripe, which is only to be expected. Well, my

---

* The Royal Navy attacked the French fleet at Mers-el-Kébir on the coast of Algeria on 3 July 1940. The raid resulted in the deaths of 1,297 French servicemen, the sinking of a battleship and the damaging of five other ships. The raid followed the Franco-German armistice of 22 June.

darling, Sunday is very near, and until then I send you all my love and kisses.

Look after yourself very carefully,

Yours ever

Mary

16, Prideaux House
Prideaux Place
W.C.1
July 11, 1940

My darling David,

Thank you so much for your letter this morning. I was terribly sorry that you had to camp out on Sunday night but I hope you had a chance to make up your sleep. I bet you did. What a lovely story about the man from Lough. I hope Admiralty London ask for you.

I am sending you 5/- to help out with the collar problem, and I hope that it will do some good. The pyjama situation sounds bad, and I don't think I can do anything about the wasp-patterned model, but the blue ones will come from the laundry on Saturday and I will forward them straight away. Couldn't you drop a hint to your Mother that, instead of tins of toffee, pyjamas would be more acceptable?

I went to the hospital today and was served with a potion containing all the evil-smelling drugs known to the pharmacopoeia for sleeplessness and was also told that it was advisable for me to have junior in a hospital because it is a first baby, and therefore wayward. So I think I better stay near the U.C.

Only eight more days and as things stand you will be with

me and life will be good. Hurry up and write to me and love me always.

    Yours ever with love,
      Mary

                        16 Prideaux House
                         Prideaux Place
                              W.C.1
                        July 14th, 1940

My darling David,

I do so hope that you achieved the air raid shelter in time since your last writing and that you are whole and safe. There is a new development in the flat situation – Kay wants to stay on and share the flat with me. This means there will be three rooms between us and kitchen and bathroom etc for 17/6d per week. Do you think that we can afford this rent and that I should stay on in London? I don't think that I should even find another flat for 17/6d with such advantages – in fact I'm sure of it and I could bring the rest of the furniture back from Elgin Crescent and furnish the third room right away. Financially it will be difficult, specially for this month because I have the electricity bill for the quarter to pay and didn't anticipate paying 17/6d for the one room I now occupy, but in the long run I think it will be worth it. Anyway, what do you think? I must decide soon, so write by return.

Tom has at length been transferred to a trawler – H.M. Trawler Cape Melville, c/o 'H.M.S. Watchful', Great Yarmouth – and is at sea for quite long periods now. He isn't too overjoyed about the change as he was fond of his little yacht and living in Yarmouth.

I am praying that nothing happens to cancel your leave next

Friday and that we will soon be together again for five complete days. I have missed you so much and the Skegness period makes the change now seem more than ever vacuous. Write soon and love me always as I do you.

> Your own,
> Mary

RNB Pompey
Monday, July 15th, 1940

My darling,

Thanks very much for today's letter. I'm glad to hear that Kay has come to some definite conclusion about the flat. I agree with you completely that, if it is financially possible, there could be no nicer and no more convenient flat than where you are. It has all the advantages of space, running hot water, light and air which you would not get anywhere else for 17/6 p.w. The question of whether you should stay in London has been settled – you want to stay and will be happier if you stay, and that is the only consideration. So it means, then, paying another 6/- a week for the use of the other room, which is very reasonable. The decision as to whether it can be afforded must rest with you as you are the one who has to deal with the domestic economy at the present. You'll be getting another 6/- p.w. when the child is born and even if I don't get a commission, you'll get an extra 7/- on Sept 5 when I get rated as a writer. It's the intervening period that will prove difficult, but I say that if you think you can manage it make arrangements with Kay right away. Incidentally what has happened to make her change her mind about taking a house in Watford?

Did you read James Agate on Sunday? He had a very pungent

criticism about 'Distant Point'* at the Unity Theatre, but quite a complimentary one. There was also an obituary by Dilys Powell to French films. Very touching.

Friday draws nearer very quickly, only four days now. I'm not sure what time the train arrives but expect I will be home about 3.30.

I've got another appointment with the dentist tomorrow to have a fourth tooth stopped. It's nice to have it done for nowt.

Well my darling, write again and tell me how you are. I send you all my love and hope that it will keep you well and happy.

    Your very own,
    David

                                IDD Mess
                                  RNB
                            Portsmouth
                 Friday, July 26th, 1940

My lovely darling,

It was really such a marvellous break to be with you again so long, even if it makes it harder to come back. We were very lucky too, as this morning an order was issued to the effect that all leave in excess of long weekends was to be cancelled as from that day, so all those who would have started their five days from today are very disappointed.

I went before the Board yesterday and had a good interview but none of the nine candidates know the result yet. We do know though that if successful we shall appear before the Admiralty Selection Board on Monday, and if successful again there, the die is cast and we must then wait to be drafted to an officers' training centre.

---

* *Distant Point*: Play by Soviet playwright Alexander Afinogenov.

The questions asked were for the most part routine such as 'Where did you go to school', What is your father', 'What sports do you play?', etc. The only two different ones were when the Training Commander asked if I realised what it meant financially. He estimated that it would cost £8 per month to live in the ward room, but the Paymaster Commander disagreed by putting it at £5. (Here a slight argument ensued with me a polite spectator.) However, Sub-Lieuts don't live in the ward room and have a restricted mess bill and if it cost £5 or £6 to live in the ward room it won't be too bad as to qualify for ward room I would get a 50 per cent increase in pay as a Lieut. in rank.

The other question was 'Do you get much time for reading and what books do you read?' I mumbled something about [Leonard] Strong and [Aldous] Huxley and fortunately the question was not furthered. Well, I'll let you know the result when it is made public.

When I arrived on Thursday I found the King here, which entailed waiting about for some time before I could be checked in. Then Len came up to my mess and told me all about himself. He is trying to get into the gun crew of a merchant ship (D.E.M.S.) but so far has not been successful. Part of 219 class arrived this evening, Pat and company and everyone except Harry, who committed the unforgiveable sin of missing the train at Waterloo!! Pat has the records with him which solves that problem.

I hope you were able to rest yesterday afternoon after all your labours and that the hospital was not too exasperating.

Keep well. Above all keep sleeping during the night. Write to me quickly and I'll write to you and let you know the news as soon as it is available.

With all my love darling and remember I'll love you to the end of my days.

    Goodbye

    David

16, Prideaux House,
Prideaux Place,
W.C.1
July 29th, 1940

My dearest love,

Sorry that you had to wait so long for a letter, but I hope that you are reassured now. I wasn't so well after you left but am feeling quite fit today and looking forward with more confidence to the advent of the playboy of the western world (junior F). I suppose by now you are out out of suspense regarding that blasted commission. Whatever happens, my best wishes and all my love go with you.

Dick has his medical tomorrow at Edgware at <u>8.15am</u> (barbarous naval hour) and is hoping for the navy. I am glad you have met some of the Skegness louts again as they were a good bunch.

I succumbed to temptation and went to see 'The Grapes of Wrath'* on Saturday. The critics haven't lied or exaggerated, it is a terrific film. It doesn't evoke emotion or pity – it is beautifully unemotional – but rather anger as the book did, and the photography has learnt a lot from Russian films – unadorned close-ups of human faces, the use of space and darkness and silhouettes. Like the book it is more a magnificent piece of reportage – than which there can be no better literature in my opinion, as it is the material that present life is made from. There was spontaneous applause at the final speech of the film, which stated that all the experiences which the characters had gone through only served to toughen them and they were the PEOPLE and therefore couldn't be crushed, but would go on forever.

Write immediately you hear anything about the 'C' and don't

---

* *Grapes of Wrath* (1940), directed by John Ford, starring Henry Fonda, Jane Darwell and John Carradine.

be too disappointed if they are stupidly unenterprising enough
not to make you an admiral.

　　With all my love, my own darling,
　　　Mary

Only 3 more weeks!
Are you coming up on Sunday?

CHAPTER 12

A Child is Born

Cadet rating 842
HMS King Alfred
Hove. Sussex

Sunday Aug 11th 1940.

My darling Mary,

This certainly is some place.
After two more days of it, I'm beginning to
appreciate good living again.

Yesterday we had a lecture on
gases, followed by another visit to a gas
chamber to test the efficacy of our gas masks—
which constituted our morning's work. In the
afternoon I went with another rating to a
golf course up on the Downs and had an
excellent game, although exposed to wind,
sun and rain. (Today I have quite a tan!).
We must have walked about 10 miles in
all, and were very tired at the end of it all,
but a dinner in the ward room of steak and
fried potatoes, welsh rarebit, fruit, biscuits &
cheese & coffee, soon put us on our feet
again, and we ended the evening with
successive games of table tennis and billiards.
Today, the routine is very short and much the
same as Skegness: up at 8 o'clock, breakfast
8.45, divisions 9.40, church 10.15 and free
after church to go ashore.

The food is absolutely irreproachable

On 9 August 1940, Cadet rating D. H. Francis, apprentice paymaster, is posted to HMS *King Alfred*, in Hove, Sussex, an onshore training establishment set up to produce a new kind of officer commissioned into the Royal Naval Voluntary Reserve to swell the ranks of the rapidly expanding wartime navy. It was housed in the newly built Hove Marina requisitioned for the purpose.

German bombing starts to pick up in intensity. A few days after David leaves Portsmouth, the city, and particularly the dockyards, is badly hit.

The day of the predicted birth comes and goes amid growing impatience and discomfort for Mary as the London Blitz gets under way and she has to struggle down to the air shelters in her heavily pregnant state. Finally, on 31 August, the great day arrives and to some initial consternation it is Andrea Rosheen who is delivered at University College Hospital.

★

Cadet rating DHF
HMS King Alfred
Hove. Sussex
Sunday Aug 11th 1940.

My darling Mary,

This certainly is some place. After two more days of it, I'm beginning to appreciate good living again.

Yesterday we had a lecture on gases, followed by another visit to a gas chamber to test the efficacy of our gas masks – which constituted our morning's work. In the afternoon I went with another rating to a golf course up on the downs and had an excellent game, although exposed to wind, sun and rain. (Today I have quite a tan!). We must have walked about 10 miles in all, and were very tired at the end of it all, but a dinner in the ward room of steak and fried potatoes, welsh rarebit, fruit, biscuits and cheese and coffee, soon put us on our feet again, and we ended the evening with successive games of table tennis and billiards.

Today, the routine is very short and much the same as Skegness: up at 8 o'clock, breakfast 8.45, divisions 9.40, church 10.15 and free after church to go ashore.

The food is absolutely irreproachable and is very plentiful, and in addition one can get a cup of well-nigh perfect coffee for 1d to finish off any meal. Coffee is also served during the stand-easies, and is had at breakfast instead of tea.

However, although everything sounds very luxurious and living conditions are excellent, there's no doubt about it that the course is going to be no picnic. Our syllabus includes the whole gamut of paymasters' work (correspondence, ciphering, looking after confidential books, pay, victualling and naval stores), and in addition instruction in gunnery, torpedo work, navigation, semaphore, and morse and seamanship. There will be class examinations at the end of the course, which everyone must pass, and the fact that one has arrived here is no guarantee of getting a commission. One has to reach a required standard in the exams and, furthermore, must show oneself, by one's actions and more particularly by the way in which one handles the class when class captain for the day, capable of being an officer. So it's quite obvious that a good deal of extra work will have to be done by all of us if we want to be successful.

We rise normally at 7 o'clock and at 7.15 have quarter of an hour's PT, which is very strenuous indeed. Breakfast is at 8, and divisions at 8.45. From then until 1 o'clock are periods of instruction, which recommence at 2 and continue until 4.30, from which hour one is free to go ashore, except on Thursdays, which is guest night, making attendance at dinner essential. Our class gets a duty day once every 12 days on which days we cannot go ashore or go on leave. We are on duty this Friday, so I shall be with you Saturday lunchtime.

Oh, by the way, S.S. Brighton is now closed, but Chatfields* continues on! So there will be no ice skating for me.

Most of the lads down here are RNVR or RNVWR, and are not all the public school types so beloved of some Admiral RN (ret) in this week's 'Picture Post'. There are also a few petty officers who have been recommended for commissions and one or two others from the regular navy.

Well how have you been keeping since Thursday? I hope the doctor was able to do something about the cough and cold. Is your Maw staying at Prideaux Place now? Please write quickly and tell me all the news.

> With all my love darling
> Yours eternally
> David

---

* S.S. Brighton: Sport Stadium Brighton, a celebrated leisure centre opened in 1934 containing an ice rink but closed to help the war effort. Chatfields: a luxury hotel in Brighton.

HMS King Alfred,
Hove,
Surrey
Monday, August 12th, 1940

My dearest Mary,

A thousand apologies for having to send two letters at once –
I ran out of envelopes yesterday and so missed the post.

Today we had our first day's full instruction and most of us are
frustrated by this time (6pm). P.T. at 7.15, breakfast at 8, fall-in
and divisions at 8.45. At 9 o'clock we marched to our first lecture,
which had hardly commenced before the air raid siren went,
which meant doubling to the shelters. Half-an-hour later back to
the classroom for a lecture on Lewis guns until 10.15. Then a
lecture on pilotage until 11.20 at which time there came the
quarter-hour stand easy. 11.35 we started an hour's drill in the
drill shed, which left us with just enough energy to eat lunch.
After lunch we had a period of morse (during which I and 7
other telegraphists did semaphore) followed by a lecture on the
use of rifles. Then divisions again at 4.30 for dispersal. So you can
imagine that all I wanted to do after having some tea was to sink
back in an easy chair and relax until dinner time! Which I did.

The weather is absolutely lovely and the sea looks really
marvellous, so clear and clean. The terrace outside the ante
room is very pleasant as it catches the sun all day.

Evidently we are only the third paymaster cadet class since
the introduction of the idea of promoting ratings from the lower
deck. The first came in at the end of March only 5 strong and
the second came at the end of May and passed out last week –
there were only 18 of them. So the Boards must be held when
each class is finishing the course. Executive boards seem to be
held every three weeks as there are classes at various stages of
development in the 10 weeks course.

The Grapes of Wrath is on this week so I must certainly go along and see it. I'm so glad you got the dole all right. The extra 3/- is useful. I'm very glad I had that extra money as I've had to buy a manual on navigation and there are two or three other books it is advisable to buy.

I managed to get another pair of shoes, a pair of pyjamas, 2 first-quality ties and also 2 towels (1/- each) for you. As expected, the standard of living here is highish so I'm going to make a determined effort to get rated up.

Well my darling, please write again quickly and remember that I love you always.

Your very own

16 Prideaux House,
Prideaux Place,
WC1
August 13th, 1940

My darling David,

Your two letters received this morning have impressed me enormously with the luxury of the life you are leading and the strenuous course before you. Both of these things seem all out of portion to anything else you have experienced in the navy. But don't let either of them get you down. D'othing ain't 'appened yet, and I'm growing manic-depressive about the whole thing, as I don't believe it is a baby, only something that I (or you) ate. I haven't heard from Thomas for ages. I presume his time must be divided between enemy mines and La belle Swallow

Oh to be with you on the Sussex Downs and to see that lovely <u>real</u> sea at Brighton and to get tanned and then tight at Chatfields! Enjoy life as much as you possibly can for both of us, but don't stop thinking of me or loving me as I can bear anything if I <u>feel</u> you are loving me a lot.

I hope the time spent in air raid shelters is not overlong or dangerous. My mother takes up residence today. I have had a blow today in the form of Gas Bill for Fittings etc . . . <u>14/6d!</u> This is a dirty trick as I thought the weekly pennies were the gas payment, and this outrage is to take place every ten weeks, shared of course by Kay. So I will have to make my budget a little more elastic. With the usual luck that does attend these budgets still operating, it ought to be all right.

I haven't any news at all really, so I will go out and shop for my lunch now and look forward to your letter tomorrow.

    With all my love my own darling,

        your very own Mary

                  HMS King Alfred
                      Kingsway
                        Hove 3
          Tuesday August 13th, 1940

My darling,

You must be feeling very glad that there are so few days left before the long awaited birth. I've thought of you so much these last few days and felt for you every time the sun shone too heatedly, knowing how you hate the heat – at present anyway. I'm keeping my ears open for any announcement of a telegram for me so that I can be with you at the first possible opportunity when the time comes. Anyway I'll be with you on Saturday about 2 o'clock to make the time pass more quickly for you. It will soon be all over and that delightful stomach will revert to its normal slimness once again. The getting back to dresses and costumes again will be something worthwhile.

Today has been another busy day. Apart from the periods of instruction, which included 1 on torpedoes and 1 on semaphore, we had 2 on air raids, one very early in the morning and another at tea time, both lasting about ¾ of an hour. We have all been issued with rifles, bayonets and steel helmets which lie beside our beds and have to be collected and donned in the event of an air raid. Eventually, after thorough instruction in the use of short-range firearms we shall be issued with pistols.

I see from the papers that Pompey caught it properly yesterday, particularly the dockyard area and some brewery in that neighbourhood. It seems I left in good time.

Well my honey, keep well always and please love me always as much as I'll love you.

Yours with a kiss to your 'cuir' perfumed hair

H.M.S. King Alfred
Wednesday August 14th. 1940

My darling,

Thanks so much for your letter. Don't get depressed about junior, and if it is something you ate, it's a bloody long time being digested!

The gas bill is a bit of a blow. Wasn't there some rebate from the meter to compensate?

Today has also been very busy and included our first lesson in Paymastery. We had another raid at lunch time but nothing developed, fortunately. So far in the course things I learned at Skeggy are proving invaluable. We have to attain a standard of proficiency in flashing and semaphore; the former I can do at a speed in excess of the final requirements and in the latter I am beginning to achieve a speed as I knew the alphabet before. This gives me an advantage in that I need not spend any spare time learning them up and can concentrate on accounting, pilotage, torpedo, gunnery and seamanship. In addition the field training we do here I learned in the last few days at Skeggy. So I can count my blessings!

Yesterday I had my first sea bathe. It was lovely; today, however, bathing has been cancelled for some reason.

Tonight I'm going to sacrifice my dinner to go and see Grapes of Wrath; the times are really bloody awkward.

It isn't long to Saturday now, and I'll be with you the following week as well, if not before!

Write again my darling and let me know how everything is going.

With all my love as always,
Yours eternally
David

H.M.S. King Alfred
Kingsway, Hove 3.
Monday August 19th

My darling Mary,

I arrived here all right; about 10 o'clock! When I got to London Bridge I found that there were no through trains to Brighton as the line between East Croydon and Purley had been bombed the previous day. Fortunately there were five others in similar circumstances, so after a visit to the R.T.O.'s office to get an affidavit to show we <u>had</u> been there at 6.16, and a cup of tea in the station, we caught a train at 6.45 to East Croydon. There we got a bus (provided by the S. Rly*) to Purley, where we were entrained once again and finally got to Brighton station just after 9.30. Fortunately no questions were asked when we arrived as it was already understood that the line had been bombed; so everything was quite all right.

I felt very tired during the day so I went to sleep from 4.30 to 6.30 and awoke so energetic that I collated three-quarters of my arrears of notes, wrote a fiery letter to the Portsmouth laundry and am finishing the day by writing this at 10.30.

Well it's almost Tuesday so in another four days I'll be with you once again, mirabile dictu, even if not before. Time passes very quickly, and it's amazing to think that on Friday we shall have been here ¼ of the course period.

It was so lovely being with you at the week end, and it will be repeated again very soon. Keep well and above all don't get depressed. And always go down into the shelter when the sirens go.

> With all my love my darling
>> and thinking of you always
>>> your David

> H.M.S. King Alfred
> Kingsway, Hove 3.
> Thursday August 22nd, 1940

My darling,

Thank you so much for the letter today. I'm terribly pleased that your Maw and Paw are looking after you so well and not letting you out of their sight!

Today at lunchtime I saw a telegram on the mail board which

---

* Southern Railway.

I thought <u>must</u> be from you, but it was for someone else. I expect the hospital will be able to tell you today whether to expect M.J.* within a few hours or a few weeks. Still I don't think it will be too long now.

Today three classes passed out at the end of their course and have gone on indefinite leave, with the exception of 6 who have been assigned to some special job. All passed the exams, the lowest getting 515 out of 1,000 marks! (50% being the pass mark). There's hope for us yet.

It must be tantalising for you to have to sit around wondering when the future leader of generations is going to leave the comparative safety of your womb. I wish I could be with you every hour before the event to look after you and to make you realise each minute how much I love you. You must remember always that I love you to an infinite degree, and that any pain or mental distress you feel, I feel too. And so I want you to have the easiest possible delivery and to be constantly aware of my thoughts and love for you, when perhaps the world seems rather dark and sickening to you.

Write please if today is not eventful, but hoping that it will be.

> Yours devotedly
> David

Wednesday [probably 21 August]

My darling,

I have just returned to Prideaux House and found your two letters waiting for me. It was just as well, in the circumstances,

---

* M. J.: i.e. Michael Julian.

that you were in time to catch the train that didn't run, even though it was desperately hard to throw you out of bed at that barbaric hour.

Tomorrow is the prophesied day, although at the moment I do not feel as if anything will happen. But one never knows from one moment to the other, and anyway I have an appointment at the hospital tomorrow, it being Thursday, so I may be influenced by the atmosphere and do my stuff. Mammy will wire you immediately. She and Pa are staying the night with me in case of emergency. Dad's job is to run out in the middle of the night and telephone. He has postponed his trip to Crewe in case tomorrow happens to be 'Der Tag'. He likes the flat very much and is to be introduced to the Percy Arms in due course. I am absolutely sure that he would like some tobacco as he has to pay 6½d for his Woodbines these days.

In case the wretched Junior has inherited his papa's idea of punctuality and keeps me waiting, it is a lovely thought to have that you will be here on Saturday. That stops old man depression from gnawing at my vitals, already violated by Michael Julian's big feet.

I hope that when you next hear from me everything will be over, but if not, restrain yourself in patience and continue to love me and write to me constantly.

With all my love my own darling

Your Mary.

P.S. I hope that the dentist does a good job and doesn't hurt, and that the air raids leave you in comparative peace (not pieces).

16 Prideaux House,
Prideaux Place,
W.C.1
Tuesday [27 August 1940]

My darling David,

Just a scribble to let you know that I am still floating around
and Michael Julian hasn't yet made a sign. I am staying over at
Elgin Crescent today and have had a very nice day, going for a
walk in the park this morning with my father and resting,
reading and eating apples this afternoon. He is going to Crewe
tomorrow and sends you his congratulations and best wishes. I
hope you weren't too tired on Monday after the early morning
rising and that everything was all right when you arrived, and
that everything is still alright. I am feeling quite well and still
don't believe in the blessed event, but maintain that it is
indigestion. There have been no more raid warnings, thank
goodness, but Dad has some hair-raising stories and bits of bomb
fragments to back up his tall tales. Tomorrow I will write longer
and more fully. This for the meantime will bring you all my
love and thoughts.

Yours for ever
Mary

H.M.S. King Alfred,
Kingsway, Hove 3
Tuesday August 27th, 1940

My darling,

How goes it? I'm still anxiously scanning the letter rack (as
opposed to covering the water-front) for the summoning

telegram. I hope you went down into the shelter yesterday evening as I see from the papers that London had a six-hour raid. That must have been awful for you, sitting in a cramped position all the time. I wish I could have been with you.

We had it pretty badly last night, too. The raids started at 9 o'clock and continued intermittently until 4 o'clock, during which time we were in the shelters. Two of our class have been badly affected by the bad air and are in sick bay today. However, in future we shall not go into the shelters at night until there is real danger of attack: everyone now sleeps in lower berth with a sort of protection on top.

Evidently a large number of incendiary bombs were dropped here on Saturday night and started fires comparable to London's. Furthermore, the Army got panic and decided to evacuate King Alfred, so everyone was paraded at 4 o'clock, complete with knives, forks, rifles, clean underwear, shaving gear etc etc etc, already to be rushed in Army lorries to the Portslade Brewery! After waiting about for about a couple of hours the Army changed its mind and all and sundry returned to bed. Then I couldn't understand why everybody was in a bad mood when I arrived!

Well I must rush away now and see what the dentist can do about my lil tooth. Be back later darling.

. . . Well I've seen the old buzzard. He's just taken an X ray to determine whether the tooth can be crowned or not. If the tooth is affected I shall have to go a) toothless or b) have a plate. If it isn't affected, I can have it crowned at a price. So I'll have to see how the X ray comes out.

One of the previous Paymaster class came back yesterday before going to his appointment to Second Sea Lord's staff at the Admiralty. He said he took no notes, went ashore every night and did no extra work, and yet came fifth in his class!

So far, of his class, only 8 have been sent to appointments, 6 to Lyness (Home Fleet CinC's office), 1 to the Hood, and himself. The rest have not yet returned from leave, which started the day before we arrived. Nice work, eh?

Well, perhaps I'll be seeing you tomorrow . . .

Keep happy and remember I always love you

16 Prideaux House,
Prideaux Place,
W.C.1
28th August, 1940

My darling,

Wednesday, and still nothing has happened! I am so disappointed and I am sure that you are tired of waiting. It seems that this can go on forever. I have to go to hospital again tomorrow for my weekly visit, and that will be a week overdue. Still, I suppose it will have to be born soon. We had another night of warnings last night, but I didn't get up for the second warning and still live to tell the tale. Tom went back to Yarmouth this afternoon and life has to settle down again, the waiting for leave again, and as a diversion, for the arrival of your lazy son.

I am so worried by the air raids you are having. They seem to be the real thing and not just the 'nuisance raids' that London is experiencing. For heaven's sake keep your head down. The tooth is a bastard too. I hope he can 'crown' you.

I hope to have better news for you tomorrow, my darling, and to see you soon.

With all my love
Yours ever
Mary

16 Prideaux House,
Prideaux Place
W.C. 1
Thursday
[29 August 1940]

My darling,

It's probably all a hoax – d'othing ain't 'appened yet. The doctor said this morning that one couldn't be sure of the day exactly but it could happen any time now, and will probably be in the next day or so. I am very well and everything seems to be in order. So if you don't receive a telegram before Saturday, you will probably be able to come to the hospital with me.

I am so sorry that your tooth is such a beast. It must have given you HELL, poor darling. Keep your mouth well wrapped up at night and don't get a cold in your teeth. Pa went to Crewe this morning. I hope he doesn't find his lil' ole hometown bombed off the map. Ma is staying with me in Prideaux and all is peaceful now between us, which is a great relief. In fact she is very kind and useful in this time.

The looking out for telegrams must be as great a strain as waiting for de pangs, but don't let it get you down my darling, as it will soon be over, and we will be together.

With all my love, forever
Your
Mary

P.S. Your old friend Arthur P is in the L.D.V.s*!

---

* L.D.V.s: Local Defence Volunteers, later called the Home Guard.

H.M.S. King Alfred
Kingsway, Hove 3.
Friday August 30th, 1940

My darling,

Thanks so much for your Wednesday letter which didn't arrive until this morning – it must have been delayed by the air raids or something.

This child really is tantalising! Still, perhaps the visit to the hospital yesterday will have produced something more definite, and so I'm eager to hear from you.

Yesterday's guest night was full of bright lights, from A. V. Alexander down/up to Renee Houston.* The former made quite a good speech on the value of the King Alfred, how excellent it was that ratings from the lower deck should be given the opportunity to take commissions etc etc. And to illustrate it he had brought along the first Admiral to reach that position from the lower deck itself, a very pleasant old boy. There was also the 2nd Sea Lord and one or two other Admiralty celebrities to adorn the High Table.

The entertainment was pretty good, too, with Renee Houston poking fun at the Admirals. She turned to our section of the ward room and said: 'Why the red rope? Is that not dangerous?' Apart from her, and a couple by name Wheeler and Wilson, two Canadians gave an excellent turn called Midnight Blues (tune Frankie and Johnnie), an ode to the midnight curfew for officers of the establishment.

Well, tonight I'm slipping out for a haircut as the Officer of the Day made remarks about it, but I won't stay out too long in case the telegram arrives.

With all my love my darling and don't get too exasperated.
bye,
David

---

* Renée Houston (1902–1980), Scottish comedy actress.

16 Prideaux House
Prideaux Place
W.C.1
August 30th, 1940

My darling,

I am still at home as you will see, but this evening I am going
to see whether the hospital will take me in before labour
actually starts as I have had a lot of pain today and don't think I
could stand another night in an air raid shelter. Seven hours on
Wednesday night – it nearly killed me and the sirens have gone
three times already today. I went to hospital yesterday for the
usual examination, but all they told me to do was to take castor
oil and go away – which adds to my misery. I expect
confidentially that I shall see you this weekend as all this pain
today must be leading up to something. The all-clear has just
sounded (I came back before it) and Mam and I will now
proceed to U.C. and ask to see the doctor.

I may see you before you read this letter. I sincerely hope so.
With all my love, darling David.

    Your
      Mary

H.M.S. King Alfred
Kingsway. Hove 3.
Monday [2 September 1940]

My lovely darling,

How does it feel now that everything is all over? I bet it feels
good! Seeing you lying there on Sunday looking so peaceful and
so well almost made me forget that you had had any connection

at all with child birth! You looked too beautiful for anything so painful.

The baby is beautiful too. The momentary disappointment about the sex disappeared completely when I saw its grumpy indignant face and perfectly shaped head and body. It's certainly going to be some child.

All the folk are very pleased about it. The inmates of Prideaux House are all very interested; Anthea and Phillip may come round and see you this week; Hetty is coming on Friday; Mr Funnell, whom I met sitting on his porch on Sunday, sends his congratulations and sundry others all send you their love and hope that you get well very soon.

Your Maw, who has been really marvellous, should have brought you a parcel of food, sweets, reading material etc today, and I will bring you lots more when I come tomorrow at 7.30.

I wrote to Tom, your Pa and my mother yesterday giving them the full details, and yesterday evening we sent off a telegram to your grandmother. There will also be an announcement in the Daily tomorrow to let all the scattered coms know the good news.

Have you thought about the name any more? It will have to be decided tomorrow otherwise the dear girl will have to be known as Miss X!

What about: Anthea Mary, Judith Caroline, Judith Mary, Sheelagh Rosaleen, Romola, Sabrina Beatrix etc etc.

Try and hit on a good name. You have more opportunity seeing the child feeding so often. Does she feed well?

I'm looking forward so much to seeing you tomorrow, and in the meantime get all the rest you can. You certainly deserve it.

With all my love my dearest Mary and please love me as much as I love you always.

Your own
David

224

H.M.S. King Alfred
Kingsway, Hove
Wednesday, Sept 4th [1940]

My lovely darling,

I'm so glad to have seen you yesterday, and to find you well and getting stronger. The baby name is a wow and has impressed your Maw considerably! I've told her to bring along some things today which you said you needed and some money. Philip said he would drop four books in at the hospital today, so you should have enough to read. Anything else?

Today is a glorious one here. The sea is looking more Mediterraneanish every day. The heat is quite tropical.

I'm afraid I missed my train last night and the one I caught was late on account of the raid. So instead of arriving at 11.45 I got here at 1.15! I was severely censured in the morning by my Divisional Officer and dismissed with a caution: 'Don't let it happen again!' However, all is well. Today I'm going to work like hell to bring my notes up to date so that I can come and see you on Friday.

Did Andrea Rosheen take her milk properly today? And has her weight increased?

You'd better write and tell Jill the good news. What is Cyril's address? If you like I'll drop them a line. The Daily advert appeared with Francis spelt with an -es, so we get a second insertion free!

Well my honey bunch, get stronger every day and we'll see if you can be really strong when I see you on Friday. Until then, with all my love and I do love you so much, my darling.

Yours always,
David

CHAPTER 13

Shrapnel and Baby Socks

poro 9(MA)
Oct 22

32, Kenon Rd
Bushey
Tuesday.

My darling,

No letter from you yet,
but I suppose a batch will arrive
together (I hope). Roleen and I are
still here, and holding our end up,
against an increasingly fierce
barrage of C.S propaganda, and
overwhelming kindness. How soon our
next destination will be decided!
It is rather frightening to think
that on Friday life changes once
more for you, and maybe for me
who seems destined to move in
your orbit. Talking of orbits, I
completed absolutely — unaided
the S.T. crossword. Did you?
Ha, ha. I knew you didn't

London starts to take a pounding as the Blitz develops in intensity and it is decided that Mary and the baby will move out of the capital to stay with David's parents in Bushey until the bombing dies down.

Mary is coming to terms with motherhood.

Towards the end of October 1940, David completes his exams and training in Hove, gets his commission and is moved to his first real posting, HMS *Lucifer* in Swansea.

★

H.M.S. King Alfred
Kingsway, Hove 3.
Thursday Sept 5th, 1940

Hullo my darling,

How are you today? Getting stronger? Had a telegram today from Grahame congratulating us on the birth, and wishing us all the best etc.

Did you get the things which your Maw and Philip promised to bring? I do hope so because it will help to pass the time away.

We had a very pleasant time today out in Portslade Harbour, handling first of all a whaler and then a motor boat. Both were great fun, the second particularly so as each of us had to take the part of bow-man, coxswain, telegraph boy and captain. Not at once of course!

Has the registrar called around yet? I expect he'll just goggle at our name! See that he gets everything down all right.

I shall be seeing you tomorrow night and then will go out to Bushey on Saturday afternoon. I hope the eggs have arrived and haven't been forgotten. It will be good to see you again so soon, and I hope the sister will allow us an extra ½ hour!

I've sent a cable to Keith giving him the news, as a letter would take about six weeks to reach him. I should think he'll be very pleased to be an uncle.

Well, my honey, I'll see you tomorrow evening. Meanwhile keep well and remember that I'm loving you and thinking about you always.

> Good night dearest one,
> David

Monday [9 or 16 September 1940]
H.M.S. King Alfred
Kingsway, Hove 3.

My darling Mary,

I certainly feel very relieved that you are safely ensconced at Bushey and are not dashing to and fro from the shelters all day. The change of atmosphere should be good for you and even if it's not the same as one's own, or <u>our</u> own, home it is a comfortable and relatively safe substitute. Please be as happy as you can there and perhaps the draft will be another marvellous stroke of luck.

Yesterday evening was absolutely hectic. I got to Victoria by way of Piccadilly and South Ken only to find a) that the station was closed and b) that trains were running from Balham and c) that there was a terrific barrage in process! Try as much as I could, there were no conveyances of any sort whatsoever to Balham, so I had to resign myself to wait in the shelter outside Victoria Station until the all-clear went. Fortunately there were three others in the same plight. But we cursed at having to wait until 5.45 in a cold and draughty shelter in the teeth of a tremendous din from anti-aircraft fire and occasional bombs! However, we all survived, as usual, despite interruptions to our already indefinite sleep by people bursting in with great lumps of shrapnel in their hands saying 'Look what I've found'!! We all managed to get into a taxi when the all-clear went (having increased our number by two) and got to Balham in time to catch the first train to Brighton and were thus in by 8.30 (only just!). How was it at Bushey? I hope it was quiet.

I'm now the proud possessor of a front tooth at last. The dentist fixed it in this evening after much manoeuvring so I am complete once again.

Well, it isn't long now until Saturday when we shall be together again. I hope the wise Andrea gave you a good night's rest yesterday and didn't howl too much!

Tonight I'm just going to have dinner, have a bath and early to bed – got to catch up on lost sleep.

Well my dearest darling Mary, keep happy and remember that I shall love you until the end of my days (even on Stornaway or the Faroes!). Eat a lot, sleep a lot, read a lot and do everything you want to.

Yours always with all my heart
David

P.S. Your letter of last week has arrived.

32 Vernon Road,
Bushey
September 18th, 1940

My darling,

No letter from you yet. But I suppose it is on its perilous way. We are still here and are both settling down now. We walked into Watford yesterday, at least I walked and the babe rode in her pram, and got hopelessly lost on the way back, and a most indignant and hungry baby roared protests which made the streets of Bushey ring, and embarrassed me considerably. Today she is sleeping in the garden and I am sitting on the step writing this letter. From all accounts London seems to be still too hot to be considered, and it is delightful to undress and go to bed at a normal time, even though I am roused twice nightly by the hungry yells of your devil-child, who grows enormously and looks even more like you. Your mother keeps commenting on the resemblance and has gone so far as to say that she looks like your father, which made that unfortunate man grow pale. My mother has rung me up and seems to be well. If you see her on Saturday, give her my love and the babe's. There are several things to be collected from the flat if you have time to call there:

a) My brown shoes
b) Milk ticket
c) Baby clothes and washing

and some things that Helen Kaye has brought for the child. I still haven't got anything to wear and Watford doesn't seem to be productive in this way, although it sounds as if there are no shops left in London.

I am only living for Saturday, my darling. Last weekend was so short and there was so much to do that I was hardly able to establish you in my life again. Let's go for a terrific walk together this weekend and talk and talk and talk some more.

With all my love for ever and ever

Wednesday Sept 19th, 1940
H.M.S. King Alfred
Kingsway, Hove 3.

My darling,

Thanks so much for your letter – I'm so glad that you're settled in and that both you and Andrea/Rosheen are finding things pleasant. That's bad news about the thumb; if it is spreading you had better see a doctor just in case there is something wrong. It seems peculiar, though, that a burn should poison a finger.

The all-day raid doesn't sound so good. Still there is compensation in not having to rush to the shelter each time the alarm goes. Get out as often as you can though and get plenty of fresh air. It will do you an awful lot of good.

I think everybody managed to arrive back in time on Monday, so leave this week should be quite O.K.

Last evening I couldn't write before the post went so I thought I'd ring you up this evening instead. That's if the telephone service is still working. Most of the communication services seem to be very much dislocated at the moment.

Yes, Brighton was bombed quite heavily over the weekend, mostly in the Kemptown area. A cinema was hit there causing several casualties. There is also a time-bomb about ¼ mile away along the front from here; the whole area around it is, of course, roped off.

We were told yesterday that the final exams were to

determine not so much whether we pass out or not but rather to give the authorities some idea as to what subjects we were good in, in order that the appointments could be best arranged. The marks also determine our seniority as Pay Subs, in that No.1 of the class will be senior to all the rest and therefore normally the first to be considered for promotion. Personally I hope that the war won't last long enough for any of us to be promoted. Won't it be wonderful when we can live together again quite normally, with no worry about having to rush back or about air raids? (Even if we do have to live on watercress occasionally.)

I ordered my uniform from Hector Powe yesterday; they will be all ready for the passing out day, which will be Friday October 4th. There is to be yet another Board, which will include no less an august personage than the Paymaster Director-General himself, together with one of the three captains who constituted the Final Board.

Well, my honey, it's not long from Saturday now. Will you send me a list of all the things you want brought down from the flat so that I shall know what to pack up. And could you also send me 5/- towards the fare as my resources are low after the repayments.

The sea has been frightfully rough these past few days – the balconies have been covered in spray. It looks a really lovely sight.

Have you heard from your Ma again? I hope she reached the sanctuary at Miss Smith's before the siren went.

Well, please write quickly and please try and keep happy. I'm really terribly relieved that you are safe at Bushey when each morning's paper reveals even <u>more</u> extensive and indiscriminate bombing in London.

Hoping to speak to you this evening and sending all my love to you as always

David

Give my love to the famille

32, Vernon Road
Bushey
Herts
Thursday [26 September 1940]

My dearest love,

I have just fed and watered our angelic child and laid her firmly on the bed, and am endeavouring to ignore her indignant protestations. It was a marvellous day yesterday. I received <u>two</u> letters from you and spoke to you on the phone. Today has so far produced nothing, but I am hoping you might still telephone. Tomorrow we go up to town to see what is left of London. My mother promised to telephone but I haven't heard from her since Tuesday, so I hope she <u>is</u> still there.

The days pass pleasantly and monotonously and the nights are at least spent in bed, even though more 'land mines' were dropped last night. I think the barrage in London must drive the bombers (and their bombs) back to the further suburbs. Your mother has been to town today. This morning she tried to convince me that I hadn't really given birth to a child and it was only my belief. A bit difficult to look intelligent and yet say nothing committing oneself to any opinion, but I get by.

You sound as though the commission is in the bag. By the way, your father has asked me to send on the enclosed, and makes the stipulation that he will only be a guarantor <u>if</u> you get the commission. I explained that the idea was no commission, no uniforms, therefore no guarantee in those circumstances.

You will soon be here, I shall be happy again. They say that beauty is the lover's gift, but you give me much, much more – life and joy.

    With all my love
      Your
        Mary

H.M.S. King Alfred
Kingsway, Hove 3.
Saturday, Sept. 28th [1940]

My darling,

The bulk of the examinations are now over. Yesterday we had Ships Office Work and Victualling, two papers that were pretty straightforward and simple. Most people seemed to do well and I am quite confident that I had a fair margin over half-marks. Today we had Captain's Office – a real bastard – with one enormous question containing at least 20 traps; needless to say, no one got it right so I imagine the marking will be on how many mistakes we didn't make. Monday we have Field Training and Signalling theory, which shouldn't give much trouble.

Yesterday I went out for the first time for weeks and saw an old film 'Desire', with Gary Cooper and Marlene Dietrich. Very amusing and delightfully witty. Did you see it in the good old days? This afternoon a party are going to seek the solitude of the greensward in the direction of Devil's Dyke – it's a long time since we had any real fresh air. Afterwards the Regent cinema (which shows that Brighton hasn't forgotten its benefactors) seems to be the place. – Ginger Rogers in 'The Primrose Path' (no connection with Desire). Then tomorrow more swotting of notes on Naval Stores, Pilotage and Coding.

Note of tragedy. One of the last class to pass out as executive subs. was killed in an air raid while on leave. Terribly bad luck.

The weather has quite changed for the better. No more cold winds and raging seas. Raiders have been rather active over the past two days – dropped an enormous one last night near Portslade.

Did you enjoy your visit to London yesterday. I hope no more bombs have hit the flat! Did you get home safely and without mishap.

A.R. is one month today. Does she continue to gain weight? Perhaps as she gets fatter she will lose her energy for crying. J'espere.

>All my love,
>David

32, Vernon Road
Bushey
Tuesday [22 October 1940].

My darling,

No letter from you yet, but I suppose a batch will arrive together (I hope). Rosheen and I are still here, and holding our end up, against an increasingly fierce barrage of C.S.* propaganda, <u>and</u> overwhelming kindness. How soon our next destination will be decided! It is rather frightening to think that on Friday life changes once more for you, and maybe for me who seems destined to move in your orbit. Talking of orbits, I completed <u>absolutely</u> and <u>unaided</u> the S. T.† crossword. Did you? Ha, ha. I know you didn't.

Commander Waters appeared on Sunday (with Esther and Bunty!) embarrassedly clutching a large silver spoon for the child. A kind and generous man.

Pera and I abandoned Rosheen to your mother's only-too-willing clutches (she'll never let us take that baby away) on Sunday and saw 'Pinocchio'. Absolutely delightful and Jiminy Cricket is the nicest thing I have ever seen on the screen. A sort of insect W. C. Fields.

★ C.S.: i.e. Christian Science.
† S. T.: i.e. *Sunday Times*.

I have the whole house to myself now and have been doing the washing. The nights are still noisy and the Caledonian School has been hit again. Monotonous aim the Germans have. I will take the baby out in her carriage to post this letter and maybe walk around a bit as it is a lovely Autumn day blue, brown and gold, with enough wind to excite, but benevolently warm.

I am knitting the baby a pair of socks; that's apropos of nothing, but just to let you know.

I hope there will be a letter from you before the day ends, to make it a <u>good</u> day.

    With all my stored up love, sweet David,

      Your Mary

CHAPTER 14

Swansea

32. Vernon Road
Bushey, Herts
Nov. 5th, 1940

My darling David,
        Thanks for your
second letter. I hope the Chinese
lady holds her man, as the all-
electric house sounds the very
thing. But don't rely upon it, as
I am longing to come, and the
all electric lady might delay
unduly. Everything goes well here —
the Nazis are not so violent as
last Friday night; Rookie is
very well & very talkative
these days. She sends you her
love, & a milky kiss. I have
moments of feeling very well, &
others when I feel bloody.
The eye trouble appeared again

David gets his commission and is swiftly transferred to HMS *Lucifer*, an onshore naval base at the mouth of the Tawe River in Swansea. *Lucifer*, commissioned on 1 November 1939, was home to a minesweeping trawler fleet whose main function was to safeguard crucial British shipping lanes by keeping the Bristol Channel clear of mines.

David's few letters before Mary and Rosheen join him describe his efforts to find suitable accommodation and his first impressions of his new companions, surroundings and Welsh weather.

He eventually finds suitable accommodation in a house in Mumbles, a seaside village in Swansea Bay on the edge of the scenic Gower Peninsula. It will be the only year in which they live a 'normal life'.

★

HMS Lucifer,
Swansea S. Wales
October 30th 1940

My darling,

So much has happened during the last few days that it's rather difficult to know where to begin. Anyway, I'm here, if not settled, and everything has gone very nicely.

I arrived about 5.30 after quite a tiring journey and reported right away; I was introduced to the Captain who is in charge here (the Admiral being in Cardiff) and to the Pay Lt Commander who is to be my boss and to the Pay <u>Lt</u>, who I am relieving (a compliment there!). Having made my presence felt and known I was advised to go to the Mackworth Hotel (where I am at the moment) for the night as it would be impossible to find any digs anywhere then. An RN dropped me at the hotel and so for the day, as far as 'Lucifer', was concerned it was ave atque vale (Hail brother, farewell.).

Today I reported at the office and spent the whole morning being introduced to the officers and personnel of each department – a very long and memory-tiring business – and then was whisked off to a local dive for numerous rounds of drinks on account of the Pay Lt's farewell. The Lt Comm asked me back to his digs for lunch where we had an informal talk about the work etc etc.

He, funnily enough, retired after the last war as a Pay Sub Lieut and became a practising chartered accountant. He has his own firm now but was called up last June because the navy, like the elephant, never forgets, and was given the rank of Lieut Comm. When it was known that the Pay Lieut (his assistant) was leaving, he asked Admiralty for a CA or an articled clerk to replace him, as he thought that a little commercial efficiency would make things run smoothly. <u>So</u>, he and I are obviously going to get along fine!!

During the afternoon, or rather what was left of it, when he and I returned from lunch about half-past three, I had more routines explained to me, and as I hadn't got any digs, came back here for the night. And here I am.

The work should be very interesting. The base is quite large and its biggest job is looking after the minesweeping flotilla, which is responsible for cleaning the whole of the Bristol

Channel. In addition there is the job of looking after gun crews on merchant ships, harbour defence, anti-invasion organisation and a thousand other odd jobs connected with a pretty busy commercial port.

My job is assistant to the Lieut Comm who is Captain's Secretary. It consists, as far as I can see, of being the co-ordinating link between the officers responsible for each department; of supervising filing and correspondence; of personal distribution of all secret documents, and lastly, of mustering the confidential and secret papers and books of the sweepers once in three months. This last job consists of going down to the docks and boarding the vessels at a surprise moment!! Rather like an unannounced cash count.

Swansea itself is quite pleasant although there is a vast industrial area. There is quite mountainous country to the rear and the coastline beyond the town is very like Cornwall. The town itself is pretty self-contained; there are several cinemas, a theatre, a few dance halls etc etc. There have been a few air raids when quite a bit of damage has been done, but it is not even as badly hit as Watford, or even Bushey. Alarms are very few. Last night, for instance, the only one was at 9.15 and lasted half an hour. Planes are said to go over occasionally, but their job is laying mines not dropping bombs.

All the married officers have their wives down here – it's definitely the thing to do. I have one or two addresses to go to for accommodation, and I don't think it should be difficult to find. Unfurnished flats in houses are very rare but furnished rooms or parts of houses are said to be plentiful. My chief lives in a delightful house. He has a very pleasant room, nicely furnished, use of the drawing room and garage, gets all his meals there (and I can vouch that they are bloody good meals) for which he is charged 47/6 a week. On the other hand the laddie I'm relieving has two rooms (large), use of kitchen (his wife does all the cooking) and of course this including gas, electricity, bath etc etc, but no meals, and he pays 35/- per week. This latter is known to be excessive and is not the general rule. Tomorrow I have booked the staff car and am going to look up the addresses to see what's what.

Well my honey darling, I'll write again tomorrow and report on any further progress. Soon we'll be together again and then we'll lead a normal life.

Give my love to your Ma when you see her, give Roshie a kiss, and for you nothing less than my love, all of it, to make you happy.

Goodnight my darling. Thinking of you always and loving you without cessation.

Yours eternally
David

Love to the old folks at home.

H.M.S. Lucifer,
Swansea
S. Wales
Friday Nov 1, 1940

Darling,

So sorry I couldn't write yesterday but I didn't leave here until nearly 8 o'clock. I managed to get 2 hours off yesterday morning to look for digs, but the two places I saw didn't suit immediately, so moved into a small but quite comfortable hotel (much cheaper) until such time as I find good digs. The first I saw was not suitable as the woman wanted to let the whole house only, but the second is a distinct possibility. The house is in a nice quarter

(No 2 London-y-Coed!) and is small but beautifully furnished; the woman has a flair for decoration and a passion for things electrical. She has an electric cooker, electric clothes boiler, iron, water heater and everything that a good housewife could require. She would under the circumstances (which I will explain) let us have a nice bedroom and the dining room to ourselves and use of the kitchen etc etc, and use of whole house when she is away, which is quite frequent. The only trouble is she can't give me a definite answer yet as to whether she can let part of the house or at what price. The issue is complicated by the fact that her husband (a traveller or something), to whom she has been married for 25 years, has gone off with a Chinese woman and refuses to say when he's coming back to the old homestead. <u>So</u>, she is writing to him to find out if he intends staying away and, if so, for how long. If he <u>is</u> staying away then the rooms are ours; if he comes back – no go!! Personally, I hope he stays away for some time, as I'm sure you will like the house; it would suit us perfectly. She is to let me know in about 10 days' time. However, I'm not relying on anything and I have four more addresses to go to in various parts.

Actually, I think you'll like Swansea. It ain't exactly a pretty town, but it has plenty of character and plenty of life. It has a funny little railway called the Mumbles Railway, which runs all the way along the front from the docks. Actually it's only two trains joined together, but any suggestion that it is a tramway is enough to give you the cold shoulder for the duration if you live in Swansea!!

Work goes very well. All the staff are very easy to get on with if a little lazy. And bit by bit I'm picking up the work in my department. How goes it at Bushey? I hope it won't be too long before you come down here. Just as soon as I find the right place you must come. It's difficult to know what to do with the furniture, but perhaps you have some news after seeing your mother on Thursday. Please write soon to me – at the base is the best thing – and tell me all your news.

All my love to you and Roshie.

Goodnight my honey.   David.

32, Vernon Road
Bushey, Herts
Nov 5 1940

My darling David,

Thanks for your second letter. I hope the Chinese lady holds her man, as the all-electric house sounds the very thing. But don't rely upon it as I am longing to come, and the all-electric lady might delay unduly. Everything goes well here – the Nazis are not so violent as last Friday night; Roshie is very well and <u>very</u> talkative these days. She sends you her love and a milky kiss. I have moments of feeling very well, and others when I feel bloody. The eye trouble appeared <u>again</u>. My mother says it is because I am feeding the baby and I need a tonic. Swansea ought to be the very livener that I need. In your next letter tell us what things we shall need to supply ourselves so that I can go to town and pack.

It's good that we don't have to worry about the rest of the furniture, and the removal will not be as expensive as I had anticipated. How are you for money?

It's only a week since you went away and it seems an eternity. I hope a letter from you arrives this afternoon and brightens the day. Who are you voting for today, Roosevelt or Wilkie?* (or Guy Fawkes?)

---

* The US presidential election on 5 November 1940, in which the Democrat Franklin D. Roosevelt defeated Wendell Wilkie, a Republican.

I am going this afternoon to collect my ring and <u>my watch</u>, which I found, from Mr Walker of Watford (jeweller), who is mending them.

Write soon and tell me to come.

With all my love, Mary

HMS Lucifer, Swansea.
Thursday Nov 7th 1940

My darling,

Thanks so much for your letter today. Thank God the raids are lessening in London; nevertheless the quicker you come down here the better. So far nothing nicer than the Mumbles house has turned up. But I'll give Fate until Monday. I've arranged with the secretary (heaven rest his soul) that when I have definitely decided on digs he will fix it with the capitaine to let me have time off to come up to Town to collect you! Quelle etablissement!

So will you reckon on coming down during the week Nov 17th to 24th? And will you let me know whether you approve of the Mumbles house so that if I don't find anything better I can give them a definite answer. I'll arrange the tenancy on a monthly basis, so that if it doesn't suit we can look around for another place. It wouldn't be difficult to move from one address to another in Swansea if the situation should arise.

It won't be necessary to bring much down in the way of household goods. The Mumbles dame assured me that she had ample supplies of everything, and things such as pillow slips, sheets etc are included in the rent. I think though that we should have an ample supply of towels.

Will there be anything to collect from Prideaux House? It

will probably be best to remove all personal belongings, clothes and a selection of books; I'll also write to E.M.G. and have them collect the gramophone and records (if they will do it). Having the gramophone would considerably brighten life down here. The furniture, linen, crockery and the remainder of the books, had best remain at Prideaux for the meantime. Have you made any arrangements with Kay for the safekeeping of things like crockery, blankets, linen etc?

Well, anyway, it won't be long now until you're down here. I think you'll like the place, and I'm certainly longing for the moment that you arrive. It's very quiet, and out in Mumbles the air is very fresh but seldom cold; and the seashore is very close by.

Moving expenses shouldn't be very high actually. I'll get a warrant to come up and fetch you and you can travel down here at reduced rate – it'll be 1st class, but that doesn't amount to very much for single fare. When I come I'll bring my trunk empty and perhaps we can borrow another from home; that should take all yours and the baby's clothes etc, and the bassinet and pram can come with us.

The last two nights have been very moonlit and on each night there have been raid warnings in number. There are planes about but they are far more interested in laying mines in the Channel than dropping bombs. Swansea itself is not too safe, but Mumbles is perfectly O.K., being well away from military objectives. Yes, my darling you must come down quickly and lose that eye infection; the sea air will do you good.

My finances are very low. It's a pity I didn't find the hotel on the first day as the first three days at the Mackworth cost me more than a week's stay here. Could you send me £5 about Monday of next week? If you can't spare it, say so and by return and I'll get a sub from the Ship's Office.

Fortunately the cheque at the end of the month will be larger than usual, as I can claim marriage <u>and</u> lodging allowance for the month; one is allowed also about two weeks' grace before reporting that one's wife is permanantly resident in the same place.

Well, my honey bunch, please write soon and continue to love me as completely and lastingly as I love you. Give Roshie a tweak.

    With all my love my darling
      David

P.S. Love to the old folks.

33 Vernon Road,
Bushey, Herts.
Monday. Nov 11th, 1940

My darling,

I am sending you a money order for £5, and hope it reaches you in time to save you from starvation, or a debtors' prison. It is cheering news to hear that your cheque will be larger than expected this month, as our banking account isn't what it was.

When are you coming up to get the babe and me? Jill rang up yesterday and proclaimed that she and Arthur were coming, willy nilly, next Sunday to see the Madonna and child act. I asked (your mother) whether they could come and was told that as <u>you</u> were probably coming (which would entail a lot of work) they couldn't come for the day. I compromised by telling them to come after lunch and they will have to go early anyway. So if you are here, you and Arthur can have another instalment of the eternal feud. Anyway, your uniform will dazzle him, even though Jill states he has grown very artistic in his dress, and hankers for a pair of corduroy breeches.

Everything here goes on apace, the common task, the daily round, except for the disconcerting fact that the good Annie has given notice this morning. Lord knows why. Perhaps she too has a little secret.

The nearness of our setting up home together enthrals me. I feel like a bride and have been sewing coloured ribbons on my underwear (gosh!), also reading a book on SEX which I found in a bookcase in the nursery. If I knew then what I know now . . . The things that go bump in the night are still bumping, but the homestead still stands and we are intact as to arms and legs etc.

Rosheen continues to flourish, but is confined to barracks today because of persistent sneezing. She is very nice and I love her a lot. Almost as much as I love you.

Hurry up and let me know exactly when we are to move, and continue to love me, even though we are going to degenerate into normal married life.

Yours ever with love,
Mary

H.M.S. Lucifer
Sunday, Nov 17th, 1940
Swansea

My darling Mary,

It's only 7 days now before I shall see you once again, and only 10 more before we shall be living as near a normal married life as we have achieved to date! Today I saw the woman of the Mumbles house and got further dope about the house; and saw the room by daylight.

One thing I remembered was cupboard space. In the bedroom there is a wardrobe and small chest, so, if that is not sufficient, we can share part of the good woman's wardrobe in her bedroom. The pram can be stored in the scullery to which there is a back entrance. There is a warming cupboard which can be used for the baby's clothes. Rent will include cleaning, light (as much as we want to burn as it only costs ½d a unit here), hot water etc etc, but not coal. She will keep our coal for us and bring it in, and will let us know how much it costs each week. As regards cooking arrangements: we can either do all the cooking ourselves, or we can give her the food and she will do the cooking for us, or lastly, she will feed us at a rate to be fixed or worked out between us later. Personally I think it would be a good idea if we compromised and had her cook breakfast for us (which would avoid your having to get up too early in the morning) and then do our own cooking for the rest of the day. However, that is something we can decide upon when you are down here.

This afternoon I went for a good walk past Mumbles head, where the coastline becomes very wild and rocky: it will be great fun going for long walks when the Spring comes and exploring the myriad of bays and coves along the Gower Peninsula. I think you're going to like this countryside <u>WHEN</u> it isn't raining. But, oh boy! When it rains it certainly knows how!

The difference between the bay beyond Mumbles and Swansea Bay is incredible. In the former there are criss-crossing currents, wild breakers and a howling gale, while the long sandy stretches of Swansea are calm and unruffled!

Work continues to go very well and it is really enjoyable, although often I don't leave until about half-past seven. Knowing my way about more makes the work easier and gives me more time to polish up the stuff I'm not au fait with.

The family Peach are a continual source of fun and interest. I think you'll like Mrs Peach, and she'll probably see a lot of you when you come as she has nowt to do all day. I'm glad to have made some friends already as otherwise you might have found Swansea a bit dull in winter, especially as everything closes at 9 o'clock and never opens on Sundays.

The Paymaster Director General is coming down to look over the base next Wednesday, just as he said he would. I wonder if he will remember me?

I saw 'Night Train to Munich' on Friday with my boss and liked it very much, in fact, I think it was better than 'The Lady Vanishes'. On with it was an atrocious British film, 'Room for Two', with Frances Day and Vic Oliver (remember we almost saw it at the Plaza?). Ugh!

By the way, the air is very healthy down here. It would be difficult to find a healthier lot of people than the inhabitants of this area. You'll be putting on weight (not too much of course!) and Roshie will double her weight every week. I think you could do with a seaside holiday after two months at Bushey – it'll certainly do you good.

Air raid warnings still sound on an average of one a day, but not for more than ½ hour, and then nothing happens. The people of Swansea are beginning to regain their courage.

By the way, I don't like the idea of your reading books on that wicked subject 'SEX'. It might start putting ideas into your head and that would never do.

Oh, will you wish mother many happy returns of the day for the 15th, I nearly forgot.

Has there been any news of Basil as yet? I wonder which ocean he's in.

Any news, too, from Tom? Has he appeared before the Prelim Board yet? I am very busy preparing a board here and have 11 ratings under my wing. It's rather an interesting piece of work and it's better for the lads as I know what sort of stuff goes down well. The Board will probably be next week. My other pupil, the leading writer, passed the Prelim last week and will appear before the Final Board at Pompey on the 28th. He will be loaded up with notes and messages for my old cronies in the barracks. He stands a fair chance of success but has the drawback of being 31 and married with child. However, they passed me, so they should pass him. (I'm not suggesting I'm 31!)

What is Roshie's latest weight? She should be about 13½lbs by now. Any more hair? And are her features growing more definite? Well, it won't be long before I see her and you, my lovely darling; think, a month is the longest time we've ever been without seeing one another

Please write again quickly and tell me that you love me and are looking forward to coming down to Swansea (*Vale Skegness! ave Swansea) as much as I'm longing for the moment when you arrive.

> Goodnight my dearest Mary,
>> Yours for all eternity
>>> David

(*'My tour of Britain's seaside resorts' or 'How to have your holidays with the Navee!')

> 32 Vernon Road,
> Bushey, Herts.
> Nov. 21st 1940.

My own darling,

Thanks for your lovely letter. It arrived late in the day and put an end to the catalogue of bastards that I was compiling around your sweet name (which only goes to show how much I love you). Only 3 days until you arrive here and we meet again. Yesterday a friend of yours (and mine) phoned, and is on leave, and will meet us in London on Monday – yes – Mr Berger of the Duke of Cornwall's own. I also rang up Dick and Hetty in the week and they are still alive and would also like to see us – but they both work and I don't think we shall have time to traipse around looking for them. Anyway, we shall see. I will endeavour to have Rosheen's and my clothes completely ready on Monday to be packed immediately.

I am feeling much better this week, regaining some elasticity (!) and can walk considerable distances without losing my innards. The eye complaint also has departed, and on the whole, things are looking up.

Jill and Arthur arrived on Sunday, Jill looking extremely opulent in a Harrod's suit and fur coat, and Arthur as hungry looking and dejected as ever. They behaved <u>very</u> nicely, were overwhelmed by the dauntless Rosheen (who yelled at them incidentally) and came for a long walk in Cassiobury Park with Pera and I. Pera thought Arthur just <u>too frightful</u>.

Rosheen is becoming very exuberant and yells now with pleasure, as well as anger. She is constantly trying to sit up and presses her head and heels against a firm surface and arches her back She also walks up my chest with perfect 'foot control'. People stop and admire 'the dear little boy'. Mrs Verley came today and was very impressed.

The little darling/devil weighed 13lb and then some <u>last</u> week. So god alone knows what she will end up weighing.

You are a genius in many ways, my dearest Dave, and negotiating with landladies is one of your chief talents. I am glad that you had to do it, and not I, for they eat out of your hand. The facilities offered to us at the Mumbles house ('far and few, far and few are the lands where the Mumbles live') sound

extremely good and I think we will be able to manage
extremely well.

Yesterday I went to see Pride and Prejudice and consequently
am feeling very 18th Century-ish. I have been reading quite
learned books – 'Royal George' [George III] by Vulliamy – a
very concise condemnation of the Hanoverian stock, and now
'Caroline of England' who was the wife of George II – a more
sympathetic and less erudite study. I am also struggling with an
enormous tome – 'The Thirty Years War' (the Bushey Smith's
seems to cater for those historically inclined) so the film fitted in
exactly with my condition of thought. L. Olivier as an 18th
Century buck is the most arrogant, debonair and rakehelly
creature, and therefore <u>divine</u> (oh boy) and the whole film is
permeated with the delicate, gentle yet sure satire of the
immortal Jane. Greer Garson is Elizabeth and very nice too.

Well, my chickadee, soon we shall be together and chasing
each other around bedrooms and beating hell out of each other
and having a wonderful time.

Until then

I love you madly (unquestionably, prodigiously,
extraurgently, infinitely etc . . .

Yours ever,   Mary

CHAPTER 15

A Call from the Admiralty

DC 4

24 Lloyd Square
N.C.1

December 16th

My cherished darling,

I haven't heard from you since last Monday week — have you gone on an operation? Well, as you can see, the plans have been changed again; Mountbatten has called a conference for Dec 23rd and our visit to dargs is postponed until the 31st. It has its advantages, however, as I shall get leave between 24th and 30th which is very opportune. I do hope you can come up soon as I am very lonely without you, and am anxiously waiting until I see you again. Having supper every night at the Corner House without you on the opposite side of the table is, to say the least of it, decidedly incongruous. [I must admit that one night — only one night, mind you — I migrated to dey on and a chicken chop suey, but still there was no you, and what is a chop suey without you?] Not even dey on (who is a mere ghost of

The year in Swansea had not been without incident. The city had its own blitz. Over 600 people died in German bombing raids during 1941, including one intense three-night bombardment in February which severely damaged the town centre.

In October 1941, Churchill put Lord Louis Mountbatten in charge of planning and training for Combined Operations, a vitally important military body set up to coordinate the use of the army, the navy and the air force in offensive operations against the enemy. Mountbatten set about making major changes to personnel, organisation and communications, rapidly recruiting the staff he needed.

In November 1941, David is called to London for an interview at the Admiralty on his suitability for recruitment to the newly invigorated organisation. At the time Combined Ops was working on the planning and logistics of Operation Archery, also known as the Vaagso Raid, the first true combined operation carried out by British military forces involving a daring commando raid, with naval and air force backing, against German positions on Vaagso Island off the coast of Norway.

The actual raid took place on 27 December, but before that David is transferred and made secretary to the enigmatic Captain G. A. Garnons-Williams, who was to become an important figure in British intelligence operations in Asia and Mountbatten's clandestine-operations supremo. December finds David based at the Admiralty and scouring his old haunts and friends around the Angel to find somewhere to live.

★

24 Lloyd Square
W.C.1
30/11/41

My darling Mary,

It seems to me that your old pal Dave has stepped into the world of Adventure with a capital A. The job allocated has exceeded my expectations and I'm very pleased about it.

I went to see the Deputy Paymaster Director General first of all, and after a few cordial words with him, starting with 'Ah! you're the young man who wants some blood and thunder are you? Have a cigarette!', then in to see the PDG himself, who gave me a few words of advice, and back to the Admiralty proper to meet my new boss, a Paymaster Commander R.N. whose second in command and general assistant I am to be.

He proceeded to unfold THE PLAN which detailed in quite a cold-blooded way seemed just like an everyday affair! However, it's definitely more than that.

I'm afraid I can't tell you any more as everything is very hush-hush, but I can tell that I am perfectly satisfied and greatly pleased that I have been selected for the job. My work will be of tremendous importance, so I'm going to spend every minute of my time making it a success – in fact it's got to be a success. I leave tomorrow morning for the South, where I expect to be for 4 or 5 days then I return to London and away to Scotland for a few days. I'll write often, but if you write, you had better write to this address, and I'll collect any letters between journeys.

To return to my story, after THE PLAN had been outlined, I was introduced to several commanders with whom I shall be associating. Introductions complete, I was given more detailed information and told to report back on Monday morning.

Had lunch and then saw 'Ships with Wings' (very good). I had to keep on pinching myself to make me realize that I _was_ going to do what had been outlined, as the morning's conversation seemed in the realms of fantasy! Darling, you'll laugh yourself positively sick when you know.

Philip and Arthur came round to supper in the evening. Both very much the same. Philip is a draughtsman in a Tottenham factory and Arthur a teacher in an Islington nursery school. They send their love to you.

Today I went out to Bushey and saw Mother, who is very well. Another dress for Rosheen is on its way, and also the companion bed-knob. Could you send me a) my kit bag (in bottom drawer of chest of drawers) and b) the two khaki pullovers in the wardrobe. I think I'll need them.

Later. Cancel the kit bag. I get one issued.

Goodnight my sweet. I'll love you always.

Yours eternally and irrevocably,

David

Royal Marine Barracks,
Eastney Barracks,
Southsea
Monday [1 December 1941]

My darling,

A further note. I have been sent down here as an advance guard all on my lonesome. Have made a few necessary arrangements and now have to wait developments.

It is a fantastic place. The dining hall is 40 yards long (with a table the whole length) and tonight we had a Marine orchestra to aid our digestion. The only flaw in the picture is that there are never more than a dozen people dining at once, and secondly it is run like a cafeteria. You help yourself to soup from a sideboard and when you've finished, you leap up and help yourself to fish, and then meat. Helping yourself in a palatial joint like this seems very incongruous!

I am ensconced in the Junior Officers Hutments, but have been treated very well (and in view of my job with a deal of unusual respect) being a naval officer among a flock of marines. But on the whole, they are dumber and less interesting than N.O.'s.

Tomorrow I shall have a busy day as my boss is coming down in the evening and expects a completely organised office to await him.

I hope the exhibition goes well. What news of the Mayor?

I'm thinking of you a lot and hope the separation is [not] being felt too acutely. Whatever there is will be well compensated by the tales I shall have to tell when I see you next! God, how you'll laugh!

Well my honey, must say good night now. With all my love as always to you and Rosheen. Wishing you could come with me!

Yours always,
David

P.S. If you write <u>by return</u> you can send the letter here.

[Letter from Mary to Pera, David's sister, dated Swansea,
December 2nd, 1941]

Dear Pera,

    . . . Much has happened lately. David left in a mad rush on
Friday night, called away to the Admiralty with six hours'
notice, for 'special service'. I know no more than that . . . It's
very exciting, especially as the war is moving faster and he was
awfully fed up sharing the meagre amount of work to be done at
the base with the ubiquitous W.R.E.N. I only wish someone
would call me away for special service.

I had an awfully good week in London. Somehow just
making sentimental journeys to familiar places made me feel
happy and <u>very</u> young again – you know, the place where
someone first kissed you, the place where you ate your lunch,
your first really 'posh' restaurant, and a thousand others that
only London can hold, for me anyway. We saw, David and I,
Citizen Kane and I went seule to the ballet (Sadler's Wells, but at
the New Theatre, which is full of memories of Hamlet, John
Gielgud and Peggy Ashcroft).

Rosheen is growing much prettier, but is as crazy and
amusing as ever. She can climb stairs, but her vocabulary still is
limited to DIRTY and DADDY. Some strange Freudian
connection there?

Tom comes to see me tomorrow with Evelyn, his wife, for
the first visit. I feel very nervous as I am quite scared of his
remarkable hirondelle. It is embarkation leave for Tom. He
too is sailing far away. Where, I do not know, but c'est la
guerre . . .

49 Bryn Road,
Swansea.
Dec 1st, 1941

My dearest David,

Many congratulations on the new job; you surely are the boy for getting your talents appreciated. It's like the millionth chance coming up again. I am very proud of you – full of admiration and envy, and absolutely panting to hear the full story of the job and other details.

Your loving,
Mary

24 Lloyd Square, W.C.1
11th December [1941]

Darling Mary,

Once again I've fallen on my feet. On Tuesday I received a visit from the Pay Cdr who was my boss: he settled a few outstanding points which I had, and informed me that I had been selected to act as secretary to Captain Garnons-Williams of the Admiralty Plans Division! So after getting rid of the remaining bodies at Eastney I reported for duty at the Admiralty yesterday afternoon. And that's how come I am sitting in Room No 42 O.B. surrounded by a mass of charts, papers and files containing most of the Admiralty's plans for the future!

Captain G-W is very pleasant and his job is a most important one. His visitors seem never to have less than 4 stripes and his room is never to be entered by any casual enquirers.

Today, Lord Lloyd was shown in by a messenger, and

promptly shown out again and told to wait outside! All very sinister.

G–W was originally supposed to be the chief of staff of our operation, but as it is now limited in size, he is working on something bigger and better. It's all rather a maze to me at the moment, but when I've got to know all the people who call, and the general organisation of the place, things will be much easier. On Sunday I am going up to Scotland with the capitaine to look into things up there. I gather there will be a fair amount of travelling to do.

Oh! I have two typists attached to the office, and one of them is Miss M. Moss!!! I haven't dared ask her what her first name is! They do all the typing, filing etc.

I am looking for somewhere to live at the moment. Several 'scouts' are making enquiries. Kay's house is full up and I am sleeping on the sofa. All I want is a room where I can dump my luggage, sleep and get breakfast and a bath, as I shall have to have lunch and supper out. Last night we finished at 8 o'clock.

Living is proving somewhat expensive at the moment, but I believe there is some special allowance for London. However, I shall know soon.

It would be lovely if you could come up for Christmas and spend a few weeks here. I'll ask Mother if she can put you up. I don't know what my movements will be, but I'm bound to be around some of the time.

Everything, I've come to the conclusion, is INCREDIBLE! Don't you think so? Apparently I was chosen for this job on account of the way I handled affairs down at Eastney.

Thanks for your lovely letter. I'm glad you've met and approve of Evelyn. What were the final results of the exhib? How many attended? How many new members? What press publicity? How much literature sold? Ha! Down with the Mayor!

Well, my darling Mary, write me again quickly, and I send you all my love as always. Beat Rosheen for me.

Yours eternally,

David

P.S. Had lunch with Dick on Wednesday at Eastney. He's going on the Illustrious, aircraft carrier.

24 Lloyd Square
W.C.1
December 16th [1941]

My cherished darling,

I haven't heard from you since last Monday week – have you gone on an operation? Well, as you can see, the plans have been changed again; Mountbatten has called a conference for Dec 23rd and our visit to Largs is postponed until the 31st. It has its advantages, however, as I shall get leave between 24th and 30th which is very opportune. I do hope you can come up soon as I am very lonely without you, and am anxiously waiting until I see you again. Having supper every night at the Corner House without you on the opposite side of the table is, to say the least of it, decidedly incongruous. (I must admit that one night – only one night, mind you – I migrated to Ley On and a chicken chop suey, but still there was no you, and what is a chop suey without you?).

Not even Ley On (who is a mere ghost of his former self since he was bumped off in the 49th parallel*) could console me.

---

* Ley On was a Chinese-born actor whose film credits included Michael Powell and Emeric Pressburger's *49th Parallel* (1941).

Work goes very well now that I'm beginning to grasp the essential details. Already I have been able to contribute two or three worthy suggestions to the Captain, who was pleased. Today I have been acting (and shall be continuing to act for some weeks) as Intelligence Officer and have prepared a long report. The organisation suits me very well, being highly flexible, and my office is quiet, which allows fullest concentration. Sometimes, I must admit, I look out of the window and ponder on the extraordinary luck and good fortune that contrived to establish me in 42 O.B. (Maybe reference to prefix codes used for convoys.) But me voila, so what?

I have used the influence of the alma mater to secure a cup of tea and a piece of cake for myself and G-W each afternoon from the Trade Division Tea Club, and each afternoon it is duly presented at the door, all nicely arranged on a tray, by Joy. If I had thought way back in the early thirties that 10 years later the girl who obligingly assisted me in mathmatical problems would be bringing me tea in my office – a hush-hush one at that – in the Admiralty, I should have accused myself of possessing a high-flown imagination.

I had lunch at the National Gallery yesterday. It's run on a cafeteria basis with only enough tables for half the people who go there, with the result that there is a terrific scrum. However, everything is very refined and polite; the waitresses have the accents of aristos, and no one seems to lose their tempers, which is remarkable. Food is good and well cooked, and not expensive; a sprinkling of Johns and a Nash* or two generally aid the digestion and their apple tart is served with lashings of pseudo whipped cream, which can also be put in the coffee. Mary, my darling fellow restauranteur [sic], we must visit the N.G. one day!

---

* Augustus John (1878–1961) and Paul Nash (1889–1946), British painters.

Apologies if food occupies too much space. Actually by the time I've finished here, there remains only to get supper and make my way homeward to Lloyd Square to bed. I've only had time to see one film – 'Shors' – a Soviet film of the liberation of the Ukraine in 1919; very inspiring and well acted but with a weak sound recording.

What have you been doing with yourself apart from the exhibition? I hope Swansea isn't too dull at the present.

I'll ring you this evening my honey sweet.

All my love,
David

49 Bryn Road,
Swansea,
Dec 18th [1941]

My darling David,

Fires of coal are heaped upon my head – I write you 'a snorter' and the same night you telephone me – albeit you dragged me from my bed – it was very welcome and very sweet to hear your voice. And your letter the next day – truly beeeyutiful and I am satisfied. No wonder you have me on a piece of string.

The fact that Joy is working with you is just another crazy coincidence – and fits in completely with the sort of things that happen to you. Nothing about this new job would surprise me. You're bewitched.

We went to a dance at the Pier Hotel on Wednesday having first gathered forces at Pat's to drink <u>very</u> good beer. Michael's last night in the old home, and we certainly had a super time. The keynote of the evening was craziness, so I was a succes fou,

268

needless to say. Reg also, who has been intoxicated since he became a father, was in very good form. He and I are hopelessly compromised but we know that you and Wendy trust us, don't you darling?

I had a battle royal last night with Haydn about affiliating to the WEA* and letting them boss our next series of lectures, and he put in a few very dirty stabs. For example he agreed to put the question to the group before the SCR committee had it, but presented it last night to the committee. But I, with my trusty henchman, Hert Buckett, fixed the lily-livered loon, though he still persists in thinking it's a good idea. I leave him to you.

Darling, if you are as lonely and as hungry as you sound, rush home to your Mary, who will be delighted to feed and cherish you. I am going to cook madly all the weekend – Xmas puddings, mince pies, and Pa has got a contact who might trap us a Bl. M.† turkey/fowl/chop. I am also keeping the double bed well aired and will inspect the springs. If anything stops you from coming I shall <u>die</u>. This will be our fourth Christmas together and I remember them all with such vivid flashes of happiness, laughter and love. May this one be as good! Do you remember the snowy one in Covent Garden?

Rosheen has got a minor cold, but will recover in time for the grand reunion. You've been gone three weeks! Isn't it marvellous how every change you make is 100% better than the last. I love you very much and am looking forward to the morning of Dec. 24th as the most special Christmas Eve of my life.

> Goodnight my darling
> Mary

---

* WEA: Workers' Educational Association.
† Bl. M.: black market.

24 Lloyd Square,
W.C.1
23rd December 1941

My dearest darling Mary,

I'm terribly disappointed – there is going to be no Christmas leave owing to the amount of work necessitated by this new plan, so our fourth Xmas will have to be spent apart. It's damned annoying as I had been longing to come down and be with you as long as possible, particularly after your lovely letter today. However, it's just one of those things and I'll have to hope to have some leave in January.

Your Christmas presents have been sent off today; I'm sorry that they're not spectacular, but they come with all my love nevertheless. I'll buy you a really nice present at the end of January, which should prove to be an Eldorado (miniature)!

Christmas together would have been lovely, wouldn't it? And Rosheen could have enjoyed it too. Do you realise that by the time we do see each other we shall have been separated for the longest period since we met, way back in '38?

It looks as though I shall spend a solitary Xmas day. Anne has gone down to Gloucestershire and Kay goes today to High Wycombe. So I shall have to celebrate my Xmas dinner a (or aux) Lyons [Corner House]. If we finish at midday I shall try and go out to Bushey for the night. Mother is very disappointed that you and Rosh are not coming up, but looks forward to seeing you after Xmas.

Basil, by the way, has received notification from the Admiralty that his name will appear in the London Gazette for 'courage and devotion to duty', so that looks as though he will get the B.E.M. or M.B.E. or some similar decoration. The first Francis hero!

We had a lute recital on Sunday. Diana* played us a few tunes on her instrument, which is a beautiful one. It has 19 strings altogether and is almost as light as balsa wood, specially made for her by the last surviving lute maker in England. She is very lucky from many points of view; she is the only outstanding lute player there is – taught herself from a text book in the British Museum; consequently, whenever the BBC want lute music (from a few chords to a whole recital) they always send for her and pay her well.

I must ring up this evening and speak to you once again; I hope you will be <u>in</u> and not gallivanting with that gay caballero Duckworth. And Wendy, how is she?

A slight battle is going on at the moment as I am pressing to be appointed as Secretary to the Chief of Staff of this new show (who is my boss with a new hat on). It makes a difference of 2/6d a day, which is <u>not</u> to be sneezed at.

Keith, by the way, is now a Captain. Grahame is expected back for Xmas.

Well my darling honey, it's a tragedy we shan't be together on Thursday. Enjoy yourself all the same and save a thought or so for me having a lonely table d'hôte seul . . .

　　All my love my lovely Mary. All yours irrevocably
　　David

---

* Diana Poulton, a famous English lutenist and a good friend.

[On Admiralty notepaper]
24 Lloyd Square
W.C.1
29th December 1941

My darling,

The few days passed so quickly that almost before I had time to realise I was home I was back in London again. All the same, leave like that has a tremendous thrill about it, and every moment was worth a week. It's very creditable, I think, to be so wild about one another and to enjoy each other so much after all these years. May it continue like that always. And your coming up to London in a few days' time will be something to look forward to and make plans for. We'll have a great time. All your Swansea repressions can be let loose and absorbed in the night life of Metropolis.

One thing is certain – that I love you more than anyone else in the world, and the thrill and the happiness of being with you is a feeling and an emotion in a class by itself.

I still seek a room to make my permanent headquarters – the Clark Halls may produce something on Wednesday though.

Yesterday's results were very good, but I couldn't get along because we worked until 7-ish. Attendances 12,500; collections total £1,100 odd and new members 700 odd. Everyone very pleased.

The journey back was not too bad and I managed to get quite a lot of sleep. Kay was yanked out of bed at 7 o'clock so I had to assuage her with all the morning's newspapers practically. Anne hasn't returned from her Xmas yet.

Well I must get back to work now. Incidentally I received a letter from you yesterday posted on the 10th December. Grrr! A frosty one, too.

Write soon darling and keep happy.

All my love
David

1942

49 Bryn Road,
Swansea,
Jan 1st, 1942.

My dearest David,

To wish you a happy and successful 1942, and to hope in 1943 we will be together again. Yes, the Christmas leave was super-lovely; almost worth the separation to have that excitement of being together again – and to realize that we love each other still, with the fresh and ardent love, not to be hoped for after three years of married life, and the onerous duties of parenthood.

Last night was the New Year's Eve, and I was invited once again to the soldiers' party. It was great fun, but half-way through I was stricken with a sense of inescapable loss – <u>you</u> weren't there. And I couldn't bear to stay, so went away for a lonely midnight walk in the fog, with a full moon trying to break through, and thought about you, and the strange link that is between us – for whenever I see anything that gives me pleasure, remote as it may be from you, instantaneously you are in my mind and I feel your absence then more poignantly than ever.

I had a pleasant evening on Monday. Tom came in – yes, that man again, and brought his captain and No. 1 officer, both extraordinarily nice people. No. 1 said, on seeing the posters, 'My brother's in the C. P. Will that do?' and the skipper (Neil Ross by name) had something to do with the International Brigade when in the Merchant Navy trading to Spain. Also was a member of the Glasgow Orpheus choir and was tickled to death by the gramophone. They're coming again when next in Swansea. They think they were part of the Vaagso raid, but were also cancelled. It sounds terrific from the newspaper reports, but my darling I can't help thanking Providence that you were 'cancelled'. Were the naval casualties heavy, or did the Commandos take it all?

We have had arrears of the Xmas mail. Cards from Jill and Art and also Commander Waters! He still loves us – all three. I am going to write him and re-establish contact. There was also a wire this morning with new year's greetings from Dick and Hetty which cheered me up enormously as I am feeling 'weltschmerz' today (you know – my 'but that was long ago, and in a strange country, and besides the wench is dead' mood (or do you?)). I am missing you so much since that lovely rapturous four days; like the phoenix my love arises renewed from its own burnt-out ashes (dear David). I have been playing the terribly wistful B. Mullen record

> 'Whether he loves me or loves me not
> I will walk with my love now and then.'

I hope the job continues to be interesting and exciting, and that you are enjoying your spare time enormously (I really mean that, no matter with whom), and that living quarters will spring up from somewhere, comfortable, uncramped with room for an occasional wife (<u>Me</u>).

Write soon to me my darling and for New Year's confession I will state that I love you with the same crazy, passionate, maudling, mawkish, cynical, unconsequential, inexorable, wonderful, death-defying love as ever was.

Yours ever and always
Mary.

P.S. Rosheen is grand and I have her tamed to the pot at last, which is a great relief. She sends you her affection.
P.P.S. The electricity account arrived, 19/2d for the quarter ending Dec 1941. No so bad, eh?

CHAPTER 16

Combined Operations

> D. LANG 9
>
> 29/1/42
>
> Hollywood Hotel
> Largs
>
> My dearest darling Mary,
>
> Another letter from you — eagerly awaited and much enjoyed. Your coat sounds a wow: roll along the day when I see you in it. Go ahead and get it; I'll see you get enough money to pay for it, though you'll have to wait until I can cash my cheque at the end of the month. (Theoretically I'm still in London!) What sort of hat are you going to wear with it? Get a decent one, & not another Pinock or similar beauty-killer!
>
> Rosheen's vocabulary is something to be considered, at long last. I hope she can say

David returns to London after the brief Christmas leave in Swansea and shortly afterwards is posted to Largs, an Ayrshire seaside town on the Firth of Clyde which had become a key wartime Combined Operations training centre. His first letter is dated 24 January 1942, from his base at the Hollywood Hotel, an iconic venue where five months later Mountbatten would hold a conference of the country's military leaders to begin planning the D-Day Normandy landings.

The top-secret nature of David's work as Intelligence Officer and aide to Garnons-Williams meant his surviving letters contain little information about his job, although some of the most important events of this period of the war were being prepared and planned at Largs.

Mary's letters keep him in touch with events in Swansea – social and political – and the eighteen-month-old Rosheen's progress. Her beloved brother, Tom, who is now serving on the anti-submarine trawler *Ullswater*, comes to visit.

★

Hollywood Hotel,
Largs, Ayrshire
January 24th 1942

My darling Mary,

I am wondering now where you are and what you are
doing – in Swansea or in London. I haven't heard a word from
you since leaving you, oh neglectful wife. Anyhow, I hope you
are enjoying yourself whatever (and wherever) you are doing.

Things are moving more quickly up here now, and an
extensive reorganisation is just beginning to take effect. My boss
has a dual job and is primarily engaged in operational work.
When not engaged he has to organise exercises in preparation
for operations. Either way, he is a Chief Staff Officer, so I should
get my extra gold, although 'should' is not 'will'. It means, also,
that we go back to London if an operation needs planning.

The weather up here has completely changed. Since yesterday
it has been raining solidly and all the snow has disappeared. It's
really far too wet to go out – in fact I have only been outside the
Hollywood once since arriving, which is a bad thing. The
village (or town?) is some 2½ miles away, so even to go to the
cinema one has to walk it to hire a taxi.

Food is very good and plentiful and living is quite
comfortable. The WRNS bring early morning tea, and brush
one's uniform, which is useful. However, the only diversions are
reading, ping-pong, chess, listening to the wireless and
drinking, all of which are already becoming monotonous. I
think it needs shaking up more than somewhat. Soon I shall
contact our little friends, directly I have got my bearings.

Will you send down my oilskin. I must go out and get some
exercise when it is raining, so it will come in handy. It is said
that Largs has a phenomenal rainfall, even worse than Swansea!
The Russian news is excellent, eh? Comment here is very

favourable and full of admiration, perhaps more for the Army officers than anyone else. When one hears that retreat is even the case in Libya, the Russian victories become even more important. As Kay said, it is only by a stroke of luck that we are fighting on the right side!

What else has Rosheen said, if anything? You must have a decent photograph taken soon – I want one.

Have you decided what to buy when you come to London? With a bit of luck I may be able to make it more than £7 extra, but that depends on what and how I get paid this month.

G-W had a birthday today and is very cock-a-hoop. Spent this afternoon striding up a mountain in the pouring rain dressed in his Lofoten* battle dress!

The countryside round here seems very pleasant – very mountainous and rugged. Opposite the hotel are two islands Great and Little Cumbrae which are sometimes shrouded in mist. Beyond them, only visible during clear periods, is Arran. The channel between us and the Cumbraes is quite narrow, and occasional patrol boats and M/L's come roaring past. A cruiser has been having firing practice nearby, which shakes the windows somewhat.

Having got used to Evan Williams, Bryn Thomas, Dai Davies and all, it's rather peculiar to see Hugh Colquhoun, McRobert McDougal etc etc around the place! Still, I've always wanted to see Scotland!

Write to me, your bonnie lover, when you get a moment to spare a thought for me. Yuir a guid lassie an all tha'. Och aye, and porridge fir breakfast.

All good wishes to the old folks at home, and for yourself, my

---

* Lofoten: an archipelago in Norway raided in 1941 by British Commandos during Operation Claymore and a subsequent diversionary attack to support the Vaagso raid in December.

lovely dearest darling, all my love as always. Looking forward so much to seeing you again my sweet one, wherever that may be.

Yours

David

49 Bryn Road,
Swansea.
Jan 22, 1942

My dearest David,

I received letter No. 2 this morning, and apart from the Scots dialect was very pleased – oh one point – how the hell could I write to you when you kept quite silent for days and days and days? I hope you have received my No. 1 by now. I am still in Swansea and have decided to postpone (what, again!) my London visit until your movements become more certain. If you are likely to return, even for a flying visit, within a few weeks, I can bear to wait. Swansea is <u>awful</u>. It snows, then it rains, then it snows, and so forth. I had one small crumb of consolation yesterday – a letter from little Hymie, who now that my nuptial couch (his words) no longer creaks beneath the weight of the British Navy, hastens to write to his little Mary. I <u>must</u> surely go to London. His address, if you want to know if his intentions are honourable, is: 'A' Branch, Headquarters, Eastern Command, Home Forces.

Darling, you ask me once again what I am going to buy. I have already <u>bought</u>, or at least ordered and am awaiting money to buy, the coat of my dreams. Russian Red – I have christened it 'Moscow' – with great verve and elan – a London coat finding itself by some miracle in Swansea. It gives me a tres debonair look that one feels is sadly lacking at most times. The price for all this elegance, a mere nothing, a mere bagatelle, a paltry eight guineas. So my darling husband, be as uxorious and generous as possible to your extra-va-gant wife and cough up de dough. Please. I feel very ashamed of myself, but awfully glad about the coat and I know you will approve. With black hat, shoes and etceteras I will look very, very nice.

So hurry up, and let me show you my new self. I shan't wear it until you can see it, and I can't have it until it's paid for.

Rosheen says 'MAR-MEE' in a loud sing-song shout which is very funny. She also says 'Po-Po', 'Ba-Ba', 'Drink-ee'. What a baby! The old folks are well and send you their love.

I hope that the job is as interesting as the London lay-out, but that you soon come back to London. I am missing you so much. The last parting with you was so casual and such a temporary one – but it seems to have stretched itself out in grim reality.

Are you going to make a pilgrimage to Ardrossan – to the shrine of our patron St. Edward?

Write <u>immediately</u>, <u>lengthily</u>, and <u>daily</u> my own darling to your Mary

    With all my love. x

P.S. Tom is pining for a letter from you. He asks me plaintively to give you his address: HMS Ullswater, c/o G.P.O. Write to him if you can. He loves you so much.

Hollywood Hotel
Largs
29/1/42

My dearest darling Mary,

Another letter from you – eagerly awaited and much enjoyed. Your coat sounds a wow: roll along the day when I see you in it.

Go ahead and get it; I'll see you get enough money to pay for it, though you'll have to wait until I can cash my cheque at the end of the month. (Theoretically I'm still in London!) What sort of hat are you going to wear with it? Get a decent one, and not another Pinoc[chio] or similar beauty-killer!

Rosheen's vocabulary is something to be considered, at long last. I hope she can say Po-Po at the appropriate moment.

Yesterday G-W was at a conference at Melrose so I had a relatively easy day. Today we make up for it and now (quarter to ten) I am seizing the opportunity offered by a short break to write to you for the early morning mail.

Last night I visited Largs' super cinema and had the best seat in the house for 1-4d. It's a very luxurious place inside with pictures of belligerent Norsemen all over the joint. The name? The Viking. Picture was 'Washington Melodrama'* – quite good.

This afternoon was beautiful, so I went for a walk across the hills at the back, which were lightly covered in snow. The higher hills in the distance looked wonderful – the tips catching the red rays of the afternoon sun which gave them a soft reddish hue. The sea, which is full of islands, looked more like a loch, being perfectly calm and shrouded in a wintery mist. I felt good. Everything looked good. Even the tumbling, rushing, stone-studded burn looked good – even if it is called the Gogo water!

It would have been lovely to have you there at my side, on those snowy hills, my darling Mary. Whenever there is anything really pleasant, or beautiful, or exciting, or absorbing I always wish you were there to enjoy it with me – it would treble the appreciation.

Today I was duty staff officer and had to take the salute at sundown by the army guard. Very smart.

An apoplectic signal arrived today: 'I Leading Tel. with faulty

---

* *Washington Melodrama* (1941), directed by S. Sylvan Simon, starring Frank Morgan and Ann Rutherford.

generator, reporting am tomorrow'. Some nit pencilled on the signal, 'Suggest medical officer deal with this forthwith'!

Tomorrow I will ring you my sweet. It will be heaven to hear your voice once again.

The sock situation is DESPERATE! Send 'em quick, or my last remaining pair will become one enormous hole!

I'll write to Tom tomorrow. Does he ever come up this way? I must drop Hymie a line, the dirty, double-crossing bastard. Not a single word out of him when I was in London!

To think I have been in the Navy 2 years and 12 days. How tempus fucking fugits!

Well my lovely precious Moscow Maire, I'm longing to see you in your red coat. The dough will come just as soon as is humanly possible in the speed line.

All my love, my dearest one. Write me soon again, and will me in bed with you.

David

49 Bryn Road,
Swansea,
Jan. 30. 1942

My darling David,

I hope your silence over the telephone last night wasn't due to anything more serious than bad weather or something like that.

Oh, I am missing you so much. The weekends are really unendurable now, much more vacuous and monotonous than even the week-days, and my mother being here doesn't help matters at all. In fact the less said on that subject the better, as by the end of each day, though I begin with good resolution, she reduces me to such a state of nervous irritation that I feel I cannot breathe. But this is too foolish and unimportant to really be a problem I know and I will try to overcome it.

I despatched a parcel of socks and your oilskins to you. You should receive it about Monday.

This afternoon was the first S.C.R. lecture – Dr Jarman – about 50 attended – 2 new members, collection 22/-. Not bad but could have been better. Jarman was very good. Unfortunately I couldn't go as my mother has presumed to think I go to too many meetings and wouldn't be co-operative about minding Rosheen. What the hell!

I need you so much at the moment to restore my serenity and optimism. Think very hard about me when you receive this letter and maybe some influence will come from you to comfort me.

Rosheen is being very spectacular at the moment – she is cutting 8 teeth! 4 back teeth and 4 molars all together, so it is just as well that I am at home as her nights are somewhat disturbed and she is fractious during the day, but otherwise is awfully well and good. They are forming a Nursery School Assoc. in Swansea and I went to the inaugural meeting tonight. Some child psychologist speaking so I asked her whether she thought under-two too young for a baby to go to Nursery School. She thought it was too young to break the emotional link between mother and child – bloody bourgeois guff, but maybe she's got something. I don't want to get a job, however, until we have had this long-awaited fortnight, week, or even weekend together in London. If there is the remote chance of your returning within one month or even two I will wait, as expense is still a major problem and I have spent all the money you promised me (remember?) on a red coat (still in the shop waiting to be redeemed). Let me know if we can still look forward to a bout of whoopee together and I will keep my spirits hoisted to that one hope.

Russia is the most magnificent bloody country. Did you see that Australia – read the cutting for yourself!

What can be done to save the rest of the war? Benghazi –
Singapore etc etc. Victory in 1942 says Stalin. America will have
an unbeatable navy in <u>1945</u> says Q. Reynolds!

Write to me as <u>often</u> <u>often</u> <u>often</u> as you possibly can – twice a
day if possible, as you, and you alone, in all this mad marvellous
world can influence my going and coming, my being happy or
sad, my living or dying.

Goodnight my darling

Mary

49 Bryn Road,
Swansea.
Feb 5th 1942

My dearest David,

How are you, my darling? I hope you have survived the snow
and the sickness of your superiors and that you aren't so harassed
as your last note sounded. I am glad the absence of the telephone
call was due to natural causes. I was beginning to fear that you
were snowbound, or that the rabbits you were going to shoot
last Saturday had proven tougher than anticipated. I shall still
expect the call, as it would be lovely to talk to you. It's ages
since you went away; I think the fact we didn't take the last
parting very seriously makes the separation harder this time. Still
it will be all the lovelier when we meet again.

Have you received your socks yet? And have you succeeded
in buying a cardigan? Scotland should be the place for knitted
things. But if you haven't got it yet, let me know and I'll see
what can be done in the knitting thereof.

Tom came in for a night on Monday. He is looking extremely
well and IS GOING ON 7 DAYS' LEAVE in a couple of

weeks. Ma and Pa are going up to London for 7 days in 8 days' time. I alone am faithful to Swansea. But you have not answered my question which I will now repeat. Is there a chance of our having our London holiday within the next month or so? If not, I'll go to London for a few days by myself and then come back to Swansea and start looking for a job, and forget that we ever planned to go skating or to the Café Royal.

I have a design for living:

a) To get a job in Swansea for a couple of months to save up some money.
b) Move nearer London – within distance for day travelling.
c) Get a job in London and settle Rosheen either in a nursery school outside or with my mother outside London.

But I don't want to tie myself down in a job until we have had this London holiday which has assumed such enormous importance.

So let me know if there is any chance.

I haven't got my red coat yet – still waiting for your loving husband act. Hurry up, or it will be sold away from me.

Rosheen has advanced amazingly in the last few weeks. She says MARY very clearly, and has invented a new crazy way of entertaining herself. Her shoes and socks disappear from her feet and reappear – perfectly buttoned – on her hands! She has got many, many teeth coming and is behaving beautifully.

Scotland sounds very beautiful and I hope the weather improves so that you can enjoy it. You know how I would love to be with you on those mountains, or indeed anywhere at all. I seem to have two lives – the one I live with you, and the life I lived before I knew you which seems to have caught up with me again. But with a difference in that now there is Rosheen and the lovely background of having lived with you.

Write me a long letter, or even short one like yesterday, but please write often.

Counting the mornings to receive your letters and the days until we meet again.

> With all my love
> Your own
> Mary

> 49 Bryn Road,
> Swansea.
> Feb 12, 1942

Dearest David,

I have waited for the postman to pass for the second time today before writing to you. Do you realise I haven't had a letter for a week from you! Are you still recovering from your frenzy of holding the fort, or are you deluged in more work?

If I don't hear from you tomorrow I shall start worrying and maybe send you a telegram, as I can't phone you, not knowing your phone no.

Everything here is very much the daily task, the common round. Weary, flat, stale, <u>and</u> unprofitable. Ma and Pa go down to London tomorrow for 10 days. I envy them very much.

There was a horrible hitch to the Bernals* meeting last week. The date was always uncertain and the night before I looked in the S.W.E.P. as we had promised to announce whether the meeting was to be held or not. No announcement, and believe it or not, Haydn had done bugger-all to find out whether there

---

* John Bernals was a scientist and pioneer in molecular biology who wrote extensively on the history of science. He was a supporter of communism and wrote popular books connecting science and society.

was to be a meeting or not. He feebly didn't know anything and was still waiting for the A.S.W. to inform him. On Feb 10th (the day of the meeting) I found out from the college that Bernals was not coming and managed to get an advt. in time in the papers to that effect. But I fear this has done our reputation no good, specially as the speaker for the lecture the Saturday before failed to appear. I find it impossible to work with Haydn and can only stay in the background and try for last-minute retrievals of the ground he loses.

Mrs Farrington is reported to be very ill. I must call round this afternoon and inquire.

It's difficult writing to you not knowing how things are with you. Maybe you are no longer in Hollywood. Maybe (save the mark) you no longer love me. I am just marking time, anyhow, until I hear from you. I am not going to appeal for letters this time, as that invariably has an adverse effect, but leave it to your CONSCIENCE.

Rosheen is thriving and her vocabulary now extends to PAPER (pronounced BABBER). She hoaxes everyone with her cries of Po-po like the little boy who cried 'Wolf'. She has found a marvellous way of getting out of a chair or bed – the unscrupulous brat.

The war situation is awful. Will we have to alter our slogan 'Victory in 1942'?

Any chance of our seeing London together this year? I repeatedly ask this question but receive no anwer. But then you never answer any of my letters.

On this aggrieved note I say goodbye and continue to love you, although I think you are a snake.

    Yours ever,
    Mary

P.S. Did you receive both registered letters (£3 and £8)?

49 Bryn Rd.
Swansea.
Feb 16th 1942

My darling David,

Your new address gave me many qualms the day I received your letter, especially as it was the day on which the German battleships escaped,* and therefore anxious news. But I hope you are enjoying the change and I am awaiting your next letter with eagerness in case of new developments.

I hope by now you have received letters I sent you last week, including two registered ones containing the money I was to send you. I am now the much-envied possessor of a spectacular red coat, and a hat that really does credit to the coat and to me.

I wore both yesterday as Tom came in and took me to tea on the Ullswater. Later he and Neil came back to the flat and we had an extraordinarily pleasant evening. Neil is charming. He brought me his prized Orpheus Choir records as a token, which was very touching.

You and he have a mutual friend in the Soya bean which touched him for £7 one day with an incredibly pathetic story and hasn't been seen since!

I had a Valentine telegram on Feb 14 signed H.B.! Nothing from my lawful spouse, needless to say.

Everyone seems to be in London or going (except me). Ma and Pa are there now for 10 days – Bill Laithwaite is there and Mattie, Haydn are going next weekend for half-term. Mattie's mother left today for London.

---

* A reference to the Channel Dash, a major naval engagement on 11 February 1942, in which two German battleships, the *Scharnhorst* and the *Gneisenau*, and the heavy cruiser *Prinz Eugen* escaped from Brest in Brittany and ran a British blockade in the English Channel to successfully reach their home bases in Germany.

Mrs Farrington is still very ill and the awful part of it is that probably, if she recovers physically, her mind will not be rational. Poor Ben has aged years in the last week. What a fate!

Rosheen continues to teethe and to say more words. 'BOAT' is the newest.

As for me, I grow more nostalgic daily for London and for you. I hesitate to think of you now, I grow so heartsick. God only knows when I shall see you again, or even get a letter from you. But I continue to be glad that you chose to leave Swansea and a safe humdrum existence at a time when the world is in a state of 'chassis'.

Write soon my dear David and give me some news of yourself and how you are. I feel remote and cut off from you lately. Your letters are so tense and hurried that they hardly justify the eagerness with which they are awaited. But I continue to await them eagerly, of course.

Yours ever,
Mary

CHAPTER 17

Operation Ironclad

DL 11

Hollywood Hotel
Largs. Ayr

26/2/42

My darling,

Another lovely letter from
you today, which makes today a
lovely day.

Just after I wrote to you
on Tuesday, something really staggering
happened, and at which I am still
thoroughly amazed. I'll tell you all
about it in a few days time. Its
just the old luck at work encore
une fois.

Yesterday I went for a
long walk in the hills again: it
was a delightful day - warm and
spring like and it felt good to be
alive. The countryside looked

David has been selected to become part of the planning team for a top-secret operation of vital significance for the Allied war effort: Operation Ironclad, the codename for the invasion of Madagascar.

Early in March 1942, Churchill gave the go-ahead and the planning began for Ironclad, Britain's largest amphibious assault since the Dardenelles in the First World War and the first large-scale combined air, sea and land operation of the Second. Garnons-Williams was appointed Senior Naval Officer for the actual landings, and David, his aide, was at the heart of the planning and execution of this historic operation.

David set sail on 23 March 1942. Ironclad was officially launched on 29 March 1942, and David was at sea in the large convoy heading for Africa, under the command of Rear-Admiral E. N. Syfret, aboard the *Winchester Castle*, a converted passenger ship and the headquarters ship for the Allied landings on Madagascar.

★

Hollywood Hotel
Largs, Ayr
26/2/42

My darling,

Another lovely letter from you today, which makes today a lovely day.

Just after I wrote to you on Tuesday, something really staggering happened, and at which I am still thoroughly amazed. I'll tell you all about it in a few days' time. It's just the old luck at work encore une fois.

Yesterday I went for a long walk in the hills again: it was a delightful day – warm and springlike and it felt good to be alive. The countryside looked incredibly beautiful, and again I wished you were here to enjoy it.

Sorry to hear you have a chill. Look after yourself well – we can't have anything happening to you. It's useful that your Mother is back so she can give you some 'pampering': you deserve some.

The wireless sounds rather a fiasco. I should think the best thing is to sell it, or if you can afford it, part exchange it for a good second-hand one. The problem is to get a good second-hand one you really need an expert to be present at the buying to see that one does get a good'un.

I see that Rosheen's going to develop into a bully! Hope that Anne wasn't unduly frightened by the Rosheen apparition.

A letter has just come from the Commodore here to say that I have been appointed auditor of the mess account for the last quarter! There is no escape!

Last night I took a few hours off and visited the 'Viking' cinema and saw The Face Behind the Mask* – mediocre. The

---

* *The Face Behind the Mask* (1941), directed by Robert Florey, starring Peter Lorre and Evelyn Keyes.

film of Pearl Harbour [sic] was also shown – one of the grimmest pieces of destruction I've ever seen. The poor sods inside couldn't have had a chance. That is those who weren't on week-end leave.

By the way, how is the soap rationing going to affect you? I certainly shan't use all mine so if you want any soap or soap flakes, just sing out.

I don't think it will be long before we meet again, honey. I think it will happen suddenly when it does. It will be marvellous to be with you – the last time seems now ages ago. However, we can always make up for it come the day.

Give my love to your Ma and Pa – and to you my darling Mary, all the love, the full feeling of my heart as always.

Yours eternally
David

49 Bryn Road,
Swansea,
March 1, 1942

My dearest David,

It's Sunday afternoon in Swansea, cold and bleak and boring, and I have got a new nib, so it is suggested that I write to you. I have felt a disinclination to write to you for the past few days because I felt really low – mentally and physically. I've had a horrible stomach ache for the past fortnight combined with dizziness and one complete blackout and general weak-kneedness. All caused through wearing too little underwear in my lower region. Anyway, I am much better physically but am still wanting a cure for my spirits.

Maybe your 'incredible news' will be that cure. What can it be? You really are maddening to intrigue me in this way. What key influences are at work and what new circles will you now decorate? Have you been appointed naval attaché to Murmansk, or does the luck embrace me too. I'm all agog.

I was much cheered by the news that we might be meeting soon. Not only because I long for you and need to escape from Swansea for a while, but also I want to fix my own future months and get a job either in Swansea or in London. I had written to Cmdr Waters and was going to meet him in London had I gone up when arranged, but I can see him when I <u>do</u> go.

Swansea grows more and more irksome and definitely hasn't improved since my mother's arrival. But she didn't go back to Dublin at the end of the first month and so is here for at least six months. Still, if I had a job it would be much better as I would have some other outlet.

Rosheen is very well except for a blob on the end of her nose caused by a climbing mishap the other day. It will pass if she leaves it alone. She is very smart having had a new coat, hat, trousers and shoes out of the money you sent. Moi aussi, new hat, coat and shoes, all ready for the big city. Ruth is still very ill, and having rallied through pneumonia and heart trouble has developed kidney deficiency. The mental condition is no better also, so I think her case is hopeless. We thought at the beginning of the week that she was going to recover, but things broke down again.

I had a letter from Mary Mann the other day. They are all well and Cyril is on Salisbury Plain. She is fed up where she is living and I think would like to combine with me. That would have been nice, but would be difficult now with Ma having settled with me.

Stalin's speech last week was magnificent and I was very pleased to hear the 'extermination of the Germans' doctrine squashed. What a <u>moral</u> victory for the S.U. as well as a military one.

We have now a 'Lilliput'* rejection slip to add to our

---

* 'Lilliput': a monthly magazine for humour and short stories.

collection. What shall I do with the story? Send it to a newspaper?

Hurry up darling and let me come to London. I am so ready, never more so in my life, and if I wait much longer will grow frustrated and INHIBITED. I warn you.

Rosheen can now say DOG, BOY, DRINKIE, CAKIE, CAKIE, CAKIE (at every shop that might sell cakes) and of course PO-PO. She also says POPA – for Poppamoss, but sometimes confuses the two words. She is the worst-mannered child in Swansea and is growing more like you every day. You will have to beat her hard or stand her on her head until she reforms when you come home.

What is your incredible news. Oh what?

When shall we meet again. Oh when?

Write soon and I will write more frequently now I am better. Continue to enjoy life and to love me.

With all my love as always

49 Bryn Road,
Swansea,
March 1, 1942

My dearest David,

You will be very sorry to hear that Mrs Farrington died yesterday afternoon. She had a magnificent rally, recovering from pneumonia and the heart collapse, but the kidneys also were infected and they finished her. She is going to be buried on Thursday and various organisations are going to be represented at the funeral. Ben is amazingly marvellous. He is the most realistic and honest man I have ever met and the way he has behaved and is behaving makes me admire him more than ever.

I have given a contribution to the wreath from 'a group of friends' from you as well as from myself and perhaps you will write to Ben yourself.

So much dying and so much sorrow in the world. I suppose Ruth's kind of death is one of the best ways – quick and shocking to all your friends who remember you vigorous and vital and are left with no memories of a querulous and fatuous old age.

How are you darling and what are developments regarding the news 'incroyable'? I am living for the moment I see you again. I'm afraid if we are separated too long we will grow unreal to each other – not in retrospect, but in reality. That's the way people always go for me if they are out of sight for too long. You, of course, are not 'people'. You are David, the most substantial and real person in my life, but I am a very peculiar person, so let's MEET SOON, so I can reassure myself that David and Mary did really happen.

This letter is a lot of rot, but I have been thinking of life and death, trying to find the perspective and at the moment am still in a metaphysical flight. Please forgive me and excuse me if I stop writing now.

Yours forever my darling, Mary

49 Bryn Road,
Swansea.
Sunday [no date]

My darling David,

This the strangest letter I have ever written to you – I don't know where, what or how you are, or even <u>if</u> you are, as Thursday morning was the first and last communication from you, and with what relief and joy did I receive <u>that letter</u>. Your news is very exciting and <u>tantalising</u> but I am highly delighted that it is something worthwhile and up to expectations.

Meanwhile I await (pantingly) for more news and for the story itself to break – wham – into the headlines. But if it is mortally possible I beg you to let me have a postcard, wire, telephone message, and/or, is it too much to ask? a letter <u>VERY OFTEN</u>; I need some contact with you to act as a sort of life-line, even though I'm endeavouring to be as self-sufficient and brave-little-womanish as you could wish. But I love you very much – much too much (after three years of holy deadlock) to accept your being here one day and gone the next, with unconcern. But don't worry about me because I am very busy and as happy as possible without you.

Tom and Evelyn are staying here for seven days' leave – Tom is going to a far northern destination next week. Evelyn is nice – not what I had expected at all, and I am pleased for them. The exhibition has given me a few grey hairs (mentally) as it didn't arrive on the stated day – on Tuesday midday it came after frantic phone calls to London and Paddington Station – it had probably spent the night at Fishguard. I met train after train all containing bags of fish but no photos. Nitchevo, we got them up Tuesday afternoon and though the exhibition isn't exactly a riot, it is drawing plenty of people. Real S.C.R. weather though – bloody awful. I think we will make many members from this enterprise however, as people come to find out just who is organising it, and the 'interested' forms are filling up. I will have to battle hard with Haydn, I fear, as he is all for amalgamating the S.C.R. with the W.E.A., and knowing him I mistrust his motives – laziness and pusillanimosity [sic].

Rosheen got a tooth through today and is very well. She asks querulously 'Where's Dai? Where's Dai?' 'God knows,' is the invariable answer.

The Mayor <u>ratted</u>, of course. He backed out of everything he had promised you and it's a dirty story. I have got your letter underneath my pillow and each night I wish for another letter, so try hard to let me have a word from you. I am tremendously happy for you to be doing something after your own heart. I am thinking of you constantly and I love and admire you more than anybody else on this earth.

Success and good luck, darling, and all my love always.

Mary

P.S. Give them an extra one for <u>me</u>.

[The first letter Mary wrote after their last meeting when he set sail:]

49 Bryn Road,
Swansea.
March 30, 1942

My beloved David,

You have been gone one whole week now – 7 days nearer to the day we meet again; 7 days less to await that much longed for moment. Writing to you like this, knowing that you won't receive this letter until it is very out-of-date still has the supreme satisfaction of establishing contact with you <u>at this very moment</u>. I've been cowardly all week and tried not to think about you, to be unconcerned and self-sufficient, but that's foolish, for the very thought of you stimulates me into life, and the effort of writing a letter to you has flooded me with such a wave of tenderness and love for you, my darling, that all the hard unhappiness is melting. Isn't that wonderful – at such a distance too.

Many many thanks for your wire and lovely lovely letter. I carry it around like a talisman and the promise of daily, long letters fills me with joy, although I expect I shall have them in a flood, and then starvation until the next flood.

Rosheen was very well when I arrived back in Swansea, and I hope you won't be disappointed in her when you see her. She is the most attractive little monkey, and grows more like you, especially in <u>character</u>, every day. We are definitely moving up to London, and then prepare to reorganise ourselves from there. My mother is being very co-operative lately, which is a relief. It will probably be a job for me and nursery school for the Pooch but I will keep you informed with weekly bulletins, which you will have to sort out and construct anew when you receive them.

Griff Fender have agreed to move us at the old estimate and Reg and Wendy are going to take over this flat, so that everything is being made easy. I shall put the furniture in Elgin Crescent and then look around for a charming residence in which to make a charming home for my conquering hero (that's you). In the meantime I propose to launch a captivating Rosheen on to an unsuspecting Bushey for a couple of weeks so that they can renew acquaintanceships.

So much for news here. As I say, I shall keep you posted as the plans proceed. It's your birthday on Thursday David. Where will you be spending it? Not with me, alas, but if possible I shall be thinking of you more constantly and with deeper love than even at the moment. Many, many happy returns my darling.

I find it difficult to write of little trivial small-talk items to you at this stage, so this letter will be a short one – short anyhow in ratio to the amount of love and gratitude with which it is sent.

What are a few months of waiting against a life together

which has been so much <u>fun</u>, so rich and creative and infinitely worthwhile? My darling David, so sorry once again to quote J. Donne at you, but he is always so appropriate:

> 'Methinks I lied all winter when I swore
> My love was infinite, if Spring makes it more'*

and with this I can say no more except goodnight darling; be well and happy and come back to me.

    Always until me very last breath,
       Yours
        Mary

---

* From John Donne, 'Love's Growth' (1633).

CHAPTER 18

Return to London

ML 16

32, Vernon Road
Bushey
Herts
April 16th.

My darling David.

I have
burnt my boats, crossed the
Rubicon, etc, etc. In short I
have dismantled Bryn Rd.
and am now in London.
The furniture came up last
week and was dumped
(that exactly the word) in
Elgin Crescent. How it is
to be extricated again
is a future problem. But

On 5 April 1942, with David a fortnight at sea heading for Africa, Mary writes in a moving letter that she is making plans for her and Rosheen to return to London, initially to stay with her parents in Elgin Crescent, Kensington, and David's parents in Bushey.

By the middle of April she has left Swansea for good and is looking for a flat and a job back in London. She receives a telegram from David but no other news or letters. Then, on 6 May, the invasion of Madagascar bursts into the national headlines. Mary finds a home – 12 Lloyd Square, a charming little house in the Lloyd Baker Estate, just off the King's Cross Road, and down the road from Angel House in the patch of north central London that she and David had made their own. She was to live there with Rosheen, when she wasn't at boarding school, for the next fourteen years.

★

49 Bryn Road,
Swansea,
April 5th, 1942.

My darling David,

You've been gone a fortnight and it's now Easter. Every week seems to be some oncewhile festival, full of some absolutely marvellous memories. Paris three years ago; I know you haven't forgotten – formidables and pigeons and taxis down the Champs Elysees, and the crazy day at Notre Dame. Oh David, how I love you and miss you, and how grateful I am to you for our life together. I am thinking constantly of you, even though I have no background for you, but find you, a solitary figure wandering in the fabulous geography of Xanadu. Come back soon my darling, and straight to me.

We are still in Swansea, but expect to move within the next fortnight. I have begun to organise things so that everything will go smoothly and also so that the further removal from Elgin Crescent to our future house (where?) will not be too complicated. My darling husband, with all deferential respect to you, am I destined to tote files and files of Paxton Chronicles and letters to and from former women in your life around England for the rest of my life? Can I now salvage them for the war effort? That is merely a rhetorical question and doesn't expect an answer. The truth is that I am infernally jealous because you haven't got me in a file, but only on 'a little piece of string'. Still maybe to be in a file means that one has gone out of your life and is merely a memory, and I definitely refuse to be in that category. I am in your life, even though you are at the other end of the earth, just as you completely dominate mine, by something much more powerful than physical presence.

Rosheen, of course, is my most tangible evidence of you, and I am eternally grateful for her existence. She is terribly like you to look at these days, and reminds me of you in many other ways. Her vocabulary is still far from fluent, but is very funny, and she has a charming new trick of batting her arms in imitation of birds flying. She continues to have a passion for books, and is much easier to keep amused. I hope to send her to nursery school when we reach London, but of course must investigate this thoroughly.

There is an amusing housing situation here. Reg and Wendy are moving <u>here</u> when I leave, and Bill and Mary Laithwaite are moving out to Newton when they leave. Le roi est mort, vive le roi! H. Glass was quite amenable to switch over of tenants and everything is fixed this end. I intend to ditch the plaguey, hag-ridden furniture at Elgin Crescent and then take Rosheen to see your mother for a week or so. I then find a new flat and then Rosheen and I start our new life. Come up and see us sometime.

But seriously one of the main reasons for coming to London is to provide a base for you and so that we can spend as much time together as possible. And one day, the war will end, and we will be together in London!

I am avidly awaiting the letters you have promised me, but with much more patience than I thought I could have mustered. One gets used to everything, but then I haven't really been sorely tested <u>yet</u>.

Everyone here sends you their love and best wishes, and I send you all my love, unreservedly and completely for ever and ever, and every pulse of my heart and every ounce of energy I possess, my own darling.

Yours passionately
Mary

Look after yourself for my sake, as I <u>could not live</u> without you. I have discovered that very recently. Enjoy yourself also, my dear David, if possible.

32 Vernon Road
Bushey
Herts
April 16th. [1942]

My darling David,

I have burnt my boats, crossed the Rubicon, etc, etc. In short
I have dismantled Bryn Road, and am now in London. The
furniture came up last week and was dumped (that's <u>exactly</u> the
word) in Elgin Crescent. How it is to be extricated again is a
future problem. But . . .

I may be on the edge of getting a job. The existence of
nursery schools influences strongly the choice of where we shall
live, so God alone knows where we shall find ourselves. Would
you object to Chiswick?

This is a very rambling and I fear incoherent letter, but to
write to you casually as if I wasn't overflowing with nostalgia
and longing for you is a bit of a strain. Hurry up and come back
to me my darling David and let us review our most marvellous,
absorbing acquaintance.

Please be well and happy and remember to love
your Mary

Rosheen sends you an imitation of a dog barking
a bird flying
a sheep baaing

and all her love.

32 Vernon Road,
Bushey, Herts.
[27 April 1942]

My sweet darling David,

I received your telegram, forwarded to me from Swansea, and it came like a lifebelt to a drowning man. How I was missing you – I cannot try to put my nostalgia for you into words, but now I have your telegram and the reassuring knowledge of your love to help fill the void.

I am still at Bushey and had intended to return to town tomorrow, but Basil phoned this morning and is coming out tomorrow so I shall wait and let Rosheen renew the acquaintance of uncle No. 2. Then back to London to find a flat and then subsequently a job.

News from Swansea – Reg Duckworth is in hospital; with appendicitis. The perils of civilian life!

Tom and Evelyn were in London last week and I went up twice to see them. Tom was on his way to Scotland for a course and Evelyn is going back on duty after seven days. Lucky pair. Tom sends you his very best wishes and insists on seeing you soon. Oh may it be soon!

Rosheen continues to develop in every way. Her vocabulary will astonish you, and she is getting extremely pretty. In fact she is going to outshine her old ma and pa in an embarrassing way. We'll have to stick together in a mutual aid society I fear. Her first act on arriving at Bushey was to discover where the sweets and biscuits were kept, and she's behaved like that ever since. But your mother thinks she's wonderful.

The weather here is wonderful. Breezy spring days with all the trees in flower. Bushey is a really lovely place in Spring as there are so many trees.

I wonder where you are and what you've seen and what

you've done since five weeks ago when you left me. The war news seems to be monotonously constant – still waiting for the month of destiny – as if Lyndoe and the stars controlled the war. I am counting the days and marking off the weeks and time still moves when you're not there, but monstrous slow. No letters from you have come yet, but I know they will and will be kept as talisman against the tedium and anxiety of waiting for you yourself.

Darling, this is such an insubstantial, unsatisfactory way of telling you that I love you in any time, in any place and circumstances, through hell and high water if you like and for always, but I do, and when you come home I shall devour you with my awful love.

Until that blessed moment, yours ever,
Mary

P.S. Look after yourself and enjoy life.

32 Vernon Road,
Bushey, Herts
April 28th 1942

My own darling David,

Just a note to confirm my letter of yesterday – that I love you more than I can hope to express and that I am living only for the day when you return. I have no news for you today, but I must just put this down on paper to relieve my overflowing heart.

I wish sometimes that I believed in God so that I could pray for your safety and happiness, but I can just <u>hope</u> fervently and passionately that you will come home to
Mary

72, Elgin Crescent,
Ladbroke Grove W.11
May 7th 1942

My darling David,

This time I think I know where you are – the long-awaited headline and general excitement <u>must</u> be your little lot. If only I was so sure of your safety. The Reign of Terror is now in full swing for me and not until I receive a cable saying at least you are alive will I be able to draw breath. Good work, darling, and all the luck in the world protect you. Let me have all the news you can manage <u>as quickly as possible</u>.

It must be very hot with you. The papers talk about intense heat. It is fantastically warm here for the time of the year. I have spent several hot and footsore afternoons investigating the flat situation but haven't got your superb flair for this job. Hampstead is very disappointing. The squalidest, sordidest (the superlative is justified) joints were offered me for simply fantastic rents, places where the kitchen, bathroom and lavatory were all the same place (truly) and where the fireplaces and electric fittings were all missing. When I consider the amenities and rent of Prideaux House I feel disgusted at the profiteering in these tenement houses.

I have enrolled Rosheen in the Kensington Day Nursery, although there is a waiting list, in case I have to take a flat in this district. She is very grown up – went to the hairdresser yesterday to have her hair cut and behaved beautifully. She is rehearsing 'Hello Daddy' as her party piece when she sees you again. Oh may it be soon my darling. I can hardly write with the tremor of excitement that comes over me at that prospect. How will you look? What will you say? I am remembering now your face and the moments when you are transfigured from being quite an ordinary nice-looking human into someone of breathtaking beauty; when looking at you with your hair lying over the pillow gives me all I ever got from poetry or music, and that's certainly aplenty.

I am so full of love for you I cannot bear to write any more. I will go to bed and think maybe that you will come in later on in the night when I am asleep, and perhaps I shall dream of you.

Goodnight my darling. Please be safe and well and come home soon.

Mary

72 Elgin Crescent,
Ladbroke Grove, W.11
May 24, 1942.

My darling David,

The weeks melt away, and yet time hangs so heavily. No letter from you yet. Please may it come next week! This is the last weekend I shall be writing from this address and also my last weekend of being 24. Next week I move to 12 Lloyd Square; next week I am 25; next week I, most probably, start my new job. Yes darling, that's what I said. I've been asked to go to Lawrence and Wishart* and be trained in <u>Advertising and Publicity</u>. My dream job, or so it seems at the moment. Nothing is fixed yet as it all depends on how soon I can get Rosheen to settle down in the day nursery, but very soon (I fear) I shall be a

---

* Lawrence and Wishart: a left-wing British publisher founded in 1936 through the merger of Martin Lawrence, the Communist Party's press, and Wishart Ltd, a family-owned liberal and anti-fascist publisher. In the turmoil of the late 1930s the new press was immersed in the political and cultural life of the Popular Front, publishing literature, drama and poetry as well as political economy, working-class history and Marxist classics.

working gal again. With your back turned darling, I have reorganised my whole life again, to prove to myself that I can do it. But it hasn't stopped me from wanting you and missing you and making everything just lose its essential point because you aren't there to be pleased or sceptical at the various things I have been up to.

When are you coming back? Oh please hurry as time's winged chariot is roaring very loudly at my back and our daughter is growing into a prodigiously talented young lady. I feel so madly jealous of other women when I see them walking with their men, <u>hate</u> them when they look possessive or coquettish, and every time I see a naval man about your build these times my heart turns over, and my treacherous, shortsighted eyes tell me it's you, and that you've come back to London without telling me, or that you're with another woman and have forgotten me, or that 'you and me' never existed at all. You see, I don't presume to take you for granted even after four years.

I met Helen Kaye this weekend, of all people guaranteed to bring back those hectic early days. She was up from Sheffield for a conference and was <u>exactly the same</u>. She sends you her love, and of course everyone else does that.

If I don't get a letter from you soon, I won't be able to write to you anymore. The strain of expressing oneself to a person who has just become represented by a sort of telegram that you make by sticking a pin into a list:

REGARDS
LOVE
FONDEST LOVE
MOST FOND LOVE
ABSOLUTELY FONDEST LOVE

(I couldn't understand the monotony of the 'fondest' until I worked it all out) is becoming too much for my always incoherent pen, and if I don't get a letter next week, I shall wrap myself in the nearest eiderdown and hibernate until one does come. And <u>watercress</u> won't lure me out this time.

This is an egotistical epistle, isn't it? All about me. But how are you and what are you doing and where, oh where are you? Everything is a question. Do you miss me in spite of the new and amazing life, and, <u>most important</u>, do you love me, not fondly or uxoriously, but as you did in November in Brighton, a long time ago – coldly, brightly, aquamarinishly, skating-rinkishly, Regency-monstrously? Do you? I love you with the bright, clean intensity of our walk to Hampstead Heath four years ago and I refuse to let the fact that next week I am 25, that I have a daughter who will be much more beautiful and charming than me, that you are many miles away and practically an unknown equation (what do I mean by that? God knows), change it into something 'fond' and what the Americans might call 'corny'.

By all this you will see that I am just as crazy as ever (by your standards of course, oh most logical and earth-bound materialist) but in spite of that, think of me sometimes and love me <u>always</u>.

Your Mary

CHAPTER 19

—

Mission Accomplished

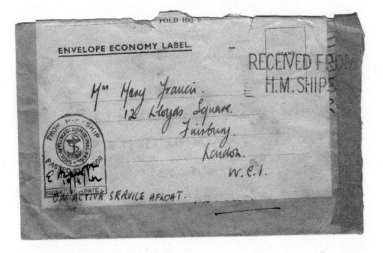

ENVELOPE ECONOMY LABEL.

Mrs Mary Francis.
12 Lloyds Square.
Finsbury.
London.
W.C.1.

ON ACTIVE SERVICE AFLOAT.

RECEIVED FROM
H.M. SHIPS

Operation Ironclad ended triumphantly on 7 May 1942, with the surrender and capture of Diego Suarez by the Combined Force after a short, sharp assault which produced minimal casualties. Churchill sent his warmest congratulations to Admiral Syfret.

After the long silence maintained while the operation was underway, David finally writes Mary a letter trying to explain the extraordinary events into which he has been catapulted.

★

At Sea,
25th May 1942

My darling Mary,

This time I write I'm not feeling quite so depressed about the future but rather resigned to what's going to happen. So my adored Mary, this will be more a narrative than an outpouring of depressed feelings.

Actually, the experience of this operation has in itself been marvellous and with that experience came the added novelty of seeing fresh parts of the world. We called in at Freetown first stop. Up to then the voyage had been uneventful, except for a few submarine scares, but on board the Winchester Castle the Staff

Office was a hive of industry – plans being re-made, preparations at advanced base considered, orders being produced and innumerable activities which occur on a combined operation.

Once at Freetown we met the Flag Officer of the Force, Rear Admiral Syfret. The plans prepared by us were approved 100%, which was a great compliment to Garnons-Williams, and quite rightly so. We only stopped there 5 days, which I think was quite enough. Freetown is pretty deadly – very hot, stuffy, and dusty. Fortunately we were on board most of the time in harbour, which at least guaranteed a slight breeze. I think, though, the most amusing thing was the first sight of Africa – a long sandy foreshore, with reddish soil sprinkled with a thick scrubby vegetation, broken by a few palms here and there. It was so completely typical of what one had always thought Africa to be like that we couldn't help being amused.

There was no shore leave given at Freetown for security reasons, and so my memories of the place are few, except that, as always, my 'staff' (I had one Pay Lt Cdr and 1 Pay s/Lt all destined for the base at Diego Suarez, as my helpers) and I had a hell of a lot to do. We left there on 7th April and arrived at Durban on 23rd. En route, we crossed the line* and had a ceremony on board: there were so many who hadn't crossed the line before that only a selection could be initiated. It was my job to draw the names from the hat, and I made the unfortunate error of drawing my own out as well! However, it was quite good fun. Father Neptune 'came on board' with his retinue and all the various initiates were called out, seized by the assistants, drenched with two powerful hoses, lathered, shaved, forced to eat an abominable pill and then drenched once again. However, I am now a proud possessor of a certificate signed by Neptunus Rex in person, showing that I <u>have</u> crossed the line. The star

---

* The equatorial line.

turn was Woodward, the Pay Lieut, who eluded the assistants by climbing up a pole and remaining out of reach for some minutes, much to the delight of the crowd. He was only captured after some difficulty.

Durban – Oh Durban will always be a high spot in everyone's minds. It's one of the most amazing places in the world. In this place, which is miles from any war zone, the people have only one thought: to do anything they possibly can to entertain any members of the Services who happen to be stationed there, or pass through by ship. The convoy arrived in the afternoon, and by the evening two large dances had been organised, free of charge, with partners provided, for all the service men who had arrived. (I should have said that it was decided to give leave in order to ensure that everyone was in fighting trim, both mentally and physically, for the actual attack on Diego.) Cars stopped in the street and gave anyone a lift into town, out of town or anywhere required. Lots of officers were approached by total strangers and invited out to dinner and to parties – were treated royally and then driven back to their ships. Everywhere the men went people just couldn't do enough to make them feel at home. Indeed, when we'd been in port four days and everyone else came back with glowing tales of the marvellous time they had had, I felt thoroughly envious. I was rather the Cinderella of the outfit, as the stay in Durban for me meant masses of work. That was some job, and one slip-up might have buggered the whole operation. G-W left it entirely to me.

I kept thinking the whole time of the moment we stood on Sacre Coeur terrace that Easter, that marvellous Easter, and looked out over the twinkling lights of Paris together. I remembered with almost a physical pain how cool – almost cold – your lips were when I kissed you. I can recall that perfectly, so that I can <u>feel</u> that kiss whenever I think of that moment. And, my God, how I wish we were back there again, to live those precious days over again. You know, my wonderful

Mary, you've spoiled me for all women for all time. However charming and gay they may seem, I always compare them to you with one inevitable result. I tell you again, dearest Mary, though you seemed to take offence the last time I told you, that the more I see of other women the more I think I must have been chosen son of heaven to have got you. So you can see my lovely that I wasn't particularly good company that night . . .

However, when the place closed we went for a drive down to Brighton Beach and sat watching the surf and talking until it was time to be driven home to the ship. Driving through the lighted city was lovely, too, and revived memories of England in peacetime.

The following day, G-W insisted that some of us had some 'fresh air' so we went off in a party to some friends of the Intelligence Officer who knew these parts. First there were drinks on the lawn of the house – a beautiful house surrounded by a shady garden overlooking the whole city of Durban. Then we went by car to a place called Klook, some 15 miles outside of Durban, where we had lunch in another delectable garden. We sat on a dark green lawn, some 100 yards long, set on the slight slope of a hill. Round it were the most fascinating selection of colours of trees, bushes and flowers.

Darling, I've suddenly got marching orders. I'll have to rush and try to continue this letter later. There's so much to tell you. Principally as ever I remain frantic with love for you. Having no word from you for so long is torture – I'll try and take desperate measures to contact you. Oh! I wonder what you are doing now and whether you're happy. G-W is shouting. I must rush.

Goodbye my most darling and beloved Mary. You're the loveliest person on earth and I love you desperately.

    Yours eternally
    David

What is Rosheen doing now?

Airgraph
Pay Lieut D. H. Francis RNVR
c/o Barclay's Bank
Nairobi, Kenya
29th May, 1942

My darling Mary,

Am up here on a few days' leave with Keith, who was thoroughly flabbergasted when I walked into his office yesterday! He sends his love. Everything has gone extremely well, as you've probably read in the newspapers, and everyone is very pleased with the success. How did you react when you heard the news? Your hunch was correct after all!

The future is very uncertain at the moment and it may be some time before I get back which is very depressing, as I want desperately to see you and Rosheen again. I'm rather anxious about you: it's so many weeks since leaving home that you may by now have moved, or got a job. Hope one of your letters catches up with me soon (none have yet) and then I can get the news.

Item of interest: my seaman steward on board is Esther Curtis's brother! He thought he knew me but was convinced when he saw your photograph! My adored darling, I hope that you are well and happy and that Rosheen flourishes as ever.

With all my love honey and in anticipation of an early day of reunion.

Yours irrevocably and eternally,
David

Mombasa
6th June 1942

My darling Mary,

So much seems to have happened since I last wrote that it seems difficult to know where to begin. However, I think the best way is to continue the narrative from where I left off.

The last letter I wrote was coming into Mombasa just before the frantic rush started, and if I remember aright, I was just about to describe our marvellous picnic in Durban. Well, my beautiful, it was a wonderful garden; set on a hillside right up in the hilly country, with great lawns bordered by a veritable galaxy of multi-coloured flowers, bushes and trees – the whole a picture I shan't easily forget. Durban is definitely a place to remember and, if possible, visit together after the war.

The ships sailed for Madagascar at the end of April, and the 7 day voyage was uneventful, although as usual there was plenty to do. My only memory of it is crystallised in 2 things. First, the amazingly colourful sunsets that were always a constant source of wonder. Secondly, 2 performances which the Royal Scots Fusiliers gave of 'Beating the Retreat'. Apparently it's quite an event and is given only rarely. The pipers marched up and down the deck led by their drum major, playing the most stirring and moving airs on the bagpipes and occasionally doing an intricate Highland dance. The setting was quite perfect – pipers silhouetted against those magnificent sunsets. A very good subject for a painting.

When the day of the assault dawned, everyone was in exceptionally good spirits. Perhaps 'dawned' is the wrong word. People were up all night before and the whole convoy steaming in line ahead right up to a hostile coast is another memorable occasion. The situation on board the H.Q. ship was very tense as we anchored on the edge of the minefield, 10 minutes before the appointed time. Sweepers had gone ahead and made sure the channel was clear and some destroyers had laid lighted dan buoys to guide the assault ships in.

Finally the landing craft were lowered, with what seemed an incredible amount of noise, and they started off for their respective beaches which were some 10 miles away. It took them about 1¾ hours to reach their beaches which were all hit at about the same time as per plan – 4.30 am. The Commandos managed to capture the personnel of the Coast Defence battery still in their beds, and only on one beach was any opposition encountered and that was very quickly liquidated. After the beaches had been captured, the rest for the Navy was just plain straightforward hard work. Once the battery had been captured the ships moved through the minefield without casualties and commenced the unloading of troops and stores at the maximum speed. This continued throughout the day without much interruption except a few low-flying French planes which didn't do any damage at all. Reports were coming through the whole time of the progress of the military who were moved up some 14 miles towards Antsirane (another name for Diego Suarez town) without much opposition and then were stopped three miles outside the town by a cleverly placed defence of machine guns and French 75's. This held them up for more than a day. Meanwhile the Commandos went straight through with their attack and actually captured Diego Suarez itself about 3 o'clock on the first day, and with it more prisoners than they themselves numbered! However, on the second night a mass attack was launched on Antsirane which coincided with a brilliant diversion by a destroyer which entered Diego Suarez Bay right under the noses of the guns and landed a party of 50 marines, who made a hell of a noise and generally spread alarm and despondency in the rear of the defenders. This worked the trick and we received the signal that fighting had ceased about

3 o'clock on the morning of the third day. There was great rejoicing I can tell you when that signal arrived.

The convoy moved from Courrier Bay a day or so later and anchored in Diego Suarez Bay the same day. We stayed there for some days, most of which were uneventful. The bay itself is enormous and could easily harbour the whole British Navy if desired. The town of Antsirane is very uninteresting, being a very dirty place, with everything covered in red dust. The French had paid little attention to the cleanliness of the place and even the Naval barracks were pretty grim.

I had myself a very pleasant evening ashore with my ex-staff, who had by then joined the Naval Officer in Charge Antsirane. Had an excellent dinner in the mess, washed down with good (looted) French wine followed by an excellent (looted) French brandy! We drank a hell of a lot and finished the evening by calling on some soldier friends at the Artillery barracks, who presented me with a saddle cloth from L'Artillerie Coloniale as a memento. I was in no fit condition to go back to the ship and had to spend the night on the couch in the Naval Officers' Mess! However, it was a good break.

Whilst at Diego I had the depressing news that G-W and some of the staff including me were definitely going on to India for appointments there. I wrote you a thoroughly depressed letter which exactly expresses my feelings on the subject. You'll probably get the letter in 2 or 3 weeks' time as it went by the ordinary mail. Actually, I'm not trying to think too much about it as the idea of not being able to see you for an indefinite period almost breaks my heart. It's probably done me a lot of good, though, as it's made me realise very forcibly just how madly and how completely I am in love with you. I don't think I ever realised it quite so much before as I did when I heard the news. Yes my lovely and passionately beloved Mary, I'm definitely very much in love with you, and I can only exist until the moment

I'm with you again. Oh my <u>darling</u> Mary! if you only knew –
if I could only get to you to tell you how much I love you, I'd
be much happier. The memory of our last unsatisfactory
goodbye, which was only for a few weeks, is always preying on
my mind. How I <u>ever</u> was with you without holding you tightly
in my arms is something I can't comprehend. My lovely Mary,
this letter will be brought to you by Butler (whom you met at
Largs), who is leaving for England at our next stop.

Incidentally, I am writing this at my desk in the Imperial
Hotel, Kampala, Uganda, before going to bed. How I got to this
place will be unfolded in this AMAZING narrative. Just now I
must go to bed, as we have to be up at 5.30 to continue an
epoch-making flight across Africa! Goodnight, my most beloved
Mary; I wish from the bottom of my heart you were here to
share this room with me.

★

Now, my honey sweet, I'm sitting on the terrace of the Grand
Hotel, Khartoum, overlooking the dirty, sluggish Nile. The air
is quite still and the temperature something fantastic.
Nevertheless, on with the motley.

We left Diego Suarez, not without some relief, on 22nd May
en route for Mombasa. When we arrived there the harbour was
not ready to receive us, so the ships were ordered to another
further down the coast for a few days. However, G-W was equal
to the occasion and had already decided that he and 4 members
of the staff (including me) should go up to Nairobi to see the
Army GOC East Africa and at the same time snatch a bit of
leave. This was appropriately fixed and we left the ship before it
sailed and proceeded next day to Nairobi by rail – a distance of
some 350 miles. The journey up was rather interesting as we
passed through an enormous game reserve containing giraffe,
elephants, hartebeast, wildebeest, gazelle and a whole lot of
other animals all of whom wandered quite peacefully beside the

railway track. Also in the early morning one got a magnificent view of snow-capped Kilimanjaro, and an 18,000 foot mountain in Uganda. It looked a wonderful picture just catching the rosy hues of the dawn.

Once at Nairobi we ensconced ourselves at the Norfolk Hotel and whilst the others went to see the Army, I wandered off in search of Keith. I found his office quite easily at Military H.Q. His face, when he saw me, was an absolute picture: he actually shook hands with me before he really realised who I was. Then he said: 'Good God, what on earth are you doing here!' Admittedly, I was the last person on earth he expected to see, but I couldn't help bursting out laughing.

Well, we had a lot of fun together in Nairobi, which is a very pleasant place, completely remote from the war. Dined in the town, went to the cinema, bought you some cosmetics and silk stockings (former already sent off), sent you an airgraph and two cables and generally saw the sights. After 2 days Keith arranged for me to go up into the Ngong Hills and stay with the District Commissioner, who is a good friend of his. There I spent another lovely 2 days in their house, which is some 7,000 feet up, going for walks and generally relaxing. They had a good collection of records, which I played to my heart's content, including Yvonne Printemps singing 'Plaisir d'Amour', which made me more conscious of you than ever, and a little sad too. You would have thoroughly enjoyed the place and I did so yearn to have you there that I was completely enveloped in an aura of loneliness for you, which, I'm afraid, made me bad company.

Well, it all came to an end all too quickly and last Sunday (31) we all returned to Mombasa. Keith, by the way, was not too happy as he has been rather shattered by Auriol breaking off their affair and returning to her husband. He hasn't got over it yet.

Once back at Mombasa, G-W set about fixing that he and the staff should fly to Bombay,* which he managed after some time. We spent 7 days in Mombasa just hanging around and finally caught the plane from there on Sunday morning 6th June. By this time we had learnt that Butler and another of the staff had to return to England, so they came with us to Khartoum and parted company there.

The first hop was from Mombasa to Kampala in Uganda. There, as I said earlier, we spent the night and this morning (Tuesday). We flew up to Khartoum, where I am writing from now.

Butler leaves tomorrow, so I am reluctantly finishing this letter now in my bedroom. The aerial journey so far has been quite an adventure, but I have been sick after lunch each day and am also suffering from a villainous sore throat, which doesn't enhance the enjoyment of a bumpy aerial journey over a torrid desert! However, I hope to recover from that soon. Perhaps tomorrow's trip to Cairo will cure it. After Cairo we go to Basra and from there to Karachi and Bombay.

I must say that when we set sail from England for Madagascar I didn't anticipate seeing quite so much of the world as I have done so far, and am about to do. I don't like it.

Well my beloved Mary, I feel I should like to go on writing this letter forever. What the future is going to bring I just don't know: it may be ages before I see you again, but I hope that a miracle happens.

This should reach you in a week or so, and I want you to know and be conscious of the fact that I love you passionately and that I can only exist until the moment you are in my arms again. Think of me often, my lovely darling and write (c/o Naval Officer in Charge Bombay) often please.

---

* Now called Mumbai.

Goodnight my one and only beloved Mary. Keep happy and look after Rosheen as you have been doing. Good luck in the flat and job hunt – which you may have by now.

With all my love, completely and utterly, my lovely darling, David

CHAPTER 20

Passage to India

Saturday 20ᵗʰ June 1942.   ℅ Naval H.Q.
                                             G.H.Q. New Delhi.

My beloved Mary,

         To use the old terminology – me voila! In this strange, beautiful, dirty, squalid, palatial, undernourished, bloated land of contrasts – me voila! This trip has certainly been an education in many ways, & has provided concrete evidence of what we always thought about India (including your deviations as a result of "Mother India"!).

         However, to revert to our air trip. That was really a wonderful experience and I'm very annoyed that my bad throat prevented me from enjoying it to the full. The throat, by the way, disappeared completely as soon as we reached India. The flying boat remained the same the whole way, so we managed to make ourselves very comfortable, all things being considered. In my last letter, which Butler took from Khartoum, I think we had reached that place in the narrative. The next morning our party split, G-W, Smyth the

David arrives at his new headquarters in New Delhi on 12 June 1942. In a letter dated 20 June he laments that he has still heard nothing from Mary since he left England. Communications are inevitably in a state of confusion, letters arriving out of order and crossing. Eventually on 27 June he receives a cable giving him some information on Mary's changing circumstances – new job, new house, Rosheen, still not two, in nursery school.

Bitter disappointment is Mary's reaction to the news of David's move to India. On the positive side, David receives a surprisingly substantial pay increase as he settles into the routine at naval intelligence headquarters in Delhi.

He receives his first airgraph from Mary (sent on 1 July) on 22 July – their third wedding anniversary.

★

Airgraph
Pay Lieut. D. H. Francis
Naval H.Q.
G.H.Q. New Delhi
17th June 1942

My darling Mary,

You will probably be bewildered at the cables, letters and airgraphs originating from <u>all</u> parts of the world! I hope by the time you receive this, that the letter sent from Khartoum will have reached you. That explains everything, although there are still two more letters arriving by sea route which give my reactions to coming out here and being separated from you for so long.

I still haven't heard any news from you since leaving England – and I'm desperate for news. Keith told me that you were staying at Bushey, so by now you're probably settled: <u>where</u> is the tantalising question. I'm anxiously awaiting a cable from you to say how you are, and how the wonderful Rosheen is. Send me some airgraphs as soon as possible to the above address (where I shall be for some little time, I fear), PART 2 follows.

from your David

Airgraph
Naval HQ
June 17th 1942
GHQ NEW DELHI

PART ii my darling . . . and tell me all your news. Those few days in London in March seem ages ago and I'm missing you terribly, lovely Mary. How long it will be before we meet again, God knows. I'm always wondering what you are doing, what changes have happened and where you are. Please hurry and tell me.

Is the new allotment working all right? How much can Rosheen say now? We flew up to Gwalior from Karachi and came up here by train. On Gwalior station I bought a magazine which contained a picture of Anthea Macinlay showing a child how to do a jigsaw puzzle!!

Delhi itself is a city of tremendous contrast, as you can imagine. New Delhi is the most spaciously laid out city in the world, I should think. Send an airgraph quickly, my beloved darling. How I wish you were here, or I in England.

Love to all, passionately to you

Airgraph
12 Lloyd Square,
Finsbury W.C.1.
June 25th, 1942

My darling David,

I have received your letters and cable from India and am completely shipwrecked by the new situation. Oh, my darling, what <u>shall</u> I do, now that I must ignore July 22 on my calendar as a date of no importance! I suppose I must just hope for a miracle, or for a second front quickly to end this war. All the surprises I had prepared for your return amount to the biggest flop in history – slap-bang, back in my teeth! A small, absurd, but exciting house in Lloyd Square. I will describe it fully in a letter coming to you by air-mail – a new bright red carpet (!), a job for me in L&W publishing, Rosheen going to nursery school and growing up so quickly that I had almost decided that we should have another baby. And all done at get-cracking speed because I wanted to surprise you. I can't pretend at this stage in the disappointment not to be heart-broken and desolate for you. Soon, I suppose, the brave little woman act will predominate, but at the moment – oh David! Anyway, darling, write to me as often as you can, and I will do the same. And be sure my own darling, to keep well and happy, and remember that I live and long for you and think of nothing else but how much I love you. I will send these airgraphs regularly, so you do the same please.

    Mary

Airgraph
June 29th, 1942
Naval H.Q.
G.H.Q. Delhi

My darling Mary,

Your cable arrived on Saturday. I'm terribly pleased to hear that all is well and you have a job as you wished. The news has made me much happier. I want to hear all the news as soon as possible, so send it by airgraph; that only takes 21–28 days against the airmails 7–8 weeks. Tell me how Rosheen is and where you are working and what the house is like. I have already sent you two long airmail letters which you will probably get at the beginning of August.

Things are going fairly well here as we settle down. Living at the bungalow is very pleasant and our one weak spot is moving tomorrow and is being replaced by a Pilot Officer whom we met when staying at the hotel. He should brighten things up a bit. Have seen one or two good films and am reading 'Berlin Diary'*

---

* The US journalist William Shirer's seminal first-hand account of events

and Nehru's autobiography.* Financial questions haven't been settled as yet, but we are optimistic that we will be paid by the Indian Government for the duration of our stay; that will be much better.

I've read and re-read your cable a thousand times. It makes the best reading I've come across. Lovely Mary, keep on missing me. I'll make up for it someday!

My love is all yours
David

AIRGRAPH
12 Lloyd Square,
Finsbury, W.C.1.
June 29th, 1942

My darling David,

I wonder where you are and what you are doing after your wonderful journey across the world. Your mother has had a letter from Keith describing your astonishing meeting! Oh darling. I am keeping my fingers crossed and hoping for our old luck to burst out again, though I have recovered from the first feeling of absolute <u>nothingness</u> that your news brought. Rosheen is very well and has informed me that her daddy is a MAN (new word). Is it possible for you to receive photographs of us? The house and the job have lost their dynamic since your news, but I suppose they will both come in useful.

Ben Farrington came into the office this morning to see me.

---

inside the Third Reich during five years of peace-time and one of war, published in 1941.

* Published by Jawaharlal Nehru, India's first Prime Minister, in 1936, while he was in prison.

335

He sends you his love. Mattie has a son. Wendie and Reg came to London for a holiday. Reg has been very ill but is recovering. I await news from you with impatient eagerness. Keep well and happy, my darling for that is more important to me than anything else, even our being together.

    With all my love my darling,
      Mary

AIRGRAPH
12 Lloyd Square,
Finsbury, W.C.1.
July 1st, 1942

My darling David,

    I received your second Indian cable today. Yes, I did get the special letter and it was <u>wonderful</u>. I will keep it forever, and I shall wear the little white bird always. Our house is rather extraordinary for London – a real, twisting gingerbread house – five rooms and kitchen and bathroom – but extremely interesting and lots of unusual features. I will describe it fully in a letter which you will receive eventually. I am working and Rosheen has settled down quite happily at her nursery. She is growing prettier and more of an individual each day and I am terribly sorry that you have missed these months of her development. Since you left London, I have been busier than ever in my life, but the tempo is slowing down now but, thank heaven, I still haven't time to sit and mope. I miss you terribly but am confident that our love is strong enough to stand any separations or trials and bring us back together as fresh and happy as in our first wonderful days. Be happy my darling, my only love.

    Mary

Naval H.Q.
G .H.Q. NEW DELHI
Sunday 5th July, 1942

My darling Mary,

This week has been quite busy in every way and we are now a properly recognised body at long last. I haven't yet heard from you except in the cable, which I must have read a thousand times at least, but if you have sent an airgraph it should reach here within the next ten days, which is something delightfully tangible to look forward to.

I miss you an awful lot these days. Do you remember this time last year, with afternoons at Caswell Bay and Rhosili, and walks in the evening through Caswell Woods and around Mumbles Head? It all makes me very nostalgic for you, my one and only precious Mary. And who would have thought that a year ahead we should be 6,000 miles apart? I think we would have made more of our time together, don't you? But I suppose that's always the way. Perhaps in some ways a regret is a good incentive to make the most of the next opportunity to arise. It will be for me anyway. Nowadays, I spend lots of time conjecturing on how we shall meet again, where it will be and, more important, when it will be. Conjecturing on what you will be wearing; if you have changed at all; whether working again has made you any different now you are not completely tied to the home. Oh, conjecturing on a million and one things about you that intrigue me and make me wonder about you, all of which sharpen the desire and urge to see you again quickly. Yes, my lovely Mary, I've certainly got you under my skin in a big way.

In a few days' time we shall have been married for three years, and known each other for four; in some ways it seems those years have flashed by despite the myriad things that have happened in them. In other ways it seems there has always been you and I – the

337

old David and Mary combination – with you to talk to about things, to enjoy things with, to have fun with, to enjoy life with. So much so that I'm never able to completely enjoy myself without you, so much so that you have become a definite part of me which is a continual deficiency when you're not there to provide tangibility. Physically I miss you enormously, and at times I crave to have you with me to hold in my arms and to make love to in our own inimitable way; a single bed is as good as a prison sentence, my darling, and any bed that hasn't got you in it is a single bed to me. I pray you miss me too that way; it will be all compensated for when we are together again. But that is rather like the second front – 1942? 1943? 1944? Who knows? However, there is still our luck, that hasn't failed us yet and even this trip may have a certain amount of compensations. All this is probably nonsense to you, but it means I still love you infinitely and utterly, and shall continue to do so always, see. And I hope the three years of legit living together will multiply and that I shall be <u>able</u> to love in the same way always.

Well, to get down to mundane things such as monsoons. It has been raining a hell of a lot this week, on one occasion for three days almost solidly. Going out meant getting a drenching that is difficult to imagine from English rain; one gets absolutely soaked through. Today, however, it is very hot again and the sun is burning down fiercely from a cloudless sky. The temperature is round about 110 in the shade. It's a sticky sort of heat and not one that is conducive to working hard. Nevertheless, this last week has been pretty busy. G-W came back from Bombay, where he had been on a tour with a major who is attached to the staff; Smyth is still down there but is due back tonight. As I say, we are now properly recognised and everything is more or less settling down on the administrative side, which leaves us able to concentrate on training and operational matters. One most important thing which hasn't yet been definitely settled is that of the rate of pay for Smyth and myself, which is important. Fortunately G-W has just got his settled, which means that ours should be quite easy. After about three months, when I have bought all the clothes and extra gear that is necessary for this climate, I shall probably be able to increase it. I hope the extra will be useful to you, as if I didn't know. Perhaps you will be able to buy things that haven't been financially possible before. This rate, of course, continues only so long as I'm in Delhi and in the service of the Indian Government, and when I return to the books of the Admiralty the old allotment of £19 will be recommenced. I hope to be able to let you know the decision by next week's letter, and shall of course cable the arrangements as soon as they are known.

Come to think of it it's rather amazing to be (here I go speaking as if the thing is definite) earning over £1,000 a year at the early age of 24. I wish that I could really say that I justifiably earned it. That I cannot do, except in relation to other officers here who don't earn it either. And the bearer of the bungalow, who works very hard, and is a very efficient combination of housekeeper, butler, maid, messenger, valet and general factotum, is quite pleased to receive the princely monthly sum of 35 rupees for his services. That is India. What is more, the said bearer not only feeds himself on his stipend but sends enough back to his wife and children in the hills to keep them as well. It's absolutely amazing, the contrasts.

My little house boy, who will someday graduate into a bearer, has the delightful name of Gopi. He brings me a cup of tea in the morning with the paper, and then lays out my clothes for the day. He pops back at various intervals to see that I'm still awake, just in case I get late. Then either he or the bearer serves breakfast. After breakfast he brings my bicycle around to the front door of the bungalow, with the tiffin tin containing sandwiches already strapped to the front and my thermos filled with nimbu pani*

---

*   A type of Indian lemonade.

on the carrier. During the day, he and the bearer clean the house, which is quite easy, and help the cook prepare the food. He also gives messages and buys anything I want; he likes an opportunity, or an excuse, to go down to the bazaar, because that gives him a chance to sit around talking to the other bearers and listening to the gossip of the town. When I get home at night, which is usually about 7 or 8, he meets me at the door; takes my bicycle and puts it away, comes and sees if I want tea or a drink, helps me to change, throws away my dirty clothes, turns on the shower and supplies a running conversation in very bad English interspersed with Hindustani. After changing he waits in the drawing room serving drinks and then helps to serve the dinner. After dinner all the servants clear up quickly and after coming in to the drawing room to give solemn Salaams to everyone present, they all retire to their quarters, which are at the rear of the bungalow. Gopi and I get on very well. He doesn't like me to touch my clothes, or try and keep them in order, as he insists that it is his domain. He explains very brokenly that Sahibs shouldn't bother with their clothes. Gopi is the one to do that and he can do it much better. So you see that I have been deprived of one interesting occupation in life. I gave him an old torch the other day, which was broken, the battery run down, the bulb smashed and the whole casing mildewed. I told him, at least so I thought, that he could throw it away as it was no good. Yesterday he proudly presented me with the torch, completely clean, new battery, new bulb and in good working order. He explained that he had had it fixed at the bazaar. Apparently everything can be done in the bazaar.

The bearer does more or less the same work as Gopi, except that he is higher in the social scale. The cook is a much older man and he more or less runs the domestic arrangements, and does all the actual cooking himself. He is a very steady bearded and mustachioed Mohammedan [sic] and thoroughly reliable

AND a bloody good cook. Apart from the dhobi*, who one does not see much of, the last remaining member of the household is the sweeper. He is quite a young lad who, by his very caste, is bounden to keep out of the way. He does all the sweeping up and cleaning of the bathrooms and lavatories. He comes from the sweeper caste, was born a sweeper, must marry a sweeper, must remain a sweeper all his life, and his children after him will also be sweepers. He is looked down on by the other members of the servery and as two of them are Hindus, he is not allowed to take food with them and has to come in after we have fed and the remains off our plates and what is left in the dishes is his portion. Sometimes he does alright, other times he doesn't, in which case he has to provide food from elsewhere because the others won't let him have theirs. The Muslims aren't so bad about caste prejudices, but the caste-conscious Hindu is the biggest menace to progress and emancipation of the Indian masses imaginable. And of course, it isn't only the Brahmins who are to blame; as I have shown you the system extends rigidly to the lower castes as well.

I've thought a lot about India since I arrived here, and having seen it I think the solution is thought of as being much too easy in England. I'm still busy collecting impressions so I won't this week delve into the matters political. There are a lot of moves going on in the higher circles of the Congress Party and the Muslim League which may produce a completely different line-up of political forces in the near future. Actually the theoretical solution to the problem is quite easy. It is that there must emerge in India a political party embracing all sects, capable of commanding support from the masses of the people, which can ruthlessly cut across all anti-social religious scruples and caste outlook; which is prepared to let India freely play its part in the defence of this Asiatic continent against Japanese imperialism; which is prepared

---

* dhobi: a person who washes clothes.

to set about quickly reorganising the economic needs of India to produce for the needs of the people and the fighting forces; which is prepared to throw off the fetters of British Imperialist economy, with a resultant drop in the standard of living of the Europeans as a ready sacrifice; which is prepared to destroy the power of the princes, and which, finally, has a practical conception of the part India should play in the economic organisation of the post-war Asia and the world. That, briefly, is my solution. But where alas is the party that can do it, and where are its leaders? That is the rub.

I've just finished reading Shirer's 'Berlin Diary'. It is very good, although a lot of what he said was entirely misconceived at the time. I'm reading now 'Put Out More Flags' by Evelyn Waugh. Very amusing. It has a few dirty cracks against Auden and Isherwood, which are quite timely. Have you read it?

★

Well my lovely, I've left the office where I have been writing this and have gone home. There wasn't an awful lot to do anyway as most departments close on a Sunday. Sitting at home in a sports shirt and pyjama trousers, occasionally sipping an iced nimbu pani, is a thousand times more pleasant.

We saw 'Louisiana Purchase'* on Friday. It's a lovely film. Bob Hope has some excellent cracks in it, including the usual anti-Democrat back slingers. Vera Zorina is very beautiful, but my God she has changed from the days of the Ballets Russes. Saw 'Remember'† for the second time and enjoyed it. Coming soon is 'The Man Who Came to Dinner'‡ – must see that.

How many words can Rosheen say now? I expect she is

---

* *Louisiana Purchase* (1941), directed by Irving Cummings, starring Bob Hope and Vera Zorina.
† *Remember the Day* (1941), directed by Henry King, starring Claudette Colbert and John Payne.
‡ *The Man Who Came to Dinner* (1942), directed by William Keighley, starring Bette Davis and Monty Woolley.

becoming coherent. I often wonder what she will look like when I see her again.

A house-to-house newspaper man has just arrived. He comes from time to time with a vast variety of newspapers and magazines from England. I've bought a selection of magazines and a Sunday Express for April 26th, a weekly edition of the Daily Mirror and a News Review of about the same date. One has to keep up with the home news, even if it's 2½ months old! A hell of a lot seems to have gone on which hasn't appeared in African or Indian papers.

Well, my lovely darling, I must close now. My thoughts are always with you and I'm desperate to hear from you. I hope it's soon. Keep happy and enjoy yourself.

With all my love, as ever, to you my sweet, and to Rosheen. Remember me to Kay, Anne and Joan, and any of our little friends.

Yours eternally
David

P.S. I forgot to tell you that yesterday I bought a solar topee!

AIRGRAPH
12 Lloyd Square,
Finsbury. W.C.1
July 17th, 1942

My darling David,

I wonder where you are now, and what you are doing. I am thinking of you all the time and hoping that you are well and happy. It grows awfully near the date when we were going to be together again, and this sense of loss without you doesn't decrease in the slightest. On the contrary, believe you me, the

nostalgia for you grows to proportions beyond enduring at
times. Oh my! Oh my! Hurry up please, <u>and come home</u>.
Everything goes well. Rosheen grows and grows and I am
managing my dual job quite well; I took Roshi to a Czech
garden party last weekend and she distinguished herself by
dancing a gloriously clumsy, gay dance to the Czech national
anthem. How you would have loved to see it! She adores music
and is always dancing. Oh, when will we three all be together
again. I am living for that day, and, in the meantime, waiting to
hear from you.

    With all my love,
      Mary

[Telegram sent to Mary for the couple's third wedding
anniversary (22 July), dated 'New Delhi 17th July 1942'.
Addressed to Mary Francis, 12 Lloyd Square, London W.C.1.
and stamped 'PASSED BY CENSOR':]

'AFTER THREE YEARS LOVE YOU MORE THAN EVER, IF THAT'S
POSSIBLE AWFULLY LONELY FOR YOU CABLING TEN POUNDS
BUY YOURSELF SOMETHING NICE FROM ME ALL MY LOVE
SWEETHEART = DAVID FRANCIS'

AIRGRAPH
12 Lloyd Square,
Finsbury,
London W.C.1.
July 18th, 1942.

My darling, much-longed-for David,

    I am at Bushey for the weekend, and here received your

two-part airgraph, which is the next best thing, I suppose, to having you yourself. Rosheen and I are very well. She is playing the piano at the moment (a terrible row!) and has been writing letters to 'Daddy' all afternoon. I wish I could send them to you but the censor would think they were coded! Have you received any letters from me yet? I wrote you a lot, and I am afraid if you don't receive them, you will find your memories of Mary growing dimmer and dimmer, and all connected with Brighton and Paris and other <u>isolated</u> happinesses, when I still very much exist, now, in the present, and demand to be remembered and loved by you forever. Yes please. I am thinking of you to the point of obsession, my darling. My magnificent obsession. Be well and happy, and make the most of the new life, but remember me. Everyone sends you their love, and best wishes. Some even envy you. Write to me and come back soon.

 Your,
  Mary

Airgraph
Naval H.Q.
23rd July 1942
G.H.Q. New Delhi

Mary my precious darling,

 Your first airgraph arrived yesterday (dated 1st July). As an anniversary present. I couldn't have asked for anything better. It certainly came very quickly – the quickest I've come across yet. I'm glad to hear more of Rosheen. I miss her a lot. Has she changed facially much? And where does she go to school?! The house sounds intriguing. It's on the borough flats side of the square, isn't it? Who do you share the house with? Is your mother still with you? Longing to hear where you are working and all details. Oh! It was so good to hear from you again my darling; and I shall look forward every day now until your long letter arrives. I'm sure too that long separation won't make any difference to us, except to make the day of our reunion so much more momentous and the more eagerly anticipated. But all the same, I wish it would come quickly! I want to be with you again so much. Send airgraphs often, my peerless Mary, and continue to love me as I love you – utterly. D

12 Lloyd Square,
Finsbury,
W.C.1.
July 23rd, 1942.

My darling David,

Yesterday, a day which I was dreading, turned out to be very happy and exciting because of your really beautiful flowers and <u>super-lovely cable</u>. Thank you, my darling. You almost fulfilled your promise because you really were with me yesterday. The flowers reminded me of the day we went to Margate and you spent your very last shilling on an enormous bunch of flowers on the way home – but these were much more lovely. How did you spend the day, and did you get my cable? Have any of my letters caught up with you yet? I hope so, because I want you to know that Rosheen and I are well and that we are missing you and longing for the day when you come back. With all my love.

For ever and ever,
Mary

CHAPTER 21

The Long Silence

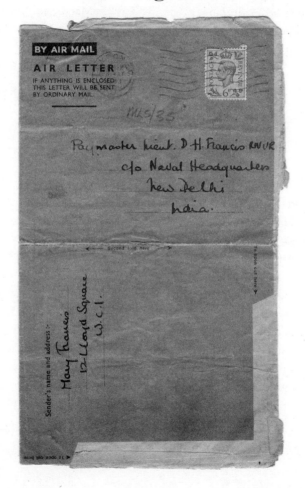

The vast distances and dislocation of the war make communications erratic and disordered. Letters, airgraphs, cables, the occasional parcel arrive out of sequence, some probably not at all. The letters appear here, as far as possible, in the order in which they are dated, or using guesswork when, as sometimes happened, they carry no date.

There is a particular black hole in the late summer and autumn of 1942 due to an exceptional turn of events which arrives out of the blue for David. He and the Garnons-Williams Combined Operations planning team were rudely yanked out of the doldrums and expedited to Mombasa to plan the second phase of the total removal of the Vichy regime in Madagascar – only partially completed – after an abrupt change of mind by the top brass.

★

12 Lloyd Square,
Finsbury,
W.C.1
August 13th, 1942

My darling David,

Your letters are a great joy to me. Today I received the one about Gopi – he seems a very nice little boy. Thank him for looking after Sahib Dopi so well for me. I hope you are looking after <u>yourself</u> well these troubled times. I am waiting anxiously now for a cable from you which will give me some idea of your whereabouts and well-being. The prospect of increased allotment is very interesting – it would seem that I could get cracking on our crazy wee house and make it into a real tasty spot – but if it doesn't materialise I can get by very well on the present arrangement. Rosheen isn't too well this week. Her back teeth have incapacitated her for a while, but she is recovering today. I am well, but missing you so much that I can't sleep, and am as restless as a flea. Hurry back and bring some peace to your Mary. I have sent you a long airmail letter today and a cable last week. Have you received anything else from me? I do hope so, my darling, as I want you to know how much I love you.   M

12 Lloyd Square,
Finsbury W.C.1
August 15th, 1942

My own darling David,

I wonder where you are today? I am thinking of you so much, even more than usual, perhaps because it is Sunday and there is more time. We have a fire in the living room today – the very first, and the room looks lovely! I have been making jam – plum and greengage (do you remember the lemon marmalade way back in the old Swansea days?) and nailing black-out shutters together. Rosheen of course has been helping in all operations. But where were you? The wireless played Brahms's 'St Anthony Choral' to complete the atmosphere and the whole day of doing pleasant, familiar things has reduced me to a woeful state of nostalgia and longing for you. My darling, I hope you are well and happy and it won't be long until you return to Mary, who still loves you PRODIGIOUSLY.

Round and about
17th August, 1942

My beloved Mary,

I have just ¼ hour to scribble this note and send you off a parcel 'by special delivery'. I'm quite OK and well – India is left behind temporarily – and there's plenty of work to be done. Probably by the time this reaches you I shall be back in India again – who knows. These last few days have been quite adventurous again, so when they're over I'll give you a full account.

Before leaving Delhi, I had received 2 cables and 2 airgraphs which I am still reading over and over again. I expect by the time I get back there will be some letters from you, which will make returning to Delhi well worth while. Longing to hear about the house and how you came to get it.

No more time to write except to say I miss you terribly still, and I love you with all the depth of feeling I possess. The day when we come together again is wonderful to think about – I hope it won't be too far away.

With all my love, my most precious darling – to you and Rosheen
Yours eternally
David

Please write, cable and airgraph often

Airgraphs [2]
12 Lloyd Square,
Finsbury W.C.1
Aug 23rd 1942.

Part I

My darling David,

Your letters are still reaching me, about a month late. Not too bad, but I wonder where you are at this present time, and how you are, and I am missing you so much. Rosheen has got whooping cough – not badly. She hasn't even whooped yet, but that's what she was sickening for, not measles. Nursery schools are a good idea – but how can you stop children 'catching things'!? Meanwhile I have given up my job for a while and am concentrating on getting Roly better. There is no need to worry about her as she is full of beans and as interesting as ever, and having to stay at home will give me the chance to do something to the house. I think also I will take Ro to the sea for a week or so and give her plenty of ozone stored up for the winter. I am feeling rather like a holiday myself as whooping corf means sleepless nights for Mary. Continued . . . P.S. I love you.

Part II (I still love you)

Hello, darling David, here I am again. Are you getting any news through from me yet? I do hope you have received a proper letter, as Airgraphs, though terribly nice, are inadequate to express all the feeling I have for you and to give you a slight idea of how much I am missing you. Darling, it's terrible! Every day I hope for news from you and one day I'll hear that you are coming home . . . that will be the day. Only make it come soon because I am developing all kinds of repressions and unorthodox ideas! India sounds wonderful, and I envy you from the bottom of my heart. You must see the Taj Mahal (I knew you'd meet an old school friend (female); it must have been an <u>awful</u> big school) by moonlight – the T.M. I mean – and spare a thought for your old pal Maire, who will probably be looking at the Albert Memorial. Cyril Mann came to see me last week and sends you his very best wishes – I still live and breathe for you alone – I truly mean that, my dearest. Your Mary.

12 Lloyd Square,
Finsbury W.C.1
September 3rd, 1942.

My darling David,

I received your cable for Rosheen's birthday yesterday, after several anxious days of wondering what had happened to you in the India debacle.* There was also an airgraph. So altogether yesterday was a good day. Rosheen became two very amiably and uneventfully. She is almost better from the whooping cough – she hasn't really been ill at all with it, but it is infectious, so I have had to keep her away from the nursery and also give up my job for a time. I hope when the quarantine time is over to go back to my job at Lawrence and Wishart or somewhere else with part-time work, as I have discovered full-time work, plus Rosheen, plus looking after a house is <u>de trop</u>, and doesn't really give good results. So the babe will go to the nursery for the morning while I am doing something, somewhere, and we will have the afternoons together; I think this will be nicer for Rosheen and me, but I am sorry to give up my present job as it is interesting, if not awfully well paid.

---

* India debacle: presumably a reference to the Quit India Movement, a civil disobedience campaign launched in India on 8 August 1942, in response to a call by Gandhi for immediate independence.

Rosheen is growing up terribly fast. She talks all day long now about 'planes', 'cars', 'boys'. She gives a realistic imitation of a dive bomber diving and can count, rather erratically, from one to ten. She is incredibly pretty – Cyril Mann came to see us and thought she was really beautiful from any standpoint. He thought also that I was incredibly changed and had grown up quite exotic – like a Matisse woman. Will you like that? I am changing, I think, as I am getting thin. It makes me more 'elegant' looking. Anyway, Rosheen and I made the supreme sacrifice yesterday and had our photographs taken, and these should reach you in time for Christmas – I don't suppose there is an earthly chance of our being together by then.

Six thousand miles – that's about the limit of my depression when I consider living without you a single week longer. Some times it grows too much for me, and I indulge in the morbid occupation of detaching myself from my environment and feeling myself slowly dying. Oh David, compassionate leave, or passionate leave, please come home!

Your whereabouts are now a mystery to me and I have lost the background of bungalow and salaaming slaves that I had for you. Are you in China, or is it the Soviet Union? What an incredibly lucky Dave!

Hetty spent last weekend with us. She is now definitely 'expectant mother' – in fact any moment now. Dick was in the Dieppe raid,* but is O.K. and still dashing around the country. Ben Farrington and Pat Clarke also called in on a surprise visit. They both send you their love. Michael was wounded three times in Libya, and is now recovering from shrapnel in the head in Egypt. It seems he is lucky to be alive, as his tank was blown

---

* Dieppe raid: a daring but disastrous Allied attack on the German-occupied port of Dieppe on 19 August 1942. Sixty per cent of the 6,000 men who made it ashore were either killed, wounded or captured.

to glory. Ben didn't look so good, and Pat tells me he is badly missing Ruth. He is getting fixations on glamour girls of 20 and such-like and I have orders to introduce him to Elinor Singer. Haven't I got frustrations enough of my own – anyway I think a nice glamour girl of twenty would do Ben a lot of good.

I can't keep telling you chatty bits of news, as the whole theme of any letter I write to you is – I miss you like torture. Have you any idea of the length of your exile; shall I reconcile myself – to celibacy of course – till 'after the war', or dare I hope that you might come home suddenly. My delight and thy delight, walking like two angels bright, I wonder if that will ever happen again. Will we know those ecstatic moments like the scintillating shining parts of the Waltz Serenade for Strings? I think we will, but how lonely I am for you at times!

It's Autumn now, and though I associate every hour of the year with some memory of you, this time is especially poignant and reminiscent of fires, and music and coming home from the pictures in the dark and reading and sleeping and going to bed with each other, and all the wonderful, ordinary things that made living together so lovely that we knew, even at the time, that we were especially happy. There are leaves blowing around the streets, and fine rain and plenty of wind. Do you remember Hampstead Heath?

I wonder if you can be missing me as much as I am missing you. Do the new experiences and friends fill your life sufficiently to perhaps blur my memory just a little. I hope they do, in a way, as I wonder is it worth wasting time and life pining for someone who isn't there, and you can't live forever in the past? As for me, I think I am doomed to love you to the end of my days, even if you never return to me, and to contrast every other person with you, to their utter rout.

I had a most extraordinary experience last night – I went to the pictures, and as that is quite an occasion (to have a free night with someone to mind Rosheen), I went to the Plaza to see 'Palm Beach Story',* which is a lovely and funny film, which you must see. I came away considerably cheered up by the film, and crossing Piccadilly Circus in the direction of Shaftesbury A. (very dark), I jumped to avoid a bus. Instead of landing on the pavement as I expected I just went on falling through space – like Alice in Wonderland, down, down, down until I found myself the dusty centre of an admiring crowd in the Underground. I had jumped into the opening of the Underground and somersaulted down innumerable stairs. I was terribly dazed and amazed to find myself in one piece, but except for dirt, bruises and scratches, was perfectly all right. Isn't that an incredibly lucky escape, as those stairs are steel edged? My surprise at being in the Underground instead of Shaft. Ave. was the strongest emotion I have felt. But you see I am getting into trouble without you here to look after me, and falling down holes and such-like; so <u>hurry up</u> and come home.

My mother and father are well and I think all your relations are thriving. Basil expects leave around Christmas time and Grahame is working on a co-operative farm in Wales. Tom and Evelyn still seem very happy and their child will arrive in November. All the little playmates in Finsbury send you their love. You ask if Hymie B. is still around. Yes, he's still around . . .

Can I send you any books? I am buying the most interesting ones that come out as I can get publisher's discount, and if you would like anything sent out I can get them for you. Is there anything you need, or anything I can do for you? I do hope there is as it's something I miss very much, 'doing things for David'. Do you miss that too, that feeling of being important to someone, and having the power to make them very happy?

Rosheen, I forgot to tell you, makes up songs. Weird little hums

---

* *The Palm Beach Story* (1942), directed by Preston Sturges, starring Claudette Colbert and Joel McCrea.

that have got words and a tune, and she can sing the same one
again if you ask her. One of them goes 'Oney, oney, twoey, twoey,
threey, oney one.' The others are too obscure for me to cipher. She
also dances to music – a bit like a baby elephant, but very gay.

I have just bought Mayakovsky's* Poems. They are incredibly
interesting as an example of my pet study. You would enjoy
reading them. I have also read Steinbeck's latest book, 'The
Moon is Down' . . . Not in the same street as The Grapes of
Wrath. Aeschylus and Athens is also being read in my more
erudite moments.

I shall have to be more economical from now on, as my job is
temporarily in abeyance, but I think that I shall soon be able to
start again, even part-time. How are you managing, and to what
astronomical flights of rupees have you now ascended? Let me
have lots of news about India and the conditions of the people,
and the things that your servants say and do, and the bazaars and
the colours and the sunshine, and the contrasting types of
English people, and all the hundred thousand things you must
be seeing and doing that could only happen in India. I love your
letters so much and read them over and over again. I am seeing
the world vicariously maybe, but I enjoy imagining you going
out in the mid-day sun. Do not impale your solar topee on a
tree, my beloved, as I think that must be a dangerous thing to
do. I also enjoy (subtle hint) visualising the lovely materials and
jewellery that one could buy in India, as it is fantastic how
quickly those sorts of things have disappeared in England,
except for the fabulously rich. Life is truly austere these days for
the ordinary people, and sometimes one longs for clothes,
perfume etc, but I suppose these things can wait.

Are my letters too inconsequential, David, or do they give

---

* Vladimir Mayakovsky (1893–1930), Russian Soviet poet, playwright, artist
and actor.

you some idea of what I am doing and thinking, and how much, oh lord, how much, I miss you. I hope your job has grown in interest and usefulness, and that you are enjoying every moment of your free time. The air is so full of possibilities – the Russians' magnificent counter attack, the chance of a Second Front, the lifting of the ban,* that sometimes I hope that the Spring, 1943, will be the end of all our misery. But I miss so much the chance of discussing all these things with you and being put straight on my deviations. Never mind. I think you will argue violently again with me before we grow very much older.

I'm going to see Othello with Jill next week . . . It's reported to be good. I am also trying to take Rosheen to the sea for a week before the summer is over, but I will let you know more about this when something has been arranged, as it is difficult to find anywhere to go.

Keep writing to me, cable as often as you can, and remember I love you very, very, much.

Rosheen sends X

   Yours to the last gasp,
      Mary

                                             12 Lloyd Square
                                             Finsbury W.C.1
                                             September 6th 1942

My darling David,

   Are you getting my airmail letters? I received your cable for

_____

* the ban: a reference to the lifting of the ban on the *Daily Worker* which was imposed by the Home Secretary, Herbert Morrison, in January 1941 and removed in August 1942.

Rosheen's birthday and an airgraph last week and was much
relieved to find that all is well with you, as I have imagined you
in all kinds of hot situations, and was rather/very worried. All is
well here too. Rosheen has practically recovered from whooping
cough – in fact she is extremely well except for an occasional
cough. I too am very well, apart from a chronic and ever-
growing attack of 'missing David'. We have had our
photographs taken for you and you will receive these eventually
to remind you of the girls you left behind you. It's nearly six
months now since we last saw each other – an all-low record in
awfulness! Have you changed? How do you look? Are you
feeling well? Do you still love me? <u>When are you coming home?</u>
Have you any idea how much I love you and miss you and how
nice I'll be to you in future (if we have any future). Your much
chastened, Mary

14th September, 1942

My darling David,

It seems such ages since I had any word from you that I
begin to feel anxious for you and rather lost without you. But
maybe there will be something from you when I get home
tonight. That is the nicest thing in the day, the chance that the
postman will bring a letter from you. Rosheen and I are very
well and quickly recovering from the effects of whooping
cough. Her vocabulary is truly prodigious and you will be
amazed. I received a delightful parcel posted by Keith. Many
thanks darling for thinking of me and brightening up 'austerity'
a bit.

September 27th [1942]

My darling David,

I wonder how you are and where you are. It's ages since I had any real letter from you and I am desperately looking forward to one. Poor 'Cuckoo' is dead. I had to take him to the vet yesterday to be destroyed as someone (not Rosheen) had given him a bash on the head and driven him crazy. We are very well and still very busy and the days grow colder and darker. It's nearly a year now since you left Swansea – a miserable anniversary to celebrate. But you wanted to go, so I'll remember that. Cable me or airmail me soon as I am very lonely for you, and time doesn't help one little bit. Mary Read has got a cottage in Sussex and Rosheen and I are going to stay with her for a week. I see plenty of people and am still working part-time, so don't worry about me being lonely – but it's <u>you</u> that I miss. With all my love. Mary

P.S. Rosheen sleeps in <u>pyjamas</u> and has got a mackintosh and sou'wester and wellington boots!

12 Lloyd Square,
Finsbury W.C.1
Oct 4, 1942

My darling David,

I have heard via Tom that you have been <u>mentioned in despatches</u>. Wretched exhibitionist that you are, tell me all about it <u>immediately.</u> Oh darling, it's been so long since I heard from you and so <u>very long</u> since I saw you, and I am more ridiculously in love with you than ever, though I've got no idea in the world where you are, or when I can expect to see you again. Still it's a great life if you don't weaken and I manage to be frenziedly busy. I am still working most of the day and Rosheen is very well and happy with my mother coming over to mind her. I came to the conclusion that she was a little too young for nursery school. Our photographs are on their way to remind you (if you need a reminder) of the girls you left behind you. You will be pleased to know that I am doing fairly good work for Kay and Joan etc, and feel much more happy about this aspect of life. Rosheen knows that you are a sailor, in a boat, on the sea etc etc. She can write Goosey, goosey, gander, erratically. With all our love. MARY

P.S. Hetty and Dick Goodman have got a son.

Oct. 27th, 1942
[Sent as two separate same-dated Airgraphs]

Part 1

My darling David,

It's a fortnight now since I had your cable and I am anxiously waiting for more news of you. I haven't written you for a long time – not that I haven't wanted to – God knows I never have you out of my mind – but I cannot bear to write to you when I don't know where you are, or anything about you. Cable me soon and let me have some <u>real</u> news of yourself. I think you probably know how much I am missing you – words cannot tell you of the awful void that your absence has made in my life. I never knew I could <u>want</u> you so much in every possible way. Keep yourself safe my darling, for my sake, because I now know, if I didn't before, that I can't live without you.

Oct 27th, 1942

Continuing . . . All is well here. Rosheen is very happy and charming and continues to be intelligent and humorous. She captivated your father and calls him 'George'. I am not working at the moment as a few crises arose and necessitated my being at home, but after Christmas, maybe, I shall get another job. I am happier with a job because I am too busy to feel war-weary, and of course, financially it helps a lot. At the moment I can just about make ends meet, which is an adequate state of affairs, but a bit restraining. Oh how I long to have a long letter from you telling me what has been happening to you through these past two months of silence. Life seems to have stopped moving for me. Start me into life again, my darling, with a word to tell me that you still are my old pal Dave and will come back <u>soon</u>.

Mary

CHAPTER 22

Madagascar Assault

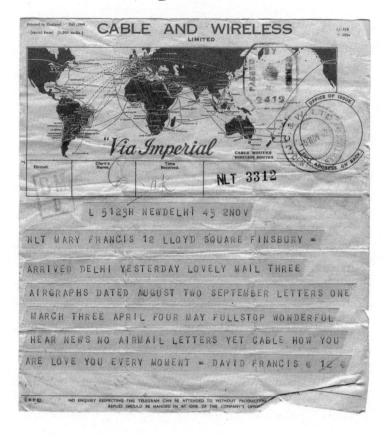

CABLE AND WIRELESS
LIMITED

"Via Imperial

CABLE ROUTES
WIRELESS ROUTES

Circuit.	Clerk's Name.	Time Received.	

NLT 3312

L 5123H NEWDELHI 45 2NOV

NLT MARY FRANCIS 12 LLOYD SQUARE FINSBURY =

ARRIVED DELHI YESTERDAY LOVELY MAIL THREE

AIRGRAPHS DATED AUGUST TWO SEPTEMBER LETTERS ONE

MARCH THREE APRIL FOUR MAY FULLSTOP WONDERFUL

HEAR NEWS NO AIRMAIL LETTERS YET CABLE HOW YOU

ARE LOVE YOU EVERY MOMENT = DAVID FRANCIS 12

NO ENQUIRY RESPECTING THIS TELEGRAM CAN BE ATTENDED TO WITHOUT PRODUCTION
REPLIES SHOULD BE HANDED IN AT ONE OF THE COMPANY'S OFFIC

The mystery of David's long silence is finally explained by him in an enormously entertaining and informative letter, originally 5,000 words, dated 5 October 1942, written from the lounge of a luxury liner on which he is one of twelve passengers en route from Diego Suarez, in Madagascar, to Mombasa. (Mary doesn't actually receive the letter until 8 December.)

★

On Tour
October 5th, 1942

My beloved darling Mary,

I should really head this letter 'I have been here before' on account of here I am again en route from Diego Suarez to Mombasa, preparing to fly off to Delhi once more. Which all goes to prove, my sweet one, that everything moves in circles.

I'm sitting in the lounge of a very luxurious liner which is at the moment carrying only 12 passengers in all; tomorrow we arrive at Mombasa very early so I'm spending the evening writing the story of the last two months. Fortunately, there is a naval officer on board who is returning to England with the ship, so he'll take the letters, which should arrive in about a month from now – much quicker than the airmail.

Well, this is how it all happened.

The last time I was able to write you a letter was at the end of July, at which time nothing in particular was happening at Delhi except the usual harassing routines of work, cinema-going etc . . . etc . . . But in the first few days of August, the Chiefs of Staff decided that the position in Madagascar needed to be 'cleaned up'. That is, they were not satisfied that the retention of Diego Garcia was sufficient to keep effective control of the affairs of the island as a whole. Therefore it was necessary to carry out major combined operations against Majunga and Tamatave with a view to engaging the capital, Tananarive, by a military drive from both sides and thereby causing the surrender of the pro-Vichy Governor General Annet, which would in turn result in the whole administration of the island coming under British authority.

We thought in India that this was very admirable, particularly as Japanese submarines had been known to be using southern Madagascan ports, with the result that ships in the Mozambique Channel were being sunk in alarming numbers.

However, about August 2nd, the Commander in Chief Eastern Fleet sent a signal to the Indian Government to the effect that Captain G-W, staff and assault force would be required to undertake these operations very soon. For two days a battle of signals between the C in C* and Wavell† ensued, the latter indicating that the loss of our force would interfere with his plans and the C in C saying bugger that, his operations were far more important at the moment.

On the morning of the 4th, it was finally decided that the C in C was right and that the force should go. Furthermore, G-W and staff were required for planning forthwith – and oh boy!

---

* C in C: Churchill.
† Field Marshall Archibald Wavell was Commander-in-Chief India.

when they said forthwith, they meant it. The rest of that day we spent in clearing up the job, packing and generally preparing to depart.

The following morning* we stepped aboard a special RAF plane at Delhi and flew off to Karachi, which we reached after 3½ hours' flying. 'We' were G-W, Group Captain Tomkinson, who was coming as observer on behalf of the Indian Government, John Smyth and myself. Stephen Vaughan-Lewis was flying from Bombay to join us at Karachi. The rest of the lads, who were not immediately required, were coming to Mombasa by boat.

Once at Karachi, we were supposed to leave the same evening by another plane, a Catalina, to go on to Aden. (See how casual I am about it all!!!) Unfortunately Stephen had very bad luck and crash landed twice on his way up from Bombay, and as we didn't know exactly how or where he was, we decided to wait a day until he arrived. This we spent in the RAF transit mess in Karachi, which was quite pleasant. There were several Americans there who didn't go much on Karachi, and bemoaned the fact at great length. G-W and Tomkinson departed to a hotel and John and I were left to our own devices. All we could do was read and wander round the building as it was raining like it can only rain in India during the monsoon period. Great thick drops that drench you in 10 seconds or so.

We heard the next morning that Stephen had crashed, was OK and was coming on another plane. By 6 o'clock though he still hadn't arrived, so we just had to leave and off we went. We learnt afterwards that he had crashed a second time in the middle of some mudflats and had had to walk some 12 miles over the flats to the nearest habitation, which turned out to be a minor rajah's palace where he was entertained right royally.

---

* Wednesday the 5th.

Unfortunately he lost all his clothes and so arrived at Mombasa a week later with a small suitcase and borrowed clothes. Actually he was none the worse for his experience except that now he is scared of flying and is not too keen or happy about flying with us to India this time.

He tells the story of his reception at the palace very well, and says it was almost worth it just to be able to tell the story of how he pressed the bell in the middle of the night and asked for something to drink – was brought a bottle of wine nicely iced which he proceeded to drink very speedily and so fell back in a drunken stupor!

However, back to the gilded staff in the Catalina. Again we had a very good journey, arriving at Aden at 8.30am the next day – a distance of some 1,600 miles. These Catalinas are quite comfortable, but this one was rather overcrowded, which meant taking it in turns to sleep. It carried a crew of 9 who were all the most incredible youths: average age of the 9 was 21, the captain being 21, the navigator 22, the second pilot 20! They were all a grand crowd, very enthusiastic about their jobs. The plane had just come from patrols over the Arctic convoys, and had then flown to Gib, Malta, Alexandria, Aden and to Karachi. This was their journey back. About 10 o'clock at night the crew produced a wonderful dish of fried steak, fried potatoes and tinned peas, followed by tinned fruit and coffee. The steak and potatoes were produced on a small electric cooking stove, which is the last thing one would expect to find on an aeroplane. I have very pleasant memories of that Catalina.

When we landed at Aden, the first call was on the RAF station to confer about our onward passage. The Catalina captain was not anxious to proceed the same day, owing to the small amount of sleep he and the crew had had on the previous days. This was generally agreed, but apparently by waiting a day we should lose a day at Mombasa, so the commanding officer of the station was persuaded to lay us on 2 Blenheim bombers for 4 o'clock the following morning, which would allow us to reach Mombasa before tea-time (distance 1,200 miles). That gave us the whole day to spend in Aden before departure. John and I had a very comfortable room where we slept until lunch time. After lunch we went to have a look around the town. The place itself is right in the middle of a volcanic rock area and the sight of these rocks and mountains rising sharply out of miles and miles of desert, is a startling one. The impression one gets is that it's looked like that for millions of years, without changing an atom – very much like the mountains surrounding the Dead Sea in Palestine. It's a sort of impression that strikes you most forcibly and I could never forget those mountains if I tried.

The harbour is a largish one and the town seems to spread over a very wide area. John of course had been there before. We watched the British troops playing the local arabs at hockey (and losing) and at football (and winning); there are quite a number of sports fields there. The shops aren't very encouraging, and the white population is practically all male, although the climate is not too bad. I should imagine there's very little to do there in the evenings though.

Well, we got aboard the planes all right, G-W and Tomky, being senior, had the front seats with the pilots, but John and I had to lie on the floor of the rear cockpit, with only a sack to lie on, for the whole of the journey. We couldn't see a thing, our only vision being blocked by the rear-gunner's back. And, my God, it was cold, so cold that one couldn't even sleep for any part of the 1,200 miles. The flight was in two hops, the intermediary stop being Mogadishu, in Italian Somaliland. This we reached about 9.30 and we stopped there for almost three hours while the planes were refuelled and the crews had breakfast. We all went down to an Italian restaurant, where the proprietor served us an excellent breakfast with delicious coffee;

he was very friendly, particularly when a few words of Italian were mustered. Mogadishu itself is a delightful little place. It looks like an Italian sea-side town transplanted in Africa. Everything is there, shops, cafes, hotels, bathing places, clubs, playgrounds, young women and children (conspicuous by their absence in Aden), in fact everything that comprises the Italian social life. The town looked very neat and clean, with brilliant white buildings and wide roads. Definitely a pleasant spot.

On we pressed and arrived at Mombasa Airport at 3.30 in the afternoon of Saturday, August 8th or 3½ days after we had left Delhi. G-W duly reported to the CinCEF and then we went away and slept until the following morning. Then we commenced the planning.

After three days at Mombasa, the whole of the planning staff moved to the Government House, which is normally the residence of the Governor of Kenya during certain months, but is now the residence of the CinC Eastern Fleet and several odd Admirals, Commodores and Captains. We were allocated two rooms there, which although sufficient at the beginning, were an absolute babel of noise by the time the complete staffs and odds and sods were there.

Government House is a lovely place. It stands right on a point at the entrance to Mombasa's two harbours, overlooking the sea. The gardens around the house are a riot of colour. But the most satisfying sight is the entrance at the top of the drive where one looks down and can see the sea through the main hallway running through the middle of the house. The sea at Mombasa is brilliant blue, and contrasting with the white of the house it makes a lovely picture.

We continued work at Government House until September 5th, about a month, when we finally set sail for Majunga.

The month passed very quickly. There was a tremendous amount of work to be done, and although I had every assistance from the CinC's staff (they were really great), including the use for 2 weeks of 2 pay sub-lieutenants and a Wren officer, it still entailed three or four all-night sessions and nights when we slept on the floor of the office. I did manage to make one dance with a small party arranged by the Wren officer (who was very charming) and a cinema, but that was all during the month.

At lunchtime, we used to take sandwiches down on the rocks and have a miniature picnic, which made a pleasant break during the day. I managed to bathe once or twice by pinching an army lorry and going down to the beach for an hour or so, but all too seldom. About 5 days before the first convoy was due to sail, the Admiral in charge of the operations began to get worried lest the orders for them were not ready in time, but he was always met with the response that the secretariat had decided the orders would be ready by 9 o'clock on the sailing day. And ready they were.

Actually, it's the biggest job I've done yet, particularly as the Admiral's Secretary had never done that kind of orders before and so looked to me for guidance. Issuing orders to a large fleet and largeish army, and ensuring that every authority had a copy of orders affecting it, was no mean job. We hit the record in bumph, there being 167 pages in all! Sounds awful, but I had no complaints.

The biggest job to contend with is alterations to shipping and plans, but we left the final running off until the last possible moment so that after the orders were issued and before the day the operation actually commenced we only had to issue ¼ of an amendment sheet. The day before we sailed (which was September 5th), I received a message that Keith was coming on the operation, and lo and behold he appeared for dinner that night on board the ship. Unfortunately I didn't have much time to speak to him at length as he was a trifle distrait. He had been sent on the operation in charge of a special wireless interception unit, which was going to listen in to all the French wireless during the assaults. With customary efficiency his sets and vehicles carrying them were placed in one ship, and he and his men in another! So, after dinner, I got hold of the appropriate Army officers and put Keith on to them with the result that the sets were transferred then and there to Keith's ship. It was very fortunate that they were transferred because the unit did excellent work during the operation and intercepted some very important messages.

On the morning of the 19th we steamed into the harbour of Tamatave, after first signalling by wireless to the governor to surrender the town. He refused, but was given first an extra quarter hour, then an extra half-hour to change his mind, but no – l'honneur and all that prevented him surrendering. By this time, all the warships were drawn up in a line facing the town and the barracks area, so his refusal was madness. Anyway, the Admiral informed the Governor that he was sending an envoy in by boat under a white flag to parley, and that if the French opened fire on the boat, military objectives on the outskirts of the town would be bombarded. The boat got within 100 yards of the shore when the machine guns opened fire on it. The Admiral kept his word. Pom-poms, Oerlikons, 37's, 4ins, 6ins and machine guns opened fire on the objectives and three minutes later the white flag was shown on the Governor's House. His honour had been satisfied by the blood of some 20 innocent spectators who had been rash enough to stand behind a machine gun emplacement to watch the proceedings. The emplacement received a direct hit from a destroyer.

The landing of troops and transport went ahead and happily enough, the civilian life of the town started again very quickly – and children were playing on the beach again that afternoon.

I had a wonderful surprise there. On the afternoon of the assault a ship arrived from Diego with some mails, including a

372

batch for me which had been kindly forwarded on from India. 4 airgraphs from you dated June 29th and July 17th, 18th and 23rd; and one cable dated 5th August. Also one airgraph from Wendy. This was lovely and I spent the next few hours reading and re-reading them, absorbing every word. I'm so glad the cables and airgraphs are arriving and that the flowers for the 22nd arrived safely. God, how I wish I had been there to give them to you myself. I got your anniversary cable two days later (in India that is), but your airgraph dated July 1st arrived in record time and was delivered on <u>the</u> day. Very nicely timed. Did you get the £10 safely. I'm afraid none of your letters have reached me yet, but I heard that a batch arrived for the Winchester Castle a day or so after we left India, so I'm hoping desperately that there will be some from you among them.

Returning to Tamatave. Once the place was ours it was merely a question of putting troops and stores ashore as quickly as possible. They continued the advance up to Tananarive, which fell some days later without much resistance, but Anmet (the Governor General) had retreated to Fianarantsoa in the south, where he is determined to resist until the bitter end. However, I don't think he'll last long down there.

Operations were carried out against Tulear and Fort Dauphin, which fell without resistance. In the former case, a Marine band was playing in the public square, much to the delight of the local populace, only ½ hour after the troops landed!

Tamatave is another very pleasant little town, and is by far the most attractive town in Madagascar. It's rather reminiscent of Mogadishu, being spaciously laid out and very neat and clean. Actually the town was completely destroyed by a cyclone in 1927, so that they had a good opportunity to plan the place properly. There were several hotels and cafes, 2 cinemas, a sports ground and race track, and very beautiful looking houses. The population consisted of some 2,000 French and 20,000 Malgache, but the white population seemed much more natural than those at Diego and Majunga. Regularly at 5 o'clock every evening the population would turn out and stroll along the very fine promenade until sunset. It looked very pleasant to see so many young people again. Actually I think a lot of them had been on holiday there as it is the most popular seaside resort, and were stuck until the 'war' is over.

The beaches are excellent. But bathing has to be done in a swimming pool on account of the sharks. I had several hours of hockey on the 'Stade', which were rather exhausting. There was one good hotel, called 'Le Cyclone', which was decorated by a local artist in a very Parisian manner with gaudy murals. The drinks were very poor, the only plentiful one being a local rum which was vitriol's kid brother; beer (Indo-Chinese) was 30 francs a bottle. However, the coffee was excellent.

On September 26th G-W was suddenly summoned to a meeting at Diego Suarez with a Brigadier who had flown specially to Africa from India to see him. Off he went in a hurry and three days later we heard that he was going to return to India with the Brigadier. On the 1st October CinCEF sent a signal to say that John Smyth, Stephen Vaughan-Lewis and myself were to report to Mombasa as quickly as possible. Next day we embarked at Tamatave in a 40-knot minelaying cruiser and after a terrible voyage (the ship rolled, pitched, tossed, vibrated and did everything one's stomach objects to – violently in my case!) we reached Diego Suarez on the morning of the 3rd. There were no cabins for us, so we had to sleep on a camp bed between the mining rails! On arrival at Diego, we three transferred to this liner, which was to leave the following day for Mombasa.

I went ashore that evening to see my ex-staff from the first assault, who are all part of the base staff. They are all much happier than when I left them, as Diego has brightened up considerably since last May.

It's morning now, and we are lying off Mombasa waiting for the pilot to come aboard. I don't know how long we shall have to wait for a plane – maybe one day, maybe five – but we shall find plenty to do here, and it will be much more fun, there being only John, Stephen and I. Later on today, I'll tell you all the things that don't belong to the story much, so until later, my most precious and beloved darling Mary.

<u>Later</u>: Thursday 8th October. We've been here two days now, my darling, and I can give you news up until tomorrow, as the ship returning to the UK doesn't leave until Saturday. We're leaving here on Sunday morning, en route for Delhi by air. There was a bit of a battle when we first arrived as C in C's staff weren't convinced of the necessity to send us by air and wanted us to go by sea.

The last 2 days have been spent moving to an accommodation ship where I stayed way back in June, clearing up our cipher log, and getting landing craft repaired. Yesterday evening we had a pleasant dance party at one of the hotels with our Wren officer typist and also, by a stroke of extraordinary fortune, with General and Mrs Smyth, cousins of John's who he saw last at Delhi. They are returning to England on another ship, lucky people. A very charming couple, they will be sending you a telegram from me on arrival in England, if they remember. General Smyth commanded one of the divisions in Burma under Alexander.

Today I am lunching with Jeremy and am going on to a bathing party on one of the northern beaches and this evening am dining with Dermot Chevenix Coote (quel nom!), the Admiral's secretary; quite a busy day.

I've sent off three parcels by the ship which contain some 'produits de Madagascar' and some things I bought locally. When you receive this letter and the parcels will you send a cable to Delhi saying 'letter parcels received', so that I shall know that you have got them. Will you also my sweet send me all your measurements and the sizes you take in shoes, stockings etc, etc; what you are short of in the way of cosmetics and anything generally; and what you would like me to bring back from India <u>when</u> I come. Also, of course, Rosheen's sizes now, I've no idea how big she is; hope the shoes fit her, if not now fairly soon. Another thing, lovely, is answers to these questions sometime:

(1) Did you receive the two large parcels of cosmetics I sent you from Nairobi?
(2) Did you receive the £10 anniversary present?
(3) Have you got my great coat and No. 1 uniform?

Well, my honey bee, I must rush off now to lunch with Jeremy and I'll write you some more ce soir. 'Bye

★

Et voila encore. It's Friday morning now and a lovely bright morning it is, too. Yesterday was a wonderful day and I thoroughly enjoyed myself. Had lunch with Jeremy, as arranged, after which John and I and 2 Wrens went off to this beautiful 'South Sea' beach and had a bathe. The water was so warm that we stayed in more than an hour. After the bathe, some sharp exercise in trying to knock down coconuts and green pineapples from some nearby trees, all to no avail. There were 6 very stately dhows, with billowing white sails moving across the horizon; against the deep blue of the sea they made a lovely picture. In the evening Coote rang up to say his ship had been ordered to sea, so I dined on board instead and after dinner saw a passable film on the quarter deck called 'Good Morning Doctor'. And so to bed early.

I'm not looking forward to Sunday at all. The idea of going back to Delhi is acutely depressing, and even though this time we shan't be there very long, the prospects after that are far from encouraging. The trouble is that now we've cleaned up Madagascar and surrounding islands, there's only one enemy left around these parts!! Still and all, we've had easy going up to now, so we mustn't grumble.

I still have that recurring fear of something happening to me before I see you again, and before I can tell you myself just how much and how often I've realised during the last few months that I love you completely and to the exclusion of all others. Remember that, because if there wasn't you, my darling Mary, the world would seem very empty and meaningless. The thought of you, and of Rosheen who is us, has been a 'constant' in a very unstable existence. I think of you continually, wonder about you, dream about you. The favourite daydream is still how we shall meet again, and I've thought up 1,001 reasons already! The only thing I don't allow myself to think about too often, is the actual <u>reality</u> of <u>when</u> I shall get home. The day seems so damnably distant that it doesn't bear thinking about too hard. I just don't see how I can get back until the war is over, unless a miracle happens, particularly now that we are a tested, successful combined operations staff, and the <u>only</u> staff in the Indian Ocean. John and I came to the rather depressing conclusion that our only future is to go on doing operations against the Japanese until we get wiped up or until the war is over, whichever is the sooner. So you see, the day of return is in actuality a remote one. Unless a miracle, a longed-for miracle, happens.

Rosheen sounds quite wonderful from the airgraphs. Has she still got that wicked smile? God, how I long to see her again. It's an awful feeling to be missing these crucial months of her development. She must look <u>lovely</u> going off to school each day.

You need never have any fear of any memory of you growing dimmer, my darling. On the contrary, because I think of you so often, my memory is being continually analysed and checked for detail, with the result that I remember more and more about you as the days go by. No, my honey, although those 'isolated happinesses' you talk about are unforgettable memories, it is the total memory, the thoughts about our everyday life and the continuous enjoyment of each other, that is treasured. And if I had to choose one moment as a perfect and lovable recollection of you, it wouldn't be Paris, or Margate, or Stoke Row, or Brighton, or Hampstead Heath, or Pwll Du, but just the way you looked lying on the bed in University College Hospital after Rosheen was born; very bright but very pale and weak, but wonderfully beautiful and lovely. I think of you that way a million and one times, my darling.

Now I must close, my sweet. Give my love to everyone in London, and anyone else you meet who is deserving of it. I'll cable you directly I reach Delhi, and send you airgraphs by the score. And you write to me and cable to me just as often as you can, honey.

Goodnight, my precious and beloved Mary; this with infinite love to you and Rosheen. Keep well and happy – think often of me please, and never fail to write and tell me that you still love me; each time you tell me is a moment of priceless happiness.

You, I love to eternity with a love that surpasses all logic or analysis, except the logic that you are Mary and I am David, and together are an inseparable unity.

Darling, darling Mary, goodnight,
Your
David.

Cable and wireless telegram. New Delhi. 2 Nov. [1942]

ARRIVED DELHI YESTERDAY LOVELY MAIL THREE AIRGRAPHS
DATED AUGUST TWO SEPTEMBER LETTERS ONE MARCH THREE

APRIL FOUR MAY. WONDERFUL HEAR NEWS NO AIRMAIL
LETTERS YET CABLE HOW YOU ARE LOVE YOU EVERY MOMENT
= DAVID FRANCIS.

[Two same-dated airgraphs]
12 Lloyd Square,
Finsbury, W.C.1
November 7 1942.

My darling much adored David,

I received your cable this morning and it has made me so
happy, as it is one month since I had your last cable and I was
feeling anxious and tense about you. <u>BUT</u> when are you
coming home? I think if I could see you for just five minutes I
wouldn't mind your leaving again. But my idea of heaven is a
railway station with your train beating in, and you jumping out
to meet me. Oh may it happen soon! I am longing to have a real
letter from you. It's been so long since I heard what you've been
doing and having done to you and I never grow tired of hearing
that you miss me and still love me as I miss you terribly and love
you more than I ever thought possible.

. . . Rosheen and I are staying this week with Mary Read in a
delightful cottage in Sussex that has been lent to her. As it is
November <u>I must</u> have a day in Brighton for old times' sake and
think of you and the two Novembers we went to that crazy place.
I am glad some of my letters have caught up with you. I'm afraid
there will be blanks for the month of October as I found writing
letters to you when you were 'on tour' too painful and depressing
to do it often. But now I am full of hope and optimism again,
having heard from you. Hurry up and come home and renew
your acquaintance with your daughter as she grows up more and

more each day, and is as beautiful, wilful and merry as a young colt. She has a whole story to tell people about you – Daddy David – on a ship – on the sea – on the water – in the bath, etc and she loves you very much – as you know that I do. Mary

[Two same-dated airgraphs]
12 Lloyd Square,
Finsbury,
London W.C.1
November 16, 1942.

My darling David,

I am still in deepest Sussex staying with Mary Read in her very old and very cold cottage, complete with paraffin lamps and chemical lavatories and wild horses at the bottom of our garden. Very much Cold Comfort Farm. The country is a very dangerous place I find, what with black-bellies (Rosheen says) hanging from every bush and irate geysers that explode when you have a bath. I now look at the world with a naked and surprised face as one of my eyebrows and all my lashes festoon the ceiling of the cottage bathroom. I hope they grow before you come home darling, as I look rather peculiar at the moment. Mary says they will be longer and more seductive than ever if I stop worrying about them, so it might have been one of those proverbial winds that blew them off. Rosheen is having a wonderful time with her old pal Sylvia.* Apart from some hair-raising battles they are remarkably good together.

. . . You wouldn't know your baby now as she is a great

---

* Mary Mann's daughter, who was the same age as Rosheen, by Cyril Mann, the painter.

380

strapping wench who insists on being called 'Alexander Beetle'. God knows why! She is a wonderful companion, however, David, as all this world is fresh and marvellous to her and consequently a little bit of the glow falls on me, although shades of the prison house closed upon me a long time ago – I'm terribly sad to think you are missing this time in her development, not to mention <u>my own development</u>; I have dreamt continuously about you all week and am elated by an insuperable feeling that it won't be long before I see you again – fool's paradise maybe, but once again I can think about you without feeling completely desolate, and I can <u>hope</u>. Have the photographs reached you yet? Cable and write as often as possible and never forget me or Rosheen, who is standing by me and talking about you at this very moment.

    With all my love darling, now and forever,
    Mary

CHAPTER 23

Tragedy Strikes

On 19 November, Tom's ship, HMS *Ullswater*, is sunk in the Channel off the Eddystone Lighthouse by German torpedo boats. All the crew perished – their names are today commemorated on the Royal Naval Patrol Service War memorial at Lowestoft. Tom's son, Michael, was born days after his father was killed

David is busy and settling into life in Delhi again but the long days are mainly desk work and he chafes to be more active.

★

Airgraph [1]

Naval Headquarters,

G.H.Q. NEW DELHI

7th November 1942

My darling Mary,

We arrived back in Bombay on Friday last after a long and rather circuitous journey around the Indian Ocean. Bombay seems another intriguing place, but as we only stayed there one day we didn't have much time to look around; a drink at the famous Taj Mahal Hotel and lunch at Bombay Yacht Club was about as far as we got. We left there on the Frontier Mail* on

---

* The Frontier Mail: an Indian train which ran from Bombay to Delhi and

Saturday evening and arrived at Delhi the following night after a 26-hour journey. G-W, wearing the DSC which has been awarded to him for our first tour of Madagascar, met us on the station and took us to our new bungalow. Actually, we are still staying with Jack Worral, but he has a new place in Lodi Road, which was allocated after the half-yearly change-over which takes place in this peculiar place. Now, John and I sleep in a bungalow just around the corner and have all our meals at Jack's bungalow. Mrs Molly Worral has returned from Simla and runs the house. The other occupants are Cooper-Driver, the Air Force Officer, and a newcomer to our organisation as signals king, one Alan Seymour-Hayden. (We seem to have a galaxy of double-barrelled names.) The Worrals have a delightful little son, who was born on August 21st 1940, and who is constantly making me feel abominably homesick for you and Rosheen. He has a bearer of his own, the lucky lad, who is really marvellous to him; in fact he is like a mother. There have been a few changes among the famous household servants. GO-1 is promoted to bearer proper, and is attached to Cooper-Driver, but John and I have engaged his uncle (incidentally all bearers are related to each other), who is called Chota Lall; the name really means, Little Lall, but he's little hell to me. The weather now is very pleasant indeed. It's like an English summer during the daytime; after 7 in the evening it's like autumn, and best of all the mornings are like clear, crisp, exhilarating Spring days.

The official rig of the day changed into blues today, but we haven't complied as yet. I think I can manage without a greatcoat; the mac will do. It's quite a long way to the office

---

on to Peshawar, a distance of nearly 1,500 miles, which it covered in 72 hours with legendary punctuality. Passengers travelled in great luxury with white damask tablecloths, silver cutlery and exquisite crockery. Air conditioning was provided by blocks of ice carried under carriages with fans distributing the cool air. The train was renamed the *Golden Temple Mail* in 1986.

every day, but in order to get some exercise we make a point of walking back in the evenings. There is plenty of work to do at the moment, particularly as we are reorganising once again. G-W goes up in importance, but not in rank, and I go up accordingly, although I am not now only his secretary. What I'm more pleased about is that a lot of things I used to curse about privately during the summer will be rectified as far as I am concerned under the proposed changes. However, that remains to be seen in actual practice. There's so much more to tell you about, so I'll go on to a part 2. But I couldn't finish part 1 without telling you that for always and unceasingly, I love you. –

Airgraph [2]
Naval Headquarters GHQ
New Delhi.
7th November 42

Hello again my lovely Mary.

The most pleasurable thing about coming back to Delhi was finding a large batch of mail from you. Letters written to me in the Winchester and airgraphs up to 14th September. There is a gap between 23rd July and 13th August, which may mean I have missed some news. Oh, my darling, it really was wonderful to be able to hear about everything that has happened to you in those four months; and to know that you haven't forgotten me in the passing of time. The fact that you still love me is one which can't be too often repeated; each time is a joy to read. I don't know how many times I've read them already, in fact these letters and airgraphs are my main reading matter these days. Rosheen sounds wonderful. It's terrible to be missing all the development at this stage. Do you think she would recognise me if she saw me now? I probably wouldn't recognise her. I envy you a lot having her with you. She must make life very gay, except when she threatens whooping cough or measles. Received one airmail letter, also dated 12th August, but that is the only letter received by air. In that, my darling, you refer just in passing to an 'appendicitis scare'; my lovely, what <u>have</u> you been doing? You mustn't get ill, if anything happened to you I think the whole light would go out of my life. Keep well, because I love you so much, and should be desperate and forlorn if you aren't well.

God knows when we shall be together again; on some far-off day when the whole world situation has changed, I suppose. I miss you mentally and physically to a degree of intensity that is past description, and it daily becomes a greater fixation. So pray for both our sakes that the day comes quickly. Rosheen's dolls sound fun; tell her to treat the sailor kindly. Is the cat a real one?

Another thing mentioned in passing is that Evelyn is about to produce an infant; first I heard about it. Am I an uncle yet? Anyhow, give her my best wishes.

Hope by now you have got my long letter and the handbag from Tamatave. Let me know when it arrives. The house in Lloyd Square sounds fun. Wish I were there now. Keep it warm for me. Thank goodness I've got your sizes at last. I'll see what can be bought. By the way, I haven't had an acknowledgement of the £10 sent in July; I hope it didn't go astray. The financial question is even now still in abeyance, but there is a likelihood that we shall get the Indian rates of pay within the next fortnight or so. If you ever get stuck for money send a cable right away as I can always get it out here.

Have you still got your job? In one of the recent airgraphs you said that you were going to give it up on account of Rosheen's malaise. I hope you've still got it, as it sounds a lovely job. Somewhere where you do some creative work. Have you been doing any more writing these days? You ought.

Well, my beloved Mary, give my love to everyone, a special kiss to Rosheen, and for you, my most cherished sweetheart, my whole heart and being.

David

Air mail letter
Naval H.Q.
NEW DELHI
16th November, 1942

My darling Mary,

I'm writing this to reach you on Xmas day. Although the sun is blazing outside here, in England it must already be cold and autumnal. And this brings all my love and all my thoughts to you and Rosheen for Xmas day. I wonder what you will be doing and where you'll be on this first Xmas we've been apart since we knew each other. Perhaps in a way it's better we should be 6,000 miles apart than 600; that would be more than unbearable. I think I shall spend Xmas day reading all your letters and cables and airgraphs, to bring you closer; perhaps by that time I shall have the long-promised photograph of you and Rosheen, which your last airgraph said was on the way. That is definitely something to look forward to.

When, oh when, shall we meet again, my beloved darling? Maybe it will be sooner than we expect. The news from North Africa is so good at the moment that perhaps it will be finished suddenly and soon. And what will the great Rosh be doing? She who sat uninterested whilst nine adults calmly ate all her first birthday cake, and whose second Xmas was spent within the confines of a high chair. I guess she'll have a wild Xmas this time.

I don't know how we'll spend it. I suppose with the Worrals and any odd people who come up from Bombay round about that time. The presence of young Ian will provide an excuse for a lot of fun. It will be strange to have an Xmas day with a boiling hot sun in the afternoon; in the evenings though we can have a blazing fire and be glad of it.

I was terribly sorry to hear about Peter Goodman – that must have been tragic for Hetty at this time. How is she, by the way? The baby must be due by now. How did the fall come about? Somehow Christmas always makes me think of the Goodmans, ever since those delightfully crazy days, and crazy parties in Angel House – flat beer, crowded rooms, big eats and bedtime. Remember the long, long afternoon we had in shopping for our first Christmas – you old nagger! That must have been the first long taste I had of your tongue – metaphorically I mean!! Wish so much I could taste it again –

Well, my beloved Mary. Continue loving me as much as I love you and I shall always be happy. With all my love to you and Rosheen for Christmas and know that I shall be thinking of you all day and wishing I were with you.

Yours devotedly
David

P.S. Darling, when we do meet again we shall have to have a honeymoon for the first time.

Airgraph
12 Lloyd Square
Finsbury,
London W.C.1
December 1st, 1942.

My darling David,

Your parcel, conveyed by 'Jimpan', arrived here quite safely,
and was very exciting. Thank you so much darling, especially
for the seashells and 'money', which was such a typical personal
touch. Rosheen grabbed the sandals and handbag and has been
wearing a fez ever since. I hope they were above reproach!
Yesterday I went to Chelmsford to see Evelyn and the new
baby – Michael Thomas Moss. He is really very beautiful and
weighed 9lbs at birth. Evelyn is behaving <u>wonderfully</u> – she
never spoke of Tom at all, and I feel that, like myself, she doesn't
believe it and won't accept it – though I know it's true enough.
Pa has gone back to Shrewsbury, but is trying to get his release
from the army. My mother, meanwhile, is staying with me. We
are all very well, all things being considered. Rosheen, of
course, is the salvation of us all.

With all my love as ever,
Mary

[Two same-dated airgraphs]
12 Lloyd Square,
Dec 9th, 1942

My darling David,

This morning I received the two airgraphs of Nov 7th and
yesterday I got the long letter giving me news for the months

when you were 'on tour'. So you are very much with me at the moment, darling, and today I have sent you a cable, and after writing this I am going to write an airmail letter in which I will try to tell you more adequately how much I miss you, and how much I love you, and how I experienced what might be called the death of the soul when I read the last page of your wonderful and precious letter and found fears I hardly dare allow in my conscious mind put down in words by you of all people, who were never depressed or ridiculously morbid but always gave me strength and courage and blew away all my fears. David, if this war drags on for 30 years I can stand it if only you come back at the end of it to me. Remember that Rosheen's brother has yet to be born, and it's up to you. I am willing you with all the strength of my mind to keep safe and well, because I know now, if I ever doubted it, that life would stop for me, physically, mentally and spiritually, for ever and ever, if anything happened to you. I love you too much . . .

. . . David, my darling, it's me again – in this section I will try to concentrate on answering questions asked in your letter. 1) I have received one parcel of cosmetics, for which many thanks. 2) I did receive the £10 for our wedding anniversary, but surely I cabled you about this? 3) I have your greatcoat and No. 1 uniform hanging nostalgically in my wardrobe and occasionally torture myself by looking at them and wondering what they would be like with your arms in those dangling sleeves, and those arms around me!

The money you sent me in answer to my cable is far too much for what I needed it for. Twenty pounds would have been plenty. Shall I pay the remainder into your account, or what? Please let me know as I feel very guilty about asking you for it now, as I know life must be very expensive for you. I'm going to get another job soon, so that I shall have money of my own again and can pay you back. Many, many thanks for your prompt and magnificent generosity. With all my love, Mary

AIRGRAPH
Naval H.Q. G.H.Q. New Delhi
10th Dec. 1942

My darling Mary,

I am still shattered by the news about Tom. Haven't had a word from you since your cable last week and I hope that everything is going all right.

Did you get the money safely. Apparently the first amount was £47-13s more than I expected, and yesterday I cabled another £20. If you have any over buy yourself a nice Xmas present from me, my lovely. Had my first pay cheque yesterday with all arrears, so that means my finances can be cleaned up.

Yesterday I received 2 airgraphs dated 7th Nov from Sussex, and one from mother explaining what Rosheen could say. She certainly seems to be picking up speech very quickly. I love all your letters and airgraphs, they seem to bring you so much closer, honey. I've often thought, too, that just to be able to see you again for a short while would be satisfying in itself and sufficient to provide a strong and tangible memory for a while longer. Still very lonely for you, my sweet, so airgraph just as often as you can. By now you should have received my long letter and handbag etc. Hope so. With all my love my darling.
DAVID

Naval H.Q.
c/o G.H.Q. NEW DELHI
16th December 1942

My beloved darling Mary,

Another fortuitous chance has arisen to write to you in time
for Christmas, so first of all, here's wishing you a happy Christmas
and all my love to you and Rosheen for that day and everyday. If
I'm not with you actually, I shall certainly be in spirit – not very
satisfactory that, is it? The first Xmas apart for five years. Still and
all, my darling, we shall have to make up for all these special days
we've missed during the last few months and we'll make up for all
the ordinary days too, because those ordinary days were just as
memorable and lovely as any of the to-be-specially-remembered
days. Think of me on Christmas Day and let's try and bridge
those 6,000 miles and be close for that day. I'll be thinking of you
all day and missing you more than usual. Remember our first
Xmas in Angel House? With Mary doing the shopping on Xmas
Eve in a ratty, efficient manner? Oh to be back in the Maison des
Anges once again, even with all its inconveniences.

I still haven't really got over the shattering news about Tom,
and am rather worried that I haven't heard from you since that
first cable. I do hope everything's all right, particularly with
your mother, to whom the news must come as the hardest blow
imaginable. Please let me know as soon as possible that all is well
with her, and you and Pop.

Rosheen sounds more and more attractive as the days go by. I
should so much like to see her again now. All the airgraphs I get
from Mother continue to rave about her, and always contain her
latest sayings and doings. It's tragic that I should be missing all
these vital days of development and progress: all the same, I
think we were very lucky to have had her first year together, as
that was the time when all the fascinating things seemed to

happen to her – the sitting up, the standing, the walking and the talking. And being together to witness that was wonderful.

You know, my beloved Mary, being thousands of miles away hasn't altered my feelings at all. While we were together you were the most important, the most real, the most tangible, the most satisfying (mentally and physically), the most enjoyable, in fact the only seriously considered woman in my life. Out here, it's precisely the same. However many women one meets out here, they all seem dwarfed in comparison with you. The most peculiar thing is that the more women I meet, the more I have to pinch myself to make myself realise that I have you, my darling. To make myself realise that I have someone like you, who seems so much more real and vital and intelligent than the flippant, butterfly-brained specimens that inhabit Delhi! Sometimes I think that maybe this adorable and, by this time, almost worshipped Mary is just a figment of the imagination, a symbol of wish-fulfilment, a woman as she should be. But no, I think a bit more, think about what we did and said together, about how we enjoyed each other, and then I realise it isn't imagination but something real, <u>but</u> damnably distant. Then comes the period of homesickness, and of wanting desperately to be home again just to see you for a short while, even, but just to see you again. My darling, my darling, just when will it be? I still can't see when.

★

John is away touring and his bed is occupied by Doc Howell (complete with D.S.C. who is up here again for a few days until after Christmas. Edward Gueritz, who was up here during the summer, unfortunately contracted a strange disease called sprue whilst in Madagascar, and was invalided home from Durban. He will be a great loss to us all. Incidentally, he's also got a D.S.C. for the Diego Suarez operations.

Although living in Delhi tends to be rather deadening, we still get a lot of fun out of life. The Worrals, Molly and Jack, are really the most charming people you could ever come across – I don't think I've ever met a more generous or more good-hearted pair. They just can't do enough for us and the atmosphere here is very very pleasant. Jack is due to become a major soon, as his work is proving very important these days. Molly, whom you would love, is delightful and sometimes even reminds me of you. She and Jack are very much in love with one another and seem to suit each other admirably. Ian, who is adorable, is only 10 days older than Rosheen, so I expect a lot of the things he does and says, Rosheen is doing also way back home.

He and his bearer, who is called Bali (Knee-high Ned to us on account of his four feet height!), are the greatest of friends and really Molly has a very easy time as a result. The bearer dresses him and gets him up in the morning, looks after him all day and finally puts him to bed at night! A regular procedure before bedtime is for Ian to kiss all his 'uncles' goodnight, so he can rely on an extra quarter of an hour before bedtime finally comes if there is a full house of 'uncles' (John, Monty, Seymour, Doc and myself)!! Peculiarly enough, he is already bi-lingual and can speak in English and Hindustani. I enclose a photograph of him so you can see what he's like.

There are some other photographs with the letter. One of the boys going to work and some views of the bungalow, one of Jack and one of Monty in the tin bath. Would you believe it that in these spaciously designed, comfortable houses (or bungalows), with water and electricity laid on, there are no baths or lavatories? The sweeper is the unfortunate one as a result of the latter lack! The garden is very pleasant with plenty of space for lawns and vegetables.

John and I still sleep round the corner with the Roes owing to the bed shortage at Molly's, but it is not inconvenient as we only go there last thing at night and leave first thing in the morning. Dicky Roe is a Civil Servant, and Peggy also works at the G.H.Q.

They have two children, a boy of about 9 and a girl of 7, both of whom have just returned from school for the Xmas holidays.

John's wife has returned from Bermuda, where she has been for the last two years. She brought her two sons back, too, and is living now in Cirencester. She is very anxious to get a job in London and will probably be coming up there very soon. I have given your address to John, who has told her to call on you if she gets the chance. Her name is Diana and she sounds rather nice. So don't get a shock if a Mrs Smyth calls on you one day.

By now you should have received my long letter written on the ocean and at Mombasa. I do hope you've received it safely together with the three parcels sent with it. Let me know as soon as possible.

*

Financial matters were settled properly just recently. I am definitely lent to the Indian Government while doing my present job, and by good fortune, the appointment has been back-dated to the 13th June. I received a cheque for something like Rs.4,500 at the end of November, but have to pay most of it back to the Admiralty on account of allotments and advances received.

I enclose my Xmas present to you my darling. Two opals I bought here in Delhi. I haven't had them made up in rings as the Indian standard of workmanship in gold is very poor, and you'd probably get better results from an ordinary jeweller in England. I suggest one for you to wear yourself and one for you to wear for Rosheen until she's old enough for one. One of them is a 'green' opal and the other a 'fiery' one.* I have a guarantee from the jeweller here that he will exchange them if you don't like them, so let me know. Actually, I think you will

---

* Many years later the opals were stolen from Rosheen's home in Highbury, north London.

like them as the colours are so fascinating, particularly in the half-light. And every time you look at them think of me, my beloved and very much missed Mary, and let them serve as a reminder that I love you very, very much.

What kind of jewellery do you like? Although there is a tremendous selection here, much of it is trashy, and most of what is good is terribly expensive. Would you like a bracelet? As regards other things, I've only got so far as some Chinese silk and some dress materials. I'm going to get my Chinese shoemaker to make you some shoes, too. By the way, what size shoes does Rosheen wear?

Well, my lovely darling, I must say goodnight as it is very late and I have to wend my way back to the sleeping bungalow. This letter has to be handed in to my friend, who is returning to England by tomorrow midday, so I'll write a few more notes tomorrow. Goodnight, my passionately adored Mary; I'm still thinking of you every conscious minute and missing you painfully and distractedly every moment of the day.

*

The weather is still delightful, but much colder. During the daytime it is very warm and bright, no clouds in the sky ever, and the evenings are sharper, so that one is grateful for a warm fire. The early mornings still have that delicious spring-like freshness that makes it a pleasure to walk around to the living bungalows for breakfast. That's always the time to see the brilliant green parakeets (like parrots) flying about in the sun. There are a number of jackals in the area and at night one can hear their rather unearthly shrieks all over the place.

Just down at the end of the road are the Lodi Tombs surrounded by glorious lawns and gardens which are very pleasant to walk through. There are two very fine old tombs there which contain Mohammed Lodi and brothers. We cycle through the gardens every day on the way to work.

Another beauty spot we visited is a place called Qutab, which is a high tower some hundreds of years old on the outskirts of Delhi. From the top of the tower you see miles and miles of ancient ruins and tombs which are all that remain of the 7 ancient cities of Delhi. Far away in the distance you can see the beginnings of Delhi itself. The view is wonderful. Immediately surrounding the Qutab are some more gardens which are almost nicer than those around Lodi. We had a crazy moonlight picnic there the Sunday before last – very successful indeed. The only drawback was that Monty mixed a vicious drink called Borgia's Breath which resulted in three of the company passing out very quickly. However, we had dancing on the grass and games and lots to eat and drink and everybody seemed to enjoy themselves. The bearers and the cook were there too, doing all the cooking etc, and afterwards they and the tonga wallah who brought them there had a hell of a party themselves, which finished up with all of them, including the tonga wallah's horse, spending the night in the servants' compound in the bungalow!! Knee-high Ned didn't get up until about 11 o'clock the following day.

We also had two dance parties, one at the Imperial Hotel and one at a new place called the Piccadilly. Both were great fun. Each time we took our own liquor with us, as the prices are so exorbitantly high. At the Imperial it was kept under the table and jugs of lime juice were filled up with gin at appropriate moments by Monty. All went well until Monty emptied half a jug down himself by mistake, thus causing a certain amount of amusement to all and sundry. The Piccadilly was more discreet.

Apart from these odd nights we lead a very quiet life, just going to the cinema when there's a good film on. The rest of the evenings we spend at home reading, listening to the wireless or playing the gramophone (which we bought as a pre-Christmas present for Jack and Molly). We've seen 'Pride of the Yankees'* –

---

* *Pride of the Yankees* (1942), directed by Sam Wood, starring Gary Cooper, Walter Brennan and Teresa Wright.

very good indeed; 'Next of Kin' – excellent; 'Pardon my
Sarong' – passable; 'Shadow of the Thin Man' – weak; 'Babes on
Broadway' – good; 'Nothing But the Truth' – excellent; and
one old and mediocre film with Leslie Howard and Bette Davis
I can't remember the name of. There seems to be a good
selection on the way, including another Bob Hope.

★

I often wonder what you are doing with yourself all day and
what you're doing at particular times of the day. My thoughts are
constantly straying back to England and in imagination I already
know what 12 Lloyd Square looks like, and what you look like now,
and how the wonderful Rosheen is and what she does. Honestly, my
darling, I just don't see <u>when</u> the great day of return is coming. It
may be years yet. However, I always live in hope and pray that it
may be very very soon. Because my wonderful Mary, I miss you
terribly and am incredibly lonely for you. That's why your letters are
so satisfying in a way and why I love reading them over and over
again. They bring you very close and near when I read them. So
please send me lots more, particularly letters. But above all, let me
know how you are quickly – I want to know that you are all right.

Now I must close my beloved. I do hope your photographs
arrive very soon – I'm looking forward to seeing them. Give me
some news of Kay, Joan, Hymie, Anne, Ben, Reg and Wendy,
Haydn and Mattie, and Pat, and Bill Laithwaite, if you have any.

Enjoy yourself at Christmas, my darling Mary, and think of me.

All my love to all at the house and to you and Rosheen my
special and warmest love for Xmas and every day and all day.
Still love you eternally and unceasingly –

Bye bye, my sweetheart
David

P.S. Do you know it will be nine months since I've seen you on
Saturday?

1943

12 Lloyd Square
Finsbury W.C.1
Jan 5th 1943.

My darling, much-desired and much-missed David,

I haven't heard from you since your Christmas cable – please write soon as I miss you frantically, more even than when you went away, so long ago. Do you realise it's thirteen months since you saw Rosheen – half her age – and that she is no longer a baby but a very self-possessed little girl? She weighs 33 pounds, for your information, and is 40 inches tall (I've just measured her). By the way, have our photographs reached you yet? If they have been lost I've got a duplicate set I can send you. I sent two packets, one containing a wallet with a small portrait of R and me inside and the original 48 of R. Another one of two studio size portraits of R and myself. My poppa is at the last stage of getting his release from the army and meanwhile my mother is going into a nursing home for a couple of weeks' treatment for her nerves. She is very well though, all things considered, and has been staying in our little house these last few days. Mebbe you will come and see it one day and some aspects of it will please you immensely. Nursery school seems to be in constant state of quarantine for violently infectious diseases so am immobilised for indefinite period.

With all my love, all my thoughts, all my hopes,
Your Mary

Naval H.Q.
G.H.Q. NEW DELHI
Friday, Jan 7th, 1943

My darling Mary,

I'm writing this sitting on the verandah at the bungalow, stretched out on a long sofa-like piece of furniture, watching the setting sun throw its lazy shadows over the garden; the air is very peaceful and the birds are singing haphazardly. I'm very lonely for you at this time, my sweet one. It's a time of day when just to have you beside me would be nothing short of ecstasy. I managed to get away from the office early today as I worked all Sunday and definitely need some fresh air. No one else is here at the moment except Ian, who is very much here! He is sitting beside me asking 'What's dis', 'What's dat' picking up the paper and the pencil and putting his grubby hands all over the letter. Now he's examining my shoes and demanding an explanation for everything, including why I bought them. He's a very amusing little boy, and very good looking. He has already picked up an extraordinary number of Hindustani words – it seems very peculiar when he says things at his young age which one cannot even understand. Now he's parading his teddy bear around the verandah in a topee. Pardon me a moment – he wants to fight . . . Right, now that's settled!! I expect Rosheen is acting just the same and doing the same sort of things. God how I wish I could see her though. Ian knows I am writing to Auntie, which he keeps repeating. Bedtime at last – he's been taken off by Bali the bearer (knee-high Ned). So I can write more or less uninterrupted.

It seems an awful long time since I wrote to you last, so there's lots to tell you. Before I begin, your two delightful Xmas telegrams arrived yesterday, but were appreciated just as much as if they had arrived by Xmas day, because every word, letter, telegram, airgraph, or what you will which I receive from you is treasured equally as a thought from you – a repetition that you are still thinking of me after all these months. So thank you darling, and thank you Rosheen, and send me lots more please.

Christmas wasn't really Christmas without you, my sweet. Although all things being considered we had lots of fun, it still wasn't really Christmas. At frequent moments I was seized by an overpowering nostalgia for you, and fell a-thinking of the crazy but wonderful times we used to have at Christmas. I think the most memorable one was the first. It's the one I always reminisce about mentally. And now it's already 1943, and in a few weeks I shall have been away from you for a whole year – it seems terrible to think about and seems more than depressing when I do think about it. In some ways I don't regret having come away from you, because it has shown me anyway just how terribly much I am in love with you, and how much I want you and need you. Sometimes I am surprised myself that I am so completely and utterly yours, but Mary, if I haven't told you a thousand times already, I'm still illogically crazy about you. When I think of our flippant conversations at Largs, or the frightening inadequacy of our last few minutes together in England, I almost get heart failure. I do love you so much, my precious and unequalled Mary, so please forgive me for repeating it in each airgraph and letter I send. But each time I sit down to write, the first thing that comes into my head is that I love Mary eternally and without cessation so I can't help telling you each time. My only consolation is to think about that already much dreamed about day of re-union and to swear to myself that I will be your humble and devoted lover for always when we come together again. Speed the day, and the kind fates that watch over us preserve us both safely for that day.

Well, my darling, the sun has sunk and it is getting dark (7 o'clock) so I must move back into the bungalow. The others have come back and want an early dinner as we are going to see the Soviet film 'Defeat of the Germans near Moscow', so I'll finish tomorrow . . .

★

Saturday: The Soviet film was excellent and we feel that all of us here are really wasting our time compared with the <u>total</u> effort the S.U. are putting into the war. This country knows little of war, Indian and British alike, and a few bombs, to which every town in Britain has become accustomed, only serves to panic an entire city here. I personally don't feel I'm doing enough to justify my pay at the moment, although very occasionally there are some extremely interesting jobs to do. It's the long in-between-whiles that get me down completely and produce a feeling of frustration and impotence. I think I'd rather be anywhere than here and I imagine that if life back at the bungalow wasn't so amusing and full of fun I'd pass away from acute depression. However . . .

On Christmas eve we had a very enjoyable dance at the Piccadilly. Quite a big party consisting of Jack and Molly, Doc, Monty, John Dicky and Peggy Roe, Anne someone (a friend of Molly's from Simla – has a broad Glasgow accent), a friend of Doc's called Haley (Sq Leader), a pleasant but rather young female staff captain called Sheila Whitmarsh, and myself. We danced until 10'clock or so and then finished up with coffee and hamburgers with the manager, Mr Sox, a Greek who used to keep a joint in Rangoon. He's great fun – a real film restaurant manager – and he's very good at winking his eye at any liquor we bring in with us.

Christmas day I had to work, but the main dinner was in the evening, and what a dinner! The Konsamo (phonetic!) really excelled himself (which is saying something!) and produced a marvellous repast. Goose was the main dish (mit stuffing!) and we practically ate ourselves into a stupor. We had a largish party

round for dinner – two people called Olliphant, Horley, two Air
Force friends of Monty's, the whole family here and G-W's
personal assistant and stenographer, who is called Christabel Hoy
(short title Shipper). After dinner we danced a bit, but there
wasn't much of the good old Christmas spirit and we were
quietly tucked away in bed long before 1 o'clock.

The following day Molly and I went down into Chandni
Chowk,* which is right in the middle of the native bazaar, to
buy you some dress materials. We had a lovely time and
managed to get some good stuff after a lot of bargaining, but it's
very expensive. Apparently, no one out here thinks of buying
Indian materials as they are generally of very poor quality – the
colours run, they crumple easily etc – so we bought English and
American ones instead. I also got you some hairpin things,
which I believe are very expensive in England.

The bazaar itself is fascinating, full of narrow streets
absolutely crammed with native shops selling everything under
the sun from sweets to dress materials and bicycles to kitchen
utensils. There were some excellent shops for brassware of all
kinds, which looked well made. But that sort of thing is much
too heavy to buy. Most of the good commodities in the shops
are, of course, exported from England. It's rather tricky to know
exactly what to buy, but so far I've confined my purchases to
some dress materials, cosmetics and native jewellery, but if
there's anything else you need please say so and I'll see what can
be done.

Our tonga followed us all the way, which was useful, and we
had a horde of little boys with raffia baskets on their heads
waiting to carry all our purchases. It was rather like going on
'safari' in the bazaar, with thousands of interested natives as

---

* Chandni Chowk: a seventeenth-century market in Old Delhi.

onlookers. Molly was really marvellous at bargaining with the shopkeepers, and always managed to beat them down.

Well, my honey, here we are at page 4 and I've a hundred other things to tell you about, so I'll have to continue in another letter. Write to me as often as you can, my precious darling, as I love your letters and airgraphs. All my love to you, dearest one, and to Rosheen.

Your devoted and all too lonely David

Naval HQ
c/o GHQ NEW DELHI
January 16th 1943

My darling beloved Mary,

Tomorrow G-W and our new Signals Officer are departing on a liaison visit to England, so another golden opportunity has arisen to get a letter to you quickly. They should reach home within 10 days, so you'll get this before the end of the month. They're both very lucky to get this trip. I'd give anything to come back and see you again, even for a short time. Jack Mansell, the signals officer, is a very pleasant person and I have asked him to call on you when he gets to London, so don't be surprised if a Lieutenant Cmdr suddenly appears on the doorstep! He says he definitely will call. They expect to stay in the region for a fortnight, so if you see him, make arrangements to send me back a letter through him when he returns.

Today, my darling, I received your cable dated 31st December, saying that the second cheque had arrived safely, the new allotment is OK and the flowers and groceries were properly delivered. I'm so glad. That clears up all my questions about safe delivery now, with the exception of a special Xmas letter which I sent back with another envoy about a week before Christmas. Did you receive that safely? Apart from the letter, there were a number of photographs and two opals, one for you and one for Rosheen, enclosed. Let me know as soon as possible by cable that they have all been received safely.

Since I last wrote we have been very quiet indeed, although life in the office has been very hectic this week. G-W heard that he was going about Wednesday and since then everything has been done in rather a rush to ensure that he takes the right papers home. Today, at 11 o'clock, he suddenly realised that he hadn't a passport, and I had the rather amusing job of getting him one (as a civilian). By 4.15 I had him photographed, photographs developed, application form signed and witnessed and passport made out and signed by the Chief Commissioner, which I think is an all-time record! It's the first time I've seen a passport actually being written out. The man who did it was an extraordinary person altogether. He had no legs, but moved around at incredible speed on his spine, and could quite easily lift himself onto a chair. He surprised me more than somewhat by leaping up onto the window sill and opening the window. In fact he moved at such incredible speed that I was all lost in admiration for him. Very helpful sort of person, too.

I went to quite a pleasant dance on New Year's Eve at the Gymkhana Club with a largish party; there were too many people seriously engaged in 'having fun' to make it at all good. That club always makes me want to laugh or pinch myself to accept the fact that it is real, and really exists in this year of grace 1943. A galaxy of very plain, over-dressed, under-intelligent women and uniformed (some gorgeously) men with that perpetually degenerate look which characterises our ruling, and would-be ruling, classes would just about sum it up. Whenever I enter its not unattractive portals I always quote your much-repeated phrase

'Que fais-je dans cette galere'* to myself and laugh. If they only knew!! However, as I only visit it about once a month or so, perhaps I shouldn't complain. Went there yesterday evening with Mansell and his friends just to say goodbye in a proper and fitting manner. I do so hope he's able to get along and see you – it will establish some form of personal contact.

There's been quite a deal of movement here in the house recently. John has been away in Calcutta and only returned last Wednesday. Stephen has been up for a few days, and also a captain of the security side called Annis, who was with us in Madagascar. He succeeded on each occasion there in getting everything laid on in all respects – partly by his language, partly by his job, and partly by his handsome appearance!! At one time he had a contract with Warner Brothers in Hollywood and made a number of films there (mostly in small parts). He's quite interesting about his experiences there.

Last Sunday, Molly, he and I went out to tea with Molly's sister. We were having tea on the verandah when a man passed by in the road with a performing bear, rattling a drum. I asked casually what the bear did, and without further ado the bear was summoned into the garden to do his stuff. It was rather pitiful to see the way he danced around on his hind legs and played about, finally ending with a fight against his owner – all to the accompaniment of the drum. However, that was the first occasion in my life when I have had a performing bear brought in especially to amuse me!

Molly and I have had two fascinating and amusing trips down the Chandni Chowk, the road running right through the native bazaar. We bought quite a number of materials and oddments which I have described fully in my last letter. Now I have quite a

---

* 'What am I doing in this nightmare/mess?' Colloquialism taken from a Molière play, *The Impostures of Scapin* (1671).

store of dress materials and cosmetics to bring you back, come the day. I hope it's OK to bring you back dress materials rather than the made-up dresses, as it's very chancey getting them to your measurements here. If you like, I will get them made up. Let me know about this as it is a rather important question. Also let me know if there's anything you specially need which I can get you. A few days ago I gave some materials for underclothes to a native embroiderer from Kashmir, who is now busy making you a glamorous nightdress and some panties. If they are OK I'll give him the rest of the georgette and Chinese silk to make up. Please let me know exactly what you want, my precious darling and anything you need for Rosheen. The financial situation is quite healthy at the moment. Having my appointment backdated to 13th June at full Indian rates was a stroke of good fortune, as after paying back the Admiralty for all the advances, allotments and victuals which I had received from them since that date (I had to pay back something in the region of £275!!) I had a substantial balance to hand. Most of this I sent to you as I don't see the point of trying to spend money out here. I just keep enough to cover my expenses and buy you and me things and that just about covers my pay. After paying income tax and allotment I'm left with about 570 rupees a month. Living with the Worrals, including a party about once a fortnight, and people to dinner costs about 240 rupees, and the bearer, dhobi, cigarettes, fares, dinners at restaurants, cinemas, cables, postage, teas in the office and odd expenses absorb another 200 or so. That leaves me with 170 to spend on buying you things and also on the very necessary replenishment of my clothes, which have a short life with these Indian dhobis!

All the money I've sent you is definitely yours to spend and save as you think necessary. Actually when I've bought a few more things for my wardrobe I'll be able to increase your allotment, but that depends entirely on whether I remain in this job here or not. If I move away again anywhere outside Delhi I shall go back to Admiralty rate, and that, I'm afraid, means a reduced allotment. However, it's always useful while it lasts! If you can manage to save a bit for a rainy day, well and good; if not, so what, you've spent it on something you've needed and liked and the money has served its purpose and that's that. The only thing that I would like you to do is to give Joan £3 a month towards the 'funds',* which, I imagine, she can always do with it.

So far, your long-expected photograph hasn't arrived. I'm terribly anxious to have a good photograph of you, my beloved Mary, and especially of Rosheen, whom I haven't seen now for just over a year. If it hasn't arrived by the end of the month I'll send you a cable and perhaps you could send another one by Mansell. The original one may have been lost at sea.

Well my beloved and adored Mary, it's now nearly midnight, so I must away to our sleeping bungalow. Goodnight, my sweet one, tonight I shall be thinking of you and what you're doing, and tomorrow I'll add some more lines to you. Pleasant dreams . . .

★

Things are very much a rush at the moment, my darling, so I'd better finish this before the bag closes.

Write to me often my beloved Mary; I love everything you write.

> with all my love to you and Rosheen,
>> eternally, irrevocably
>>> your
>>>> David

---

* Funds of the Finsbury branch of the British Communist Party.

12 Lloyd Square,
W.C.1
Jan 12, 1943.

My darling, darling David,

Your Christmas letter of December 16th has just arrived with
opals and snapshots safe and I am walking on air at the moment,
it has made me so happy. Oh David, what you do to me. That
little piece of string is stronger than ever (you remember the
piece you have me on). The opals are beautiful – the most
exciting present I have ever had, and I shall do what you
suggest, have them made into rings for myself and Ro when she
is older. But your letter was the most exciting and beautiful
thing of all and I shall find a lot of happiness in some lonely
future days by reading it again and again. Time and distance
have made no change to my feelings for you except perhaps to
intensify them, but it is so comforting and reassuring to hear
you say the same thing. I sometimes fear the rivalry of exoticism
and strange adventure, but if you remember me above all others,
my old pal Dave, everything is all right. As for news here, my
mother is going into a nursing home for a short treatment –
nothing serious; Poppamoss is on the last lap towards becoming
a civilian again, I have opened an account with my new
allotment at the Midland Bank, Basil is still on leave and we are
going out this weekend to see him and Pera, everybody here
(Finsbury) is working very hard, I am collaborating in the
translation of a book from French and will let you know more
about this, Rosheen is healthy and beautiful, and I continue to
love you desperately.

Your Mary

P.S. I have sent numerous cables lately acknowledging all your
presents – so many. Have you received these?

CHAPTER 24

The 'doomed generation'

CABLE AND WIRELESS
LIMITED
Via Imperial

The first line of this telegram shows:—Number, office of origin, date.
(NOTE: " Oversea " is used to denote that the office of origin has been suppressed.)

CIRCUIT   CLERK

OVERSEA

L12402N SO 29/37 11FEB

EFM MRS MARY FRANCIS

12 LLOYD SQUARE LONDONWC1 =

DELIGHTFUL PHOTOGRAPHS ARRIVED YESTERDAY WOULD
HARDLY RECOGNISE ROSHEEN STOP YOU LOOK SO FRESH AND
LOVELY THAT IM OVERWHELMED WITH NOSTALGIC LONGING
FOR YOU ALL MY LOVE ETERNALLY =

DAVID FRANCIS

ANY ENQUIRY RESPECTING THIS TELEGRAM SHOULD BE ACCOMPANIED BY THIS FORM AND MAY BE
MADE AT ANY OF THE COMPANY'S OFFICES.

Settled in the new house at 12 Lloyd Square, Mary clears up her things at her family home in Elgin Crescent, north Kensington, including the many letters.

She is excited by the new house but as the weeks of 1943 slip by her mood darkens.

Feeding this growing depression and sense of foreboding is a delayed reaction to the sudden and shocking death of her beloved brother, Tom.

Meanwhile two significant events occurred in David's life: his chief, Garnons-Williams, is badly injured when the plane carrying him back to England crashes. The other event is the arrival of an old political friend, Michael Clarke, who comes to spend a week's leave in Delhi, precipitating much debate about developments in India and the policies of Gandhi and Nehru.

★

Airgraph
12 Lloyd Square
Finsbury,
W.C.1
Jan 21st, 1943

My darling David,

Today I have sent you a cable and an airmail letter, so at three
different times in the future I shall be with you to tell you how
much I am missing you and how much I continue to love you.
So much so that it makes me inarticulate. Everything here goes
as well as it could with the whole world emptied of everything
that makes life lovely. But one can still hope and try to work
hard for the war to be won quickly. I dream of the day when
you return, the twice blessed train that brings you into the
station and the ecstatic moment when we actually meet. I have
that at least to look forward to, to make the dullest day hopeful
and expectant. Have my cables, letters and photographs reached
you? Send me more letters, airgraphs, snapshots. I am insatiable
for news of you. Rosheen is <u>very</u> well and sends you all love. All
my love for ever and ever.   Mary

Jan. 28th, 1943

My dearest David,

I received your airgraph dated Dec 18th this morning. <u>How</u> I
wish you could have surprised me on Christmas Eve. Do you
remember how my legs collapsed once before when you arrived
unexpectedly? I have been cleaning up papers over in Elgin
Crescent and reading letters, letters, letters that you have sent me
during these past years. Some fiendishly casual that have the

power to make me hopping mad, others, that by their intensity and sincere love, still make me happy in a mournful sort of way, you know. But the whole makes an interesting documentary history of our time – the doomed generation; we who carried the can back and found ourselves in a battle. My father is out of the army and arrives here today – a civilian. I shall have my work cut out looking after him and mam for a short while as they are both still staggering from the unbelievable news of Tom's death, but I'm very glad I can help them now. I've never been much use to them before. Rosheen flourishes like the green bay tree and sends all her love to 'our Daddy'. Goodbye for now my dearest and only love.   Mary

Jan 28th, 1943

My darling David,

I am sending you two airgraphs today. This is No. 2. Have any cables or airmail letters reached you and have you got our photographs yet? If not, I will send you a duplicate set. I took your Mama and Basil to see 'Watch on the Rhine'* yesterday, Very good play and I think they enjoyed it. B. has got a new appointment and is waiting to leave any time now. I saw 'Doctor's Dilemma'† and am going to see 'King Lear' next week, so you see my education isn't being neglected. I do lots of things. I have masses of friends and yet I feel that everything and everybody that had power to touch my heart are far away, dead or estranged. As a matter of fact they are. I just accept friendship and love now. I give <u>nothing</u> in return. Oh darling, come back

---

* *Watch on the Rhine*: influential anti-Nazi play written by American playwright Lillian Hellman in 1941 and brought to London in 1943.

† George Bernard Shaw's *The Doctor's Dilemma*, first staged in 1906.

and release me from this frozen hibernation before I turn into stone. My love for you even, real and vital though it is in actuality, just now seems hopeless and thwarted and blighted with unreality. So come back <u>soon</u> and teach me once again how to live.   Mary

Naval H.Q.
NEW DELHI
Friday Feb 12th 1943

My dearest darling Mary,

This is really Part 2 of a letter I started last week. Since the day I wrote Part 1, so much seems to have happened that I hardly know where to begin. There has been excitement, travel, work and everything, including an element of tragedy. Let's start with the worst first. At the most unfortunate possible time in his career, G-W has met with a serious air accident which will mean his being out of action for several months and, I suspect, he will not return here. We haven't had any details yet, but we suspect where it actually happened and when etc. He separated from John Mansell and proceeded on his own, so John will still be calling on you. You probably won't get the letter G-W took for me, though. It's terribly bad luck about G-W, as he is just about at the peak of his career and power here, and unlikely to reach the same position again. We're all anxiously awaiting full news. Curiously enough, that was the first long journey he's taken without me for a long time, so even though he was going to England, I'm glad I wasn't with him. (Two other people in the same plane were killed.)

Well now for something happier. At long last your photographs have arrived. They are lovely. Rosheen looks quite different and must have changed an awful lot in the last year. She seems to have the face of a child now and not a baby. And you, my beloved, you look so fresh and beautiful and even younger: it makes me thoroughly homesick to look at you, which I do at frequent intervals throughout the day and each time I repeat to myself 'God, but Mary's beautiful' as if I didn't already know that. I'm really thrilled with them all. Thank you darling.

On Friday morning last week, John and I flew down to Bombay for a weekend of work and tours. We had an excellent passage down, and on the first evening had dinner with another cousin of John's (these Smyths are everywhere!), our pilot, a Wing Cdr called Grant-Ferris who is MP for St Pancras, and an Army major. The place – the Yacht Club, where the food and drink are unsurpassed as yet. Saturday we had conferences all day and in the evening John and I went shopping in Crawford Market,* where we had a very amusing time bargaining with the stall holders. One of them tossed with us whether we should pay Rs 12 or Rs 15 for a despatch case! We lost, but beat him on the next toss for a couple of Indian handbags. One's for you, darling: I think you'll like it. Also bought an Indian jade necklace for you. In the evening I went out with Jack Davison to see 'United We Stand' (I was staying with Jack by the way). Sunday we spent touring ships, but in the afternoon we went to a place a few miles north of Bombay to inspect a place in my official capacity! Evening time we dined with the Captain-in-Charge Bombay once more at the Yacht Club. Monday morning more conferences and in the afternoon I went with Stephen Vaughan-Lewis to have a look at his place of work. Evening I went out with the boys to see 'Tortilla Flat', which was quite good but awfully disappointing compared with the book, which I liked very much.

---

* Crawford Market: one of the oldest and most important markets in Mumbai.

We flew back on Tuesday morning stopping en route for lunch at an RAF station commanded by a friend of John's. The passage again was excellent and I slept most of the way in order to recuperate from the very energetic week-end! Very useful tour all the same; I was very glad of it. Over to Part III or II, my darling angel. With all my love eternally, dearest Mary.

    Your

      David

Air mail letter card

Monday Feb 15th, 1943

GHQ NEW DELHI

My beloved Mary,

Whilst down in Bombay I had another extraordinary coincidence. All right, you've guessed! I met another girl from Paxton! Was having lunch with Stephen when a waiter brought a note across from another table which said 'Are you the Francis who was at Paxton?' Heigh ho, there across the room was sitting a girl from Burma called Doris de Kretser, with her father. Wasn't that amazing? They had rather a bad time in Burma as Doris contracted infantile paralysis in 1940, and although partially cured, was forced to trek out of Burma in 1941 with the rest of them, thus undoing all the benefits of the cures she had been undergoing. Now she still has to use a stick to move around with, which is very tragic. Mrs de Kretser unfortunately contracted a fever while on the trek and, like hundreds of others, died through lack of medical supplies and attention. Altogether a very tragic family. Mr de Kretser, who was a judge in Rangoon, has aged incredibly in the last 10 years, but I suppose that is no more than is to be expected if a man has lost his wife, his house, his job and has his daughter paralysed and his only son serving in the RAF in England. It was nice meeting them though.

Yesterday I had a lovely letter from you dated Dec 9th. That's the first letter I've received for what seems like months. I like your idea of going into the engineering business – that should be darn interesting. Hope the new creche will be more satisfactory than the old one. Who is it being run by? Sounds conveniently close. I would love to see Rosheen now. Her photos are fascinating and I examine them each morning when I get up and each night when I go to bed. Yours is simply lovely. That I carry with me all day and am frequently looking at it. Darling you look so young and so fresh and so unmaternal! What have you been doing with yourself.

The weather here is getting daily warmer. Now all the Spring flowers are blooming and the gardens are looking wonderfully colourful. The life of the flowers is very short, though, and in a couple of months or less they'll all be over. Last Sunday we had a grand picnic in the gardens of the Qutab (where we had a moonlight picnic in November), and had a lovely time. The gardens there are looking at their best and are most beautifully kept. There were about 20 of us altogether, including four London firemen and three children. After tea, some of us performed the energetic feat of climbing the Qutab tower. Later on, while walking round to have a look at some of the ruins, an angry swarm of bees suddenly attacked the party, and principally a girl called Sheila Whitmarsh, who was stung badly several times. I've never seen anything like that before and always thought bees to be fairly peaceful animals unless definitely enraged, but now I know better! Reg, one of the fireboys, was stung on his nose and I twice on the forehead whilst trying to knock the bees off Sheila! However, it didn't mar the party and some of us ended up the day with a bit of dancing at the Piccadilly and a cinema afterwards. After the energetic day on

Sunday we've had a very quiet week so far and aren't breaking out again until tomorrow, when we're having a chop suey and picture night. The meal was ordered yesterday after careful consultation with the prop of the Chinese restaurant.

All my love eternally to you and Rosheen, my beloved
Mary
David

Airgraphs
12 Lloyd Square,
Finsbury W.C.1
March 10th, 1943

My darling and dearly beloved David,

What an amazing sequence of letters from you are arriving! A batch dated 'November' this week and also some much later ones, including the information about G.W. I shudder to think of the oaths I first wasted on the air when I heard you weren't coming with him – and then the awful sequel. My God, darling, your lucky star is working overtime. May it continue to do so. I am still waiting for your Mansell to turn up and the letter I had written when I first heard about this is sadly out-of-date. I must revise it and try and hurry J.S.M.'s visit up, as I haven't written you a real letter for an awful long time. I will try and explain this in Part II of this airgraph. The first part ends with eternal love from Maire.

Part II

Dear D.B.D. [see part I]

The opportunity of saying something that would be really topical and fresh to you filled me with great enthusiasm, but it's been sadly delayed. Another reason has been a very 'creepy' period in my life – you know, nothing to say to you who are in a different world from me, you who belong to new people and a fantastically new mode of life – nothing to say except that I love your memory and I live chiefly for our reunion, but our present relationship fills me with a sense of futility – despair occasionally, and a queer indifference for the contact that letters can make. This is a sporadic condition, and I'm cured at the moment of writing, but you must understand why there are such awful gaps in my writing. Part 3 will give you my news, such as it is.

Mary

Part 3

My dearest and only love,

After the Oxford Group Truth* of Part 2, I give you the news. My little house is very crowded at the moment as Poppa's been discharged from the Army at last and is staying with me because Mam is in hospital. She's rather ill and I'm rather worried about her, but what's one more worry when you reach saturation point? Evelyn and Michael have also taken up residence, much against my will as they are an agonising reminder of what has happened and, temperamentally, the organising of other people's lives is not my strong point. But what can I do? She is the most helpless and least decisive woman I have ever met, and the baby is aged four months (nearly). So, by a great effort, I've just got to be a 'good organiser' and push everyone around. Rosheen, thank God, remains herself, merry, imperious and excitingly intelligent. I will write lots more.

Mary

---

* A reference to the Oxford Group, the parent of the Moral Re-Armament movement, an influential but controversial group founded by Frank Buchman, an American Lutheran pastor, in the 1920s, part of whose teachings included confessions of perceived errors or wrongdoings.

Air mail
12 Lloyd Square,
Finsbury W.C.1
March 17th, 1943

My dearest love,

Last night Mansell came to visit me and told me that I had better not rely on him to bring you all my news – so I must write you lots of letters to make up for lost time. He reduced me to a state of despair as he held out no hope of an early reunion – but today I feel more philosophical about it all. You are so infinitely worth waiting for – I have so much more to live for than many other women that I can keep the hope of our someday coming together again as a driving force to get me through the dreary months (or years – God forbid) without you.

It was very good to hear that you are well and happy and to see someone who had actually spoken to you and seen you in the flesh quite recently. I love you so much David, I needn't elaborate it as it is a very simple and elemental thing. Though you are so far away and it has been so long, nothing can qualify my love – it is a present and immediate thing and I am very happy when in your letters you tell me the very same thing.

It will be your birthday in two weeks' time. I have sent you a cable for it, but that could never express all the fervent hope that your 25th will be memorable and lovely and that your 26th will be celebrated at <u>home with me</u>.

A year ago you went away. Yesterday I took my little red coat to be cleaned – do you remember the brave red coat which I bought to say goodbye to you in? If only I could wear it to meet you <u>coming home</u>. But the war isn't over yet, so I shall try to stop dreaming these impracticable dreams and become a realist, but with the monotony, cruelty, sordidness of life made beautiful by the fact that somewhere you are thinking of me and remembering me with love and that I am inspired always with love for you and a profound faith in our eventual future together.

With all my love, forever and ever,

Mary

Airgraph
Naval HQ. G.H.Q.
NEW DELHI
19th March, 1943

Part 1

My darling, beloved Mary,

I haven't written to you for almost two weeks now, which is most reprehensible, I know, but has been caused by 2 disturbing factors: (a) the arrival of Michael Clarke on seven days' leave and (b) my being confined to bed for several days with a severe chill! Michael arrived on Friday 5th and was able to stay until Saturday of the following week, and we had a grand time. It made all the difference in the world to be able to discuss reasonably intelligent matters once again. We talked a great deal about our impressions of India, and found we agreed on quite a number of them, and particularly on Gandhi and the general political situation here. Possibly we were somewhat heretical, but that remains to be seen! Michael is practically recovered from his wounds, which fortunately have left no visible mark, and is in remarkably good spirits. He seems to have seen much more of Indian life than I have, principally because he lives in a smaller town where the residential areas are less segregated and is doing darn well at Urdu. We had a busy week. Saturday we saw a very enjoyable film, 'The Talk of the Town' with Jean Arthur – very witty. Michael spent most of the day wandering

round Delhi and seeing the sights. End of part 1, my darling,
which comes to you with all my love as always.

DAVID

Airgraph
Naval H.Q. GHQ
NEW DELHI
19th March 1943

Part 4 [parts 2and 3 missing]

Mary most sweet,

On Saturday I started in earnest with this darn chill and spent
from Sat night until Wed midday in bed. Apart from the
discomfort, it was in many ways very pleasant. I lay in bed and
read all day, or talked to occasional visitors or just lay and looked
out on the lovely garden and thought about you and a hundred
and one other things . . . There is no doubt, my precious
darling, that there is no question of <u>my</u> having you on a string,
on the contrary I'm bound to you with bonds a million times
stronger than string – perennially. In fact, being away from you
is like putting aside one's deeper self, into cold storage if you
wish, only to be taken up again when the old combination of
Mary and David is a real one again. I thought a lot about Largs
last year, too, and read all your letters through again, which
always makes me happy, at least temporarily so . . . In fact, my
lovely and beloved Mary I am still hopelessly in love with you.

David

We went to see 'How Green is my Valley'. I liked that very
much as a film, but don't somehow think that the background
scenes and the general local atmosphere were much like South

Wales – at least the South Wales we knew! . . . Just to add to the general excitement, two bombs were thrown in the cinema. Fortunately both exploded harmlessly, but the moment of anticipation was not pleasant. Apparently this also happened at two other cinemas, with the same result.

We have talked a lot about the terroristic methods being adopted by certain sections of Congress* and we are appalled by the absurdity of the policy. Naturally our little friends† are doing everything in their power to combat this policy and achieved quite good results in Calcutta, despite the activities of the Fifth Column. It achieves exactly nothing, but serves to alienate quite a large section of the thinking population in India.

There is still no party in India that commands mass support for a sound policy, and I suppose until there is, there will be no solution to the Indian problem. Congress, in my estimation, should only be supported because it is the mass party in India and representative of the equivalent of the 'working class' in India, and not because of the policy it is presently advocating. No well organised party could ever permit something so palpably absurd as Gandhi's fast‡ to take place and although I'm basically in sympathy with the ideals for which the Congress leaders are working in respect of Indian independence, I think them bloody fools to adopt such childish and illogical methods to achieve those ideals.

Our friends here admire Gandhi tremendously but I'm afraid that I don't share that admiration, in fact I can think of nothing better for the Congress leadership than that Gandhi should die. It would at least give the people of the Nehru outlook a proper chance.

---

* The Indian National Congress Party, founded in 1885, became pivotal in in the opposition to British colonial rule in India.

† Presumably local members of the Communist Party of India.

‡ The Indian leader Mahatma Gandhi used hunger strikes and fasts as weapons in his campaigns of peaceful civil disobedience in the struggle for Indian independence and caste issues. Others advocated less peaceful methods.

On Tuesday Seymour came back from the wilds and John came over to dinner, so we had a quiet evening at home. The following day, Michael and I took Jack and Molly to lunch at the Imperial Hotel, which we all enjoyed a lot. In the evening we had dinner with Wilson (John's secretary) and a grand evening it was too. They have a piano and Michael played all the classical pieces he could remember, including the piano version of the main themes in all our favourite symphonies. It was the first time I'd heard the piano being used for classical music for it seemed like years.

Thursday evening we had dinner with some very interesting Americans I'd met a couple of weeks before. One, by name Spingarn,* whose father was a famous professor in the United States, went to the L.S.E. His friend, who is quite different in outlook, is very amusing and witty. Talk was good that evening and very worthwhile. Another American who joined us was a Democratic Party organiser in one of the Middle Western States. Spingarn is a trifle pedantic, but as Michael said, it's a pleasant change even to meet a pedant out here.

Friday, we were going out again, but unfortunately I was seized with a feverish chill and after feeling bloody awful all day, I went to bed very early with two aspirins and an extra blanket. Today I feel much better, although not completely.

I thoroughly enjoyed last week and I think Michael did too. He did some slick work with some acquaintances of his up here, which may result in his being posted here, which would be marvellous.

About 5 days ago I received an airgraph from you dated 28th Jan. I understand only too well how you feel, my lovely darling . . . I miss you more than words can express and know I shall not start to live deeply again until we are together once more.

★ Probably the son of Joel Elias Spingarn, a famous American liberal educator, literary critic and civil rights activist.

Please write and cable often. There are lots of things I want to know more about. What are our friends doing in England? How are things locally? What book are you helping to translate and who with? How are Evelyn and Michael? Hymie, Joan, Kay, the Swansea mob? And of course give me more and more descriptions of Rosheen, what she says, what she does, how she looks etc. I still look at those 48 photographs with a certain amount of amazement, to think that I have a daughter as grown up as that . . . Your silk pyjamas are well under way now, and should be finished at the end of the week. I am also going to buy a pair of Kashmiri pyjamas at the end of next month – they're nice and I know you'll like them . . . [page missing]

I have all your letters written to me in London in 1941 and up at Largs and to the Winchester Castle, which always makes me feel happy and glad that I've got you in the world. I've got very pleasant memories of you-and-I up at Largs, particularly gambolling in the snow. Remember? It was nice just lying in bed looking out on to the garden, which is looking lovely just now. Thinking about you, my beloved darling, makes me realise more and more that you represent the most important and most substantial part of my life, into which everything else falls into categories of superficiality and unimportance. I talked a little of this with Michael, who accused me of being obsessed with triviality, which is probably quite true . . .

12 Lloyd Square
March 20th, 1943

My darling and much beloved David,

A year ago tonight I saw your train off at Euston after that dreamlike fantastic fortnight together. Scotland, snow, whiskey and teacakes, and then London – that desperate last evening and our tender farewell – 'where the bloody hell have you been?' – mutually said. This morning I received your cable 'celebrating' the anniversary and thank you very much for thinking about it and for still loving me. I sent you a cable this week for your birthday. I hope you received it in good time. I think cables from this end take longer than from your end. I sent you one the week before, just because I wanted to tell you <u>quickly</u> how much I love you and miss you. Sometimes I am overwhelmed. I have resolved to write you something every day as a penance for all the times I didn't write.

Everything here is just the same. Pop, Evelyn and Michael are still staying here. I haven't had the chance really to solve my own problem of finding an adequate nurse for Rosheen and getting a job. But I suppose looking after all these poor orphans is a good job – but I'd rather have office hours and free time when work is over . . . Anyway, it will pass.

Rosheen sends you her love. She knows all about you and we have long conversations about 'when Daddy David comes home' which are very tantalising and make me rather faint with desire for that day.

Your lists and catalogues of your shopping expeditions make me drool at the mouth. What a magnificent prospect. I shall look like the coupon-clippers dream of home! Underwear, glamorous cosmetics, jewellery. Oh David, David! Wearing your discarded striped pyjamas I dream of yellow chiffon. Exotic and erotic – oh please come soon!

The last Orson Welles film, 'The Magnificent Ambersons', is in town. No West End cinema will touch it on account of box-office flop 'Citizen Kane'. So I'm going to tour the suburbs till I find it. I missed Jean Gabin in his American film – I wanted to revive the thrill of seeing 'Quai des Brumes' with you. Going to the cinema without you isn't the same. No film seems as funny, as super-smashing as they used to. And David, wasn't going home together after the flicks the best of all? Both of us stimulated, critical, and terribly in love – much more interesting than any film. Come back soon my darling Dave.

    Yours ever,

      Mary

Airgraph

27th March, 1943

Naval H.Q.

G.H.Q. NEW DELHI

Part 1

Mary, my beloved darling,

No letters or airgraphs from you this week, but 2 cables instead – one for my birthday. I do so hope Mansell does call before he returns – he promised faithfully he would. Probably he's been touring around a lot.

It's an awful thought that in few days' time I shall be 25. It seems just a short while ago that I was 21 – four years that seem to have been absorbed by the war, or the threat of war, have just flashed by. Shall we ever recapture them?

There have been a few bright spots this week in this sterile, atrophying, aimless existence here. I've bought and played innumerable times the Toscanini recording of the Pastoral; it's very satisfying to be able to hear it again and it revives most pleasant memories of you and the days of old – makes me terribly nostalgic and dissatisfied, too. Somehow I always associate that symphony with Tom.

On Monday we saw a very amusing film, 'Take a Letter, Darling' with Rosalind Russell. I thoroughly enjoyed it and it put me in a good mood. Both the film wit and R R made me think of you – the latter because so many of her attitudes and expressions are like yours, and the former, because it was typical of the kind of film we loved seeing together. In fact this week I've been reminded of you in innumerable ways – but what brought you closest was your lovely telegram, which makes me feel that if you still love me and continue to love me, my existence in this world is forever justified. Eternally yours, David

CHAPTER 25

Last Posts

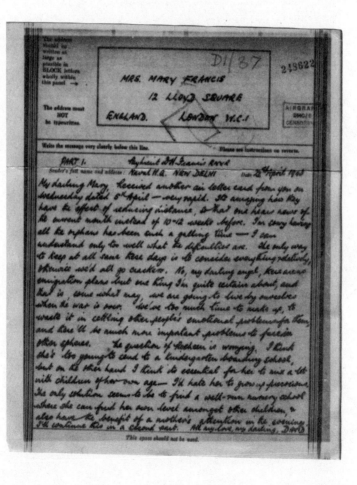

Almost exactly a year had passed since the couple had last seen each other in Largs. The strain on Mary, combined with the death of her brother and the continued presence of 'the orphans' crowded into the small house in Lloyd Square, was growing almost unbearable. She sees her situation stretching into the future without hope of relief or resolution.

Her last letter to David displays a sort of defiant jauntiness. David senses her mood and his letters are full of encouragement, gossip, tender tributes and identification with her condition. He recognises that she would be happier with an interesting job and agrees, although reluctantly, that a well-run kindergarten boarding school could be the answer.

Poignantly, his last surviving letter finishes: 'However much I love you, my wonderful darling Mary, and however much I crave to be with you again, and to resume the wonderful combination of David and Mary, there is no escape – YET.'

There was, of a sort. Three weeks later, on 28 May 1943, he died of smallpox.

★

435

Lloyd Square,
W.C.1
March 25th, 1943

My darling David,

Here I am again darling, in my campaign to write to you
oftener than ever before, to prove that a year's absence cannot
touch a single fibre, age cannot wither etc etc . . . God, how I
miss you; the longer it goes on, the worse the longing to see
you, to hear you, to feel you, gets. This is a painful subject, let's
change it, but I'm afraid it will crop up again before this letter is
finished.

Rosheen and I went to the Zoo on Monday, and it was great
fun. We kept meeting animals that originated from India. What
a ferocious place it must be, my darling. Please be careful when
you meet tigers, won't you? Rosheen didn't like the tigers or the
lions, but adored the bison which she recognised at once as 'cow
with curly hair'. She also liked the llama and penguins, but
disapproved of the monkeys. She reported back that she had seen
owls and elephants, which was quite untrue.

Do you remember Harry Rogers, Tom's great friend in the
RNVR? He came to see me the other day after 'running
around the Med' and we had a most ferocious pub-crawl
remembering Tom and the days of our great trio friendship. I
saw 'Casablanca' with him last night, as he had just come from
there, and it's an exceedingly exciting film. See it, just for the
cast alone, which is terrific. I've got a date in Casablanca when
the war is over. May I go?

My mother is improving slowly, which is something, and
maybe soon she will be able to come home and resume charge
of Poppa, Evelyn and Michael, who meanwhile stay with me.

I am writing this letter having just taken a study class – I am
progressing in that side of my education a little. But oh, how I

miss you David, in this, as in everything. You will never know how important your influence upon me – for happiness, for intelligence, for everything good – was. Come back soon darling. I miss you <u>unendurably</u> at times because I love you so very very much. Write to me often.

    Your Mary

Airmail

12 Lloyd Square, W.C.1

April 5, 1943

My darling David,

    I have gone these few days extra without receiving any news of you to make me feel rather desperate for some sort of contact or another. I received Part II of one of these airmail letters some time ago, but Part I is still on its way. Maybe it will come tomorrow and the very sight of your handwriting will act like a stimulant to my flagging spirit. At the moment I miss you to the exclusion of all other thought. Last night I dreamt that we met on board ship somewhere – a lovely dream, but alas, only a dream.

    Anyway, honey, how are you and where are you, and when are you coming back to me? My mother came out of hospital this weekend and is much better. If your post-war plans, my darling husband, include emigration a long way away from my family I shall not grieve unduly. I have had a <u>basinful</u>, but definitely, particularly as regards my dear Mama.

    Evelyn is staying here with Michael and we are mutually struggling with the problem – what to do with the children. The nursery school is out of the question, as it is inefficiently run and inadequately staffed and seems to be in quarantine constantly. As far as Rosheen is concerned, she is worrying me a lot as she is very precocious and needs other children. She demands too much from me and emotionally is too attached to me. I would like your opinion on the following suggestion – that I try to find some kindergarten boarding school run well (Dartington Hall* type) and send her there and get a job to pay the expenses? The thought of being separated from her kills me but she certainly needs a change from my all-too-tolerant care. Anyway, if I am to live months and months without you, or any prospects of you, I <u>must</u> get a job that will keep me very very busy. What do you think of all this? She is very well indeed and exceedingly sweet and charming and sends you all her love. And I also am well, if not noticeably sweet and charming, and love you to distraction and I always will. Write <u>often</u>.

Yours in all, possible ways,

Mary

c/o Naval H.Q.
Wednesday April 7th, 1943
G.H.Q. NEW DELHI

My darling beloved Mary,

Today, one of those strangely delayed letters arrived, sent by air mail on November 24th, a lovely, moving letter about Tom and the agonies of having to explain about it to Evelyn. It's difficult to really believe, at a distance, that Tom just doesn't exist any more. The reality can only be forced upon one when

---

* Dartington Hall School (1926–1987): progressive co-educational boarding school which was to have 'no corporal punishment, indeed no punishment at all; no prefects; no uniforms . . . no segregation of the sexes; no compulsory games, compulsory religion or compulsory anything else'.

the absence of a dead person causes a void in one's life. When they just aren't there to talk to, to do things with, to love or expect to see – so probably I shan't really <u>realise</u> his death until I'm back in England where I would naturally expect to see him as part of my life. But for Evelyn, and your parents and you, my darling, it must have been hell, because you are, as you said, so much the less yourselves by his death.

You know, my beloved Mary, reading through your letter makes me feel very humble and yet strangely proud. At each crisis in our lives, you've always revealed such a depth of character and understanding, and an inspired sanity, that I feel both very humble and immature beside you, and yet terribly proud that I have such a wonderful person as my wife. That sounds rather like sycophantic adoration, but isn't meant to be at all. But the more I know of you and the more I meet other people, particularly other women, so much the more am I lost in admiration for you and so much the more am I bewildered at my luck in having such an exemplary wife. This feeling is cumulative and each reminder of the depth or extent of my love and admiration for you only serves to kindle again that searing, devastating nostalgia for you and to resurrect that awful feeling of terror that something may happen to me before I've had a chance to see you again and tell you just how much I love you.

Oh darling, darling, if you only knew the agonies I go through sometimes when I think of the thousands of miles that separate us. For my own peace of mind, I repress and repress the thought of that distance, but sometimes it is quite impossible. I daydream much too much of the past, reminiscing mentally of all our wonderful happinesses together, hoping wildly and blindly that tomorrow will see us together again, by some miraculous stroke of the good fortune that used to be ours in days of old. Tomorrow is a lovely day – when tomorrow comes.

I'm afraid that when I do come back I shall be nothing but a humble and devoted lover, fearing to raise my voice lest it displease my lovely lady, or to be angry lest it distress her. Can you imagine me that way? Asked that question a few years ago, I should have replied 'Bloody nonsense', but knowing now the acute feeling of remorse that occurs when I recall quarrels and bickerings, as we only knew how, and how much I wish I hadn't said a lot of things I did say – I can only reply in the affirmative. Do you see what you've done to me, even at these thousands of miles distance? Oh Mary, my beloved darling Mary, I love you to eternity and am only existing for the day we come together again – physically, mentally, spiritually and in any other way in which we can absorb each other into the one being. Existing till the moment I can hold you close in my arms, fuse your body with mine and say: 'Time stand still', 'Time don't move', and stay locked with you till the end of eternity.

    Your DAVID

12 Lloyd Square, W.C.1
April 9th, 1943

Part II [first part missing]

My darling sweet David,

The tone of No. 1 seems a little tense on second reading caused no doubt by your reminding me of our last Friday together. I shall <u>never</u> forgive you for being so bloody cheerful and excited and for putting up such a poor imitation of regret at leaving your ever-loving wife. And the irony of it is that I haven't seen you since to remonstrate about it. But when shall I see you again – can I live through another year? Sometimes I think I can – know I can and probably will have to, but at other times the thought is unbearable.

It must be easier for you. You have your work and all your new exciting friends and atmosphere. Life in London is very drab these days – people seem to have lost their incentive to live even, never mind fight a victorious war against fascism.

Phyllis Freeman has had a baby son – incredible to relate. I feel jealous – I want a son before I am too old to make it a good proposition. What are you going to do about it?

What alarms me about this business of coming home is that you seem to have given up all hope – you regret the separation but accept it. Is it really to be till the end of the war, and then some? Let me know darling if it's worth hoping that some day – this year perhaps – you might arrive and telephone me – I'm on the telephone now, by the way – this is terribly important to me as it makes a great difference to how I spend the next year.

The address of my bank is the Midland Bank, Upper Street, Islington. I will send you photographs. I had better have new ones getooken as Rosheen has changed noticeably and, who knows, maybe I have too. Next month I shall be 26 years old – ask not for whom the bell tolls, it tolls for thee! Have you still got dappled eyes, darling, and does your hair still fall on the backs of chairs like a drowned poet? If I could only see you. Please make it soon; please fix it, my fixer who never failed to fix. Rosheen, who is well, sends you all her love and I send you all mine, forever and unceasingly. Mary

Air mail letter card
Naval H.Q.
NEW DELHI
Saturday April 17th [1943]

My beloved darling Mary,

There's not much news this week really. Last Saturday
we had a good, fast game of hockey in which we were soundly
beaten 8–2. In the evening Sheila Whitmarsh, who was just off
her sick bed, came round to dinner. Sunday was a hot day,
very hot and showery in the afternoon and sultry in the evening,
so we went to see Abbott and Costello in their latest – quite
amusing. I took Sheila to hear a young Viennese, by name Liesl
Stary, give a recital. It was a satisfying change to hear
some good piano music again. She played some lovely pieces by
Chopin and Liszt, did well with the 'Pathetique' sonata but
performed dully a piece of Bach. (Chaconne in D minor.)
Generally, I liked the concert, which, judged as one must
judge it in relation to Indian standards, was really very good.
Jack and I had dinner with Spingarn and Stewart on Wednesday
at the Imperial – we discussed the usual subjects, with
Spingarn developing a thesis about trade barriers. He is an
extraordinarily interesting person to listen to, as he has
that type of brain which is capable of formulating a complicated
theory in the simplest terms. I don't agree with all of his
conclusions, but he's very stimulating mentally, which does me
good.

Last week also I saw 'Mrs Miniver'. I liked Greer Garson very
much – she gave a lovely performance – but disliked the
background of the film which never seemed real or particularly
like middle class life during the war. I've had some tremendous
arguments with some people here about the characteristics of the
British middle class!! It's difficult to convince them that a man

earning, at the very minimum, £2,000 a year is not typically middle class!

On Thursday night, having been unable to get in the cinema, I wandered round to the fireboys' house and spent the evening chatting. Generally, they are quite sympathetic to my point of view, and fully realise the possibilities of this war in bringing about a decent sort of society to live in. One of them, incidentally, who was very fond of opera, used to go to Sadler's Wells a great deal and remembers Phyllis and me, vaguely, doing our stuff. Another of the boys – Snowy, an honest, simple type of Londoner – was talking about a bloke he knew in Old St. The said bloke, who had lived around those parts for nigh on 30 years, was one day told to go to London Bridge, but replied he didn't know where it was. Snowy couldn't get over it. Later on I was trying to explain where we lived. (He works in City Road.) Finally, to make the position clear, I said we lived behind Sadler's Wells. Snowy said very naively, 'Where's Sadler's Wells?'

The result of the Cheshire by-election where the Commonwealth candidate* was returned, is very interesting. I notice, too, that there was a close fight at Watford, of all places!! What's the attitude to the new party? Out here, one forms the impression that it merits support, even though it may be critical support! Let me know. Being detached from everything that is going on in England is hellish, particularly as all the detailed news is about three months out of date. This comes with all my love to you and Rosheen, eternally and unceasingly.   DAVID

---

* Common Wealth Party: a short-lived (1942–5, although finally dissolved in 1993) but politically significant party which was the only opposition to the government during the wartime Parliament. It put up candidates in defiance of the Labour–Conservative truce/coalition and succeeded in returning three members of Parliament during the Second World War. Its manifesto was 'libertarian socialist', calling for public ownership and morality in politics. Initially led by J. B. Priestley.

Naval H.Q.
NEW DELHI
Sunday April 18th, [19]43

My lovely darling,

The other day I went across to Old Delhi to meet a most interesting scientist, by name Sir Shanti Bhatnagar.* He is the Director of Scientific and Industrial Research in India. Quite recently he has been raised to the status of F.R.S., which is a great honour for any Indian or European scientist. We spent 2 or 3 hours talking together about a variety of subjects – you can guess – and discovered one or two mutual acquaintances and friends, including Ben. I thoroughly enjoyed the morning spent with him and am very pleased that he has invited me over to meet his wife. I must go one day this week.

Had a letter from Michael the other day: he has moved from Ahmednagar and expects to go to Karachi fairly soon. With a bit of luck we may be able to meet again soon. I hear you've seen Pat recently. How is she? By the way, Michael asked me to send you his love.

I have a feeling I shall be getting a new job soon – not out of India, unfortunately. G-W is apparently not coming back, so my presence in Delhi hasn't the same significance as it had before. G-W's absence rather breaks up the team, and now John is almost certain to go as well. At the moment, almost my main function is answering questions put by other departments, and generally disseminating information which I have at my finger tips as a result of my experience in England and Madagascar. But it's very unproductive and negative sort of work, and certainly not what I

---

* Sir Shanti Bhatnagar was a famous Indian scientist who played a prominent role in the country's development of scientific research before and after independence.

444

volunteered for. The only compensation of the job is that one knows exactly what is going on – and that is often a very depressing compensation! Anyway, the present Director wants to keep me in my present capacity and also to take over the work which my confrere, a major, is doing. That would mean no change, basically. A second possibility is that I might go to a job of the same kind in Delhi with another Naval captain. The third possibility is departing to Bombay again as Secretary to a captain. All three jobs are within the same organisation. Of these, I think I would prefer the second, but it all remains to be seen. I expect it will be settled within a month or so. Actually, if I have to stay in this benighted country, I think I'd rather be at Delhi than anywhere else, even though Bombay is more civilised. I'm just beginning to get to know some interesting people here. The first and second possibilities mean remaining on Indian rates of pay, the third returning to Admiralty rates. To be on the safe side, you had better assume that the allotment paid on May 1 is the last at £35 level, as I'll have to reduce if I return to Admiralty rates. Anyway, it's been very useful while it lasted. How are you financially? OK?

Indian income tax has gone up this year quite a bit, but it is still relatively small, although one doesn't get the same personal allowances as in England. Last year (June–Feb of this year) I paid a total of £65 tax, and this year the assessment for a full year is £125!! It sounds a hell of a lot of money, but in terms of rupees (which are valued at 1/6 but have the purchasing power of about 9d), and the absurd, artificially high standard of living enjoyed by Europeans, particularly service people, it isn't really much. A gin and lime costs 3/6, a razor blade 1/-, an ordinary dinner 6/-, a taxi to the station 10/-, a novel 12/6, a Woolworths soup plate 3/6, a pair of pyjamas 30/-, a new English bicycle £15. Still it's worse in Chungking! Will write some more.

Goodnight, my beloved darling,

DAVID

Naval H.Q.
22nd April, 1943
NEW DELHI

Part 1

My darling Mary,

Received another air letter card from you on Wednesday dated 5th April – very rapid. It's amazing how they have the effect of reducing distance, so that one hears news of the current month instead of 10–12 weeks before. I'm sorry having all the orphans has been such a galling time – I can understand only too well what the difficulties are. The only way to keep at all sane these days is to consider everything relatively, otherwise we'd all go crackers. No, my darling angel, there are no emigration plans, but one thing I'm quite certain about, and that is, come what may, we are going to live by ourselves when the war is over. We've too much time to make up, to waste it in settling other people's emotional problems for them, and there'll be much more important problems to face in other spheres.

The question of Rosheen is worrying. I think she's too young to send to a kindergarten boarding school, but on the other hand I think it's essential for her to mix a lot with children of her own age. I'd hate her to grow up precocious. The only solution seems to be to find a well-run nursery school where she can find her own level amongst other children and also to have the benefit of a mother's attention in the evening. I'll continue this in a second part.

All my love my darling,
DAVID

Air mail
12 Lloyd Square, W.C. 1
April 23rd, 1943

My darling much beloved David,

It's Good Friday today and raining as hard as it invariably does at Eastertime and here I am thinking about you and wishing so much that we were together. There must be a saturation point of missing someone. Maybe I will find it one day, but at the moment the nostalgic longing for you and the feeling of your constant half presence grows progressively with your length of absence. I went to a concert at the Albert Hall last Saturday and was thankful that no 'Fantasia' apparatus exists to analyse my emotions when I listen to the music. All my experiences, past, present and future, are inspired by you and dedicated to you, and so the sensations caused by anything beautiful or exciting are directed towards you. Oh David, David, how I love you, and what potentialities of life are ours together! Chemical affinity and personal magnetism when we are together and a more subtle, mental lifeline when we are apart. Do you feel me with you too? Sometimes I can almost walk with you. Today I lunched at Musso's, in Gray's Inn Road. Do you remember the beetles and our delightful wedding party?

I am extremely well and <u>fantastically</u> good-looking these days. Why can't you come home before I wither and the inner glow is dead? I only burn for you, however, and nothing could put that fire out.

There is very little additional news to give you. Rosheen was ill last week with an alarming temperature and all the symptoms of scarlet fever – which is rampant here – but produced no rash and was quickly herself again. She is very beautiful to look on, with incredibly feminine legs which win her admirers of all ages, and incredibly feminine airs and graces. The other day she was naughty and I had to put her tea on the stairs. As I was taking it out of the room she said, oh so sweetly, 'Mind you don't drop it, darling.' Complete victory for her. Evelyn and Michael went home to Yarmouth for a few weeks yesterday. We are now on the telephone – terminus 2978 – and I love it, as people are gradually finding out my number and it's still novel enough to be exciting. <u>Come the day</u> when your voice is at the end of the line.

Phyllis Freeman has a baby son, Jill and Art are expecting – yes, even they! How are the mighty fallen. Hymie came in the other day to see me. He is now a sergeant and expecting to go abroad 'any minute now' – but you know Mr B. I am going out to Bushey some time this weekend, as Pera and your Papa will be there. I am paying your Papa sundry allotments and wiping out old debts – you will be pleased about this no doubt.

We had another of our all-night parties last week, which are becoming a feature among a certain set of Finsbury citizens. We are a motley and fairly entertaining collection – an ex-librarian now working for A.R.P.,* a refugee doctor (and his refugee friends sometimes), a couple of medical students working on First Aid, Kate, Joyce Peacock and Evelyn and myself. That is a nucleus for a good party and I often think how much you would enjoy them. We talk, dance, drink and argue fiercely, play and sing to the guitar and the night just slips away. These people are helping me to get along as Tom's death produced an incredible sensation in me of being all washed up and finished with the pleasanter things of this world. I must get a job and stabilise myself that way and think think think of your homecoming.

---

* A.R.P.: Air Raid Precautions. Over a million volunteer A.R.P. wardens were created in the Second World War, to patrol the streets during the blackout, warning against unguarded displays of light from windows, providing first aid and fire-fighting. Many won citations for bravery.

Don't jeopardise that possibility if you can help it as I am
convinced that without you I cannot and will not live. Awaiting
your letters and hoping that you still love me as I love you –
passionately and forever. Your Mary

Airgraph
Naval H.Q.
NEW DELHI
24th April, 1943

Mary, my darling,

This has been an uneventful week altogether. The house is
very quiet these days as Molly and Ian have departed to Simla
for the summer, and Monty is still away.

Jack and I are by ourselves, although Peggy and Dicky Roe
are now messing with us, as their servants decamped in the
night, as servants are liable to round these parts. We expected
our own cook to start fleecing us, now that Molly, the Urdu
linguist of the household, has gone. So far he's been very good
and has produced some excellent food. Iced melon chunks, fresh
from the refrigerator, is perfect for breakfast! Fruit is very
plentiful at the moment – mangoes, oranges, bananas (remember
them?), melon, strawberries etc!! Food prices are rising
continuously, but there is no shortage of European food,
although that is not the case with the items of the Indian staple
diet.

Spingarn came round on Wednesday and brought some
records – Beethoven 2nd Symphony and the Mozart 'Jupiter',
which we played out in the garden. Norman Batley and Sheila
came round to listen, too. I like both the symphonies and am
getting to know them both as Spingarn has lent them to me

indefinitely. He has met someone who is reported to be ex-I.B.,[*]
so I'm going to try and arrange a meeting.

    All my love my darling,

      DAVID

Airgraph

12 Lloyd Square, W.C.1

April 26th, 1943

My darling much beloved David,

    I received your cable on Good Friday, so it served as a faster
message from you. I am so glad the airgraph cards are reaching
you. I will keep them flying. I have been to Bushey for the day
and today walked down Finch Lane talking incessantly to <u>YOU</u>.
Did you hear me, darling, and did the nice things I was saying
please you? Everyone here is very well. Rosheen grows stronger
and taller and I flourish too, as far as one can, living without
inspiration and delight, only hope for the future and our coming
together. <u>May it be soon</u>, and again and again. The wireless is
playing the Fifth Beethoven. Magnifique! Here's looking at you
kid, as they say in 'Casablanca' – and always with my undivided
love.

    Mary

Waiting eagerly for a long letter and some news of you.

---

[*] I.B.: International Brigade. Military units made up of anti-fascist volunteers
from various countries who went to fight in the Spanish Civil War (1936–9)
against Franco's nationalist forces – a great idealistic and romantic cause for
the international left.

Air mail
12 Lloyd Square, W.C.1
May 7th, 1943

My dearest and only love,

I received some airgraphs from you yesterday dated April 7th. Many thanks. Do you know it's nearly five years since that memorable, blessed and fateful day that boy met girl? Girl still likes it – and then some – what about you? At the moment, my darling, I am afflicted with the most undignified and disgusting boil at <u>the end of my nose!</u> So I am grateful, for once, that you are 7,000 miles away or else you might laugh yourself sick.

I have been having some interesting 'bumming' around London – learning to dance a rhumba (at last) in a Soho dive and going to a tea-dance (the first in my life!) at the Piccadilly Hotel – and in these interesting times picking up a motley and mad circle of continental flotsam and jetsam – a mad Polish sea captain who quarrelled with me about aesthetics violently – a hectic Czech, who really was hectic – you would have enjoyed it as much as I did – and I kept telling myself how much you would have enjoyed it, and then I didn't enjoy it so much because I was missing you. When next you think of me, think of little pubs off Baker Street, and perhaps that's where I'll be, tuning my low life to your high-tone places. Everyone gets shown your snapshot and we invariably drink your health and get very sentimental over you.

Evelyn's away at the moment visiting in Yarmouth. My mother isn't very well but that's not surprising. Papa I think sometimes regrets leaving life in the Army, but is looking for a more satisfactory job.

Rosheen is very well and is growing very tall and strong. She now has a circle of small boyfriends, with whom she swops 'comics'. I am taking her to Kew tomorrow to see the spring flowers. Everyone in the old Borough is fine and people are always asking for you and sending you their best wishes. We had a small tea party here today with some old familiar faces. This house is so charming and hospitable in shape. You will love it when you see it, especially my dark red carpet. With all my love my darling, sweet David and longing for your safe return.

Yours ever, Mary

Naval H.Q.
NEW DELHI
Saturday May 8th 1943

My beloved darling Mary,

Today I received a lovely, lovely letter from you dated 20th January, and I've enjoyed reading every word of it. Your letters have a curious effect on me – they produce a warm, lively sensation of being aware once again of the existence of a life and surroundings that are real, and colourful and purposeful, and to which I am forever attached. If I were a surrealist painter I think I could produce a magnificent masterpiece on the form the sensation takes. It's a very curious but very definite sensation altogether. I won't develop this any further as I'm already doing that in a long letter which I hope to send off by fast route next week. Anyway, I loved your letter and loved getting all the news about the neighbours. Darling, who else but the one peerless Mary could possibly describe Hymie as a 'sawn-off Peter Pan'!! What did he do?!

All the news about Rosheen makes excellent reading – she must be a lovely child, even if a bit irrepressible. Darling, please write me long letters giving the everyday news; that's precisely what I want to read just to reaffirm in my mind that this atrophying, empty, trivial, aimless and boring existence is not the <u>only</u> life to live. This life has few excitements really. In fact, life away from you, and London and party work can only have few interests and excitements – and the few are: (a) most important, operational work (b) meeting interesting and stimulating people and (c) seeing new places and new parts of the world. (a) seems to have lapsed; (c) is a dim and distant memory and (b) are few and far between.

I think I could have had pleasant memories of Delhi if I'd stayed here a couple of months, but 9 months is hell. You can't imagine the atrophying effect these surroundings and people have – they talk a different language completely. The only times when I feel at all normal and capable of discussing anything of any value at all is when I'm with Spingarn, or Sir Shanti [Bhatnager], whom I'm going to see this evening. Then it feels like breathing a new atmosphere.

Otherwise, the only way to spend one's time is in cinemas, bathing, badminton, dances and the outward manifestations of a society trying desperately to escape from the realities of war-time life. In fact we fritter away our time and life and thought in trivialities, whilst hundreds of our generation are fighting and maybe giving their lives in a war with which we are all inextricably associated. It's very depressing, particularly from my point of view, and will continue to be until either I come home to live again, or am transferred to some place where I can do something really constructive. Yes, I have accepted the separation from you in my mind darling – there's no other course. The only way to get away from India, which would satisfy my conscience, would be to get transferred to a more active theatre. This I am trying to arrange. Any other pretext, however wonderful the result might be, would be a denial of my personal ideology and of my personal association with the aims and justification of the war. In other circumstances the situation would be entirely different. Therefore, as long as my superiors think I'm doing a job which can only be done by someone with my experience, I <u>must</u> accept it. The only alternative is a more operational job, which I still have hopes of, but that doesn't avoid separation, I'm afraid. The objective view once again, and it's the only one. However much I love you my wonderful, darling Mary, and however much I crave to be with you again, and to resume the wonderful combination of David and Mary, there is no escape – YET.

Always yours
DAVID

David's headstone,
New Delhi Military Cemetery

EPILOGUE

n the odd way that life has of throwing things up, since reading and writing about my parents' story, another cache of letters surfaced, this time from my mother to David's sister.

They were written during the terrible empty months that followed the deaths of my father and her brother, Tom. I find it almost unbearable to imagine what a hell that time was for my mother. After Tom's death she wrote:

'. . . Crew missing, presumed killed. It amazes me that I can write that down and not go crazy. But I cannot believe it, no matter how hard I try to be realistic. Tom was the love of my life, if a brother may be described by such a cliché . . .'

Then, four months later, came the shattering news of David's death. I've learned that she told no one for several days. It was easier to not believe. Many months later she wrote to her sister-in-law:

'. . . Lately, the only message I have had for the outside world is that life stinks – a monotonous theme for letter writing. But now,' she continues, 'life still stinking, there is more to say.' She has had to recognise 'that I cannot look after Rosheen properly and have a career as well unless I bury us both in the country and try to eke out an existence on £5 a week'.

She had found 'an excellent boarding school' which had a nursery for 'babes of 2–4 and she can be with children like her brothers and sisters might have been'. She was certain that I would be much happier there than living 'the peculiar sort of existence we lead now, which is half and half of everything and both miserable . . .'

Maybe she was expecting some sort of resistance from my aunt and grandmother, because she continues almost defiantly: 'Rosheen will thank me more for making a career for myself and not claiming any returns for outrageous sacrifice when she is older.'

She has met a man – 'yes another, who seems to think that working in documentary films was what I was born for. His contacts in the film industry are numerous and he worked for no less a personage than Paul Rotha.* According to him they will welcome me with open arms' – which they did!

The last bit of that letter breaks my heart – again. Of the man, she writes: 'with his back turned, on a dark night, if I am sufficiently tight, he reminds me of David'.

The following year, writing from Scotland, where she was making a documentary film about stevedores, she says: 'The job is fascinating. The film biz is OK, it's all that is good in my life. Everything else is pretty flat and dreary and I feel completely detached from life as it used to be. Nothing is the same any more. Nothing even tastes the same any more. If it wasn't for Rosheen I think I would dissolve into a merciful mist of unreality.'

But she didn't. And I think it was the job and London – war-shook, shabby, warm, bohemian London – that saved her. The city was packed with soldiers, sailors, airmen from everywhere, and my mother lunched with poets at the Café Royal, fire-watched with Russian émigrés on the roofs of Finsbury and joined the motley crew crammed into Berlemont's French pub on Dean Street in Soho.

And all of those things I remember. The poet, the Russian émigré, the dashing Free French officer, they were all part of my

---

* Paul Rotha was a celebrated British documentary film pioneer.

childhood. Soho, too, for the rest of our lives was always our meeting place, even when I was living in France and she in Dublin: croissants in Maison Bertaux and drinks in the French, with Gaston bending over her hand and murmuring: 'chère Madame'.

But what I didn't remember or know about was what had happened before. Reading the letters was an extraordinary thing for me, like looking into a magic crystal ball and seeing a life unfolding that I never knew I had had. My mother, devastated by my father's dreadful faraway death, did as she did with the letters, put away the David and Mary part of her life and never talked to me about my father. I think that she thought of him as her lover, the death as her tragedy.

It was wonderful to understand that I was part of this story – their story. It had been David, Mary – and me. We had had a life together. Their letters were full of concern about my birth and my being. My pique at learning of my mother's absolute conviction that I would be a boy and their last-minute scramble to find a girl's name turned to joy when I read my father's letter written after his first glimpse of me: 'The baby is beautiful too. The momentary disappointment about the sex disappeared completely when I saw its grumpy indignant face . . . It's certainly going to be some child.' Now I know what a sweet loving father he would have been.

Of course I fell in love with the young man who emerged from the letters. How could I not? Charming, engaging, clever, funny, sunny. My father. I felt so proud of his rapid rise through the ranks. He was so insouciant about it – 'The old luck holds' – but it didn't. I knew nothing of his adventures in Africa and India and of how involved he was in some really important missions.

I was completely bowled over by how knowledgeable they both were about literature, art, music and politics, and how witty and passionate – particularly my mother – at only twenty-one.

Ironically, when I was twenty I asked my mother for permission to marry. She refused, saying that I was too young. My lover, with all the confidence of youth, shouted: 'You must never have been in love, Mary!' My mother stood up, eyes blazing, and left the room. When he read the letters many years later, my husband wept.

In 1947, my mother married again, not a film man nor a Soho habitué – far from it. She returned to her roots and married an Irish academic and writer. She didn't give up the film biz, however. It was not until 1951, when my half-brother was born, that we both came home permanently to the little house in Lloyd Square which she had prepared so lovingly for my father but which he never saw.

But she still never made any meaningful reference to my father. Until, many years later, widowed, frail and living in Dublin, when I think she had finally started looking at the letters again herself, she wrote me this letter after a visit:

My darling Ro,

Now that you have gone I realise what a joy you are to me and how you always have been. My life has been turned upside down and I don't want it to go on much longer. But when I see you and remember all the joy I have had, first with David and then with Flann, I remember that you were part of that happiness for me. So there.

Yours ever!

R.F.

NOTE ON THE TEXT

Mary and David wrote in a distinct style with a quite impeccable sense of spelling and grammar and we have stayed true to the original letters wherever possible. Some silent corrections have been made throughout to standardise some minor spelling and grammar in the interests of clarity. Not every single letter has been included in the collection for the purposes of length, whilst we have ensured that all the key information about their story remained.

You are invited to join us behind the scenes at Tinder Press

TINDER
PRESS

To meet our authors, browse our books
and discover exclusive content on our
blog visit us at

www.tinderpress.co.uk

For the latest news and views from the team
Follow us on Twitter

 @TinderPress